IFIP Advances in Information and Communication Technology

560

Editor-in-Chief

Kai Rannenberg, Goethe University Frankfurt, Germany

Editorial Board Members

IFIP – The International Federation for Information Processing

IFIP was founded in 1960 under the auspices of UNESCO, following the first World Computer Congress held in Paris the previous year. A federation for societies working in information processing, IFIP's aim is two-fold: to support information processing in the countries of its members and to encourage technology transfer to developing nations. As its mission statement clearly states:

> *IFIP is the global non-profit federation of societies of ICT professionals that aims at achieving a worldwide professional and socially responsible development and application of information and communication technologies.*

IFIP is a non-profit-making organization, run almost solely by 2500 volunteers. It operates through a number of technical committees and working groups, which organize events and publications. IFIP's events range from large international open conferences to working conferences and local seminars.

The flagship event is the IFIP World Computer Congress, at which both invited and contributed papers are presented. Contributed papers are rigorously refereed and the rejection rate is high.

As with the Congress, participation in the open conferences is open to all and papers may be invited or submitted. Again, submitted papers are stringently refereed.

The working conferences are structured differently. They are usually run by a working group and attendance is generally smaller and occasionally by invitation only. Their purpose is to create an atmosphere conducive to innovation and development. Refereeing is also rigorous and papers are subjected to extensive group discussion.

Publications arising from IFIP events vary. The papers presented at the IFIP World Computer Congress and at open conferences are published as conference proceedings, while the results of the working conferences are often published as collections of selected and edited papers.

IFIP distinguishes three types of institutional membership: Country Representative Members, Members at Large, and Associate Members. The type of organization that can apply for membership is a wide variety and includes national or international societies of individual computer scientists/ICT professionals, associations or federations of such societies, government institutions/government related organizations, national or international research institutes or consortia, universities, academies of sciences, companies, national or international associations or federations of companies.

More information about this series at http://www.springer.com/series/6102

John MacIntyre · Ilias Maglogiannis ·
Lazaros Iliadis · Elias Pimenidis (Eds.)

Artificial Intelligence Applications and Innovations

AIAI 2019 IFIP WG 12.5 International Workshops:
MHDW and 5G-PINE 2019
Hersonissos, Crete, Greece, May 24–26, 2019
Proceedings

 Springer

Editors
John MacIntyre
University of Sunderland
Sunderland, UK

Ilias Maglogiannis
University of Piraeus
Piraeus, Greece

Lazaros Iliadis
Democritus University of Thrace
Xanthi, Greece

Elias Pimenidis
University of West England
Bristol, UK

ISSN 1868-4238   ISSN 1868-422X   (electronic)
IFIP Advances in Information and Communication Technology
ISBN 978-3-030-19911-1   ISBN 978-3-030-19909-8   (eBook)
https://doi.org/10.1007/978-3-030-19909-8

This Springer imprint is published by the registered company Springer Nature Switzerland AG
The registered company address is: Gewerbestrasse 11, 6330 Cham, Switzerland

Preface

AIAI 2019 Workshops

According to Professor Klaus Schwab (founder and executive chairman of the World Economic Forum), we are living in the era of a great revolution that is rapidly bringing huge changes and challenges in our daily lives. This is the Fourth Industrial Revolution, which has a big impact on all disciplines, even in the way that we communicate and interact with each other. Artificial intelligence (AI) is a major and significant part of the Fourth Industrial Revolution. Its rapid technical breakthroughs are enabling superhuman performance by machines in a real-time mode. Machine vision (e.g., face recognition) or language translators and assistants like Siri and Alexa are characteristic examples. AI is promising a brave new world where business and economies will expand their productivity and innovation. Machine learning and deep learning are part of our usual common interactions on our mobile phones and on social media. Numerous applications of AI are used in almost all domains from cybersecurity to financial and medical cases. However, historic challenges for the future of mankind are being faced. Potential unethical use of AI may violate democratic human rights and may alter the character of Western societies.

The 15th Artificial Intelligence Applications and Innovations (AIAI) conference offered insight into all timely challenges related to technical, legal, and ethical aspects of intelligent systems and their applications. New algorithms and potential prototypes employed in diverse domains were introduced.

AIAI is a mature international scientific conference held in Europe and is well established in the scientific area of AI. Its history is long and very successful, following and spreading the evolution of intelligent systems.

The first event was organized in Toulouse France in 2004. Since then, it has had a continuous and dynamic presence as a major global, but mainly European scientific event. More specifically, it has been organized in China, Greece, Cyprus, Australia, and France. It has always been technically supported by the International Federation for Information Processing (IFIP) and more specifically by the Working Group 12.5, which is interested in AI applications.

Following a long-standing tradition, this Springer volume belongs to the IFIP AICT Springer Series and it contains the papers that were accepted to be presented orally at the following workshops held as parallel events of the 15th AIAI conference, which took place during May 24–26, 2019 in the Aldemar Knossos Royal five-star Hotel in Crete, Greece:

– **8th Mining Humanistic Data Workshop (MHDW 2019)**

– The **4th Workshop on 5G-Putting Intelligence to the Network Edge (5G-PINE 2019)**

All workshops had Program Committees and all submissions were peer reviewed by at least two independent academic referees. Where needed, a third referee was consulted to resolve any potential conflicts.

The workshops also followed the same review and acceptance ratio rules. More specifically, the 4th 5G-PINE accepted eight full papers out of 17 submissions (47%) and two short papers. In total, 15 manuscripts were submitted to the 8th MHDW workshop. The Program Committee accepted seven papers to be published as full papers (12 pages long) in the proceedings (46.6%). Moreover, four submissions were accepted as short papers (10 pages long) to be included in the proceedings.

The third workshop organized in the framework of AIAI 2019 was:

– The **First Workshop on Emerging Trends in AI (ETAI 2019)**

This workshop, sponsored by the Springer journal *Neural Computing and Applications,* was an open workshop without submission of papers.

Artificial intelligence is going through a new boom period, with exponential growth in the commercialization of research and development, products being introduced into the market with embedded AI as well as "intelligent systems" of various types. Projections for commercial revenue from AI also show exponential growth; such is the ubiquitous nature of AI in the modern world that members of the public are interacting with intelligent systems or agents every day – even though they often are not aware of it! This workshop, led by Professor John MacIntyre, considered emerging themes in AI, covering not only the technical aspects of where AI is going, but the wider question of ethics, and the potential for future regulatory frameworks for the development, implementation, and operation of intelligent systems and their role in our society.

The workshop format included three short presentations by the keynote speakers, followed by an interactive panel Q&A session where the panel members and audience engaged in a lively debate on the topics discussed.

The subjects of their presentations were the following:

– John MacIntyre: "The Future of AI – Existential Threat or New Revolution?"
– Andrew Starr: "Practical AI for Practical Problems"

We are grateful to Professor John MacIntyre from the University of Sunderland, UK, for organizing this workshop and, moreover, for his continuous support of the AIAI and EANN conferences. We wish to thank Professor Andrew Starr for his contribution to this very interesting workshop.

John MacIntyre
Ilias Maglogiannis
Lazaros Iliadis
Elias Pimenidis

Organization

AIAI 2019

Executive Committee

General Chairs

John MacIntyre	University of Sunderland, UK (Dean of the Faculty of Applied Sciences and Pro Vice Chancellor of the University of Sunderland)
Ilias Maglogiannis (President of the IFIP WG12.5)	University of Piraeus, Greece
Plamen Angelov	University of Lancaster, UK

Program Chairs

Lazaros Iliadis	Democritus University of Thrace, Greece
Elias Pimenidis	University of the West of England, Bristol, UK

Advisory Chairs

Stefanos Kolias	University of Lincoln, UK
Spyros Likothanasis	University of Patras, Greece
Georgios Vouros	University of Piraeus, Greece

Honorary Chair

Barbara Hammer	Bielefeld University, Germany

Workshop Chairs

Christos Makris	University of Patras, Greece
Phivos Mylonas	Ionian University, Greece
Spyros Sioutas	University of Patras, Greece

Publication and Publicity Chair

Antonis Papaleonidas	Democritus University of Thrace, Greece

Program Committee

Michel Aldanondo	IMT Mines Albi, France
Athanasios Alexiou	NGCEF, Australia
Mohammed Alghwell	Freelancer, Libya

Ioannis Anagnostopoulos	University of Central Greece, Greece
George Anastassopoulos	Democritus University of Thrace, Greece
Vardis-Dimitris Anezakis	Democritus University of Thrace, Greece
Costin Badica	University of Craiova, Romania
Kostas Berberidis	University of Patras, Greece
Nik Bessis	Edge Hill University, UK
Varun Bhatt	Indian Institute of Technology, Bombay, India
Giacomo Boracchi	Politecnico di Milano, Italy
Farah Bouakrif	University of Jijel, Algeria
Antonio Braga	Federal University of Minas Gerais, Brazil
Peter Brida	University of Zilina, Slovakia
Ivo Bukovsky	Tohoku University, Japan
Paulo Vitor Campos Souza	CEFET-MG, Brazil
George Caridakis	National Technical University of Athens, Greece
Jheymesson Cavalcanti	UPE, Brazil
Ioannis Chamodrakas	National and Kapodistrian University of Athens, Greece
Ioannis Chochliouros	Hellenic Telecommunications Organization S.A. (OTE), Greece
Adriana Mihaela Coroiu	Babes Bolyai University, Romania
Dawei Dai	Fudan University, China
Vilson Luiz Dalle Mole	UTFPR, Brazil
Debasmit Das	Purdue University, USA
Bodhisattva Dash	IIIT Bhubaneswar, India
Konstantinos Demertzis	Democritus University of Thrace, Greece
Antreas Dionysiou	University of Cyprus, Cyprus
Ioannis Dokas	DUTH, Greece
Sergey Dolenko	D.V. Skobeltsyn Institute of Nuclear Physics, M.V. Lomonosov Moscow State University, Russia
Xiao Dong	Institute of Computing Technology, China
Shirin Dora	University Van Amsterdam, The Netherlands
Rodrigo Exterkoetter	LTrace Geophysical Solutions, Brazil
Mauro Gaggero	National Research Council, Italy
Claudio Gallicchio	University of Pisa, Italy
Ignazio Gallo	University of Insubria, Italy
Spiros Georgakopoulos	University of Thessaly, Greece
Eleonora Giunchiglia	Università di Genova, Italy
Giorgio Gnecco	IMT School for Advanced Studies, Italy
Ioannis Gkourtzounis	University of Northampton, Greece
Foteini Grivokostopoulou	University of Patras, Greece
Hakan Haberdar	University of Houston, USA
Petr Hajek	University of Pardubice, Czech Republic
Xue Han	China University of Geosciences, China
Ioannis Hatzilygeroudis	University of Patras, Greece
Jian Hou	Bohai University, China
Lazaros Iliadis	Democritus University of Thrace, Greece

Jacek Kabziński	Lodz University of Technology, Poland
Antonios Kalampakas	AUM, Kuwait
Andreas Kanavos	University of Patras, Greece
Savvas Karatsiolis	University of Cyprus, Cyprus
Kostas Karatzas	Aristotle University of Thessaloniki, Greece
Antonios Karatzoglou	Karlsruhe Institute of Technology, Germany
Ioannis Karydis	Ionian University, Greece
Petros Kefalas	University of Sheffield International Faculty, Greece
Katia Lida Kermanidis	Ionian University, Greece
Nadia Masood Khan	University of Engineering and Technology Peshawar, Pakistan
Sophie Klecker	University of Luxembourg, Luxembourg
Yiannis Kokkinos	University of Macedonia, Greece
Petia Koprinkova-Hristova	Bulgarian Academy of Sciences, Bulgaria
Athanasios Koutras	TEI of Western Greece, Greece
Ondrej Krejcar	University of Hradec Kralove, Czech Republic
Efthyvoulos Kyriacou	Frederick University, Cyprus
Guangli Li	Institute of Computing Technology, Chinese Academy of Sciences, China
Annika Lindh	Dublin Institute of Technology, Ireland
Ilias Maglogiannis	University of Piraeus, Greece
George Magoulas	University of London, Birkbeck College, UK
Christos Makris	University of Patras, Greece
Mario Malcangi	Università degli Studi di Milano, Italy
Boudjelal Meftah	University Mustapha Stambouli, Mascara, Algeria
Nikolaos Mitianoudis	Democritus University of Thrace, Greece
Haralambos Mouratidis	University of Brighton, UK
Phivos Mylonas	National Technical University of Athens, Greece
Shigang Yue	University of Lincoln, UK
Yancho Todorov	Aalto University, Espoo, Finland
George Tsekouras	University of the Aegean, Greece
Mihaela Oprea	Petroleum-Gas University of Ploiesti, Romania
Paul Krause	University of Surrey, UK
Rafet Sifa	Fraunhofer IAIS, Germany
Alexander Ryjov	Lomonosov Moscow State University, Russia
Giannis Nikolentzos	Ecole Polytechnique, France
Duc-Hong Pham	VNU, Vietnam
Elias Pimenidis	University of the West of England, UK
Hongyu Li	Zhongan Tech, China
Marcello Sanguineti	University of Genoa, Italy
Zhongnan Zhang	Xiamen University, China
Doina Logofatu	Frankfurt University of Applied Sciences, Germany
Ruggero Labati	Università degli Studi di Milano, Italy
Florin Leon	Technical University of Iasi, Romania
Aristidis Likas	University of Ioannina, Greece
Spiros Likothanassis	University of Patras, Greece

Francesco Marcelloni	University of Pisa, Italy
Giorgio Morales	INICTEL-UNI, Peru
Stavros Ntalampiras	University of Milan, Italy
Basil Papadopoulos	Democritus University of Thrace, Greece
Antonios Papaleonidas	DUTH, Greece
Isidoros Perikos	University of Patras, Greece
Nicolai Petkov	University of Groningen, The Netherlands
Miltos Petridis	Middlesex University, UK
Jielin Qiu	Shanghai Jiao Tong University, China
Juan Qiu	Tongji University, China
Bernardete Ribeiro	University of Coimbra, Portugal
Simone Scardapane	Sapienza University of Rome, Italy
Andreas Stafylopatis	National Technical University of Athens, Greece
Antonino Staiano	Parthenope University of Naples, Italy
Ioannis Stephanakis	Hellenic Telecommunications Organisation SA, Greece
Ricardo Tanscheit	PUC-Rio, Brazil
Francesco Trovò	Politecnico di Milano, Italy
Nicolas Tsapatsoulis	Cyprus University of Technology, Cyprus
Nikolaos Vassilas	TEI of Athens, Greece
Petra Vidnerová	The Czech Academy of Sciences, Czech Republic
Panagiotis Vlamos	Ionian University, Greece
George Vouros	University of Piraeus, Greece
Xin-She Yang	Middlesex University, UK
Drago Žagar	University of Osijek, Croatia
Rabiaa Zitouni	University Tunis el Manar, Tunisia

Contents

8th Mining Humanistic Data Workshop (MHDW 2019)

4th Workshop on "5G-Putting Intelligence to the Network Edge" (5G-PINE 2019)

Preface

4th Workshop on 5G-Putting Intelligence to the Network Edge (5G-PINE 2019)

The 5G-PINE Workshop has been established to disseminate knowledge obtained from actual EU projects as well as from any other action of research, in the wider thematic area of "5G Innovative Activities – Putting Intelligence to the Network Edge" and with the aim of focusing on artificial intelligence (AI) in modern 5G telecommunication infrastructures.

The 4th 5G-PINE Workshop had a strong impact within the broader context of the AIAI 2019 Conference. The preparatory work was mainly driven by the hard organizational effort of Dr. Ioannis P. Chochliouros (Hellenic Telecommunications Organization - OTE, Greece) also coordinator of the relevant EU-funded 5G-PPP project 5G-ESSENCE, with the support of Mr. Uwe Herzog (EURESCOM GmbH, Germany) also coordinator of the 5G-PPP project 5G-DRIVE, Professors Oriol Sallent and Jordi Pérez-Romero (Universitat Politècnica de Catalunya, Spain), Dr. Maria-Rita Spada (Wind Tre S.p.A., Italy), Professor Fidel Liberal (Universidad del Pais Vasco/Euskal Herriko Unibertsitatea, Spain), Mr. Athanassios Dardamanis (SmartNet S.A., Greece), Dr. Ioannis Neokosmidis (inCITES Consulting SARL, Luxembourg), Dr. Tao Chen (VTT Technical Research Center of Finland), and Dr. Monique Calisti (Martel Innovate, Switzerland).

Apart from the aforementioned members of the workshop Organizing Committee, the entire effort was also supported by more than 70 European experts (mainly coming from the relevant EU-funded 5G-PPP projects 5G-ESSENCE and 5G-DRIVE that formed the "core" of the corresponding effort). Among the originally submitted 20 proposed papers, seven were finally accepted as full papers (acceptance ratio of 35%) and three as short papers.

The 4th 5G-PINE Workshop promoted the context of modern 5G network infrastructures and of related innovative services in a complex and highly heterogeneous underlying radio access network (RAN) ecosystem, strongly enhanced by the inclusion of cognitive capabilities and intelligence features, with the aim of improving the network management. Based on the well-known self-organizing network (SON) functionalities, the 4th 5G-PINE Workshop promoted network planning and optimization processes through artificial intelligence (AI)- based tools, able to smartly process input data from the environment and come up with knowledge that can be formalized in terms of models and/or structured metrics, able to "represent" the network behavior. This allows for gaining in-depth and detailed knowledge about the whole underlying 5G ecosystem, understanding hidden patterns, data structures, and relationships, and using them for a more efficient network management.

The 4th 5G-PINE Workshop supported the delivery of intelligence directly to the network's edge, by exploiting the emerging paradigms of network functions virtualization (NFV), software-defined networking (SDN), network slicing and edge cloud computing. Moreover, it supported the promotion of rich virtualization and multi-tenant capabilities, optimally deployed close to the user. Inter alia, it emphasized the small cell (SC) concept, so as to support improved cellular coverage, capacity, and applications in a fully dynamic and flexible manner with a strong emphasis on vertical applications, based on well-defined scenarios as promoted by the detailed 5G ESSENCE context. Another important area of interest has been the original scope of the 5G-DRIVE project promoting cooperation between the EU and China, especially by discussing the proposed context for trials according to the corresponding European policy for realizing tests and trials, as well as by promoting the context for enhanced mobile broadband (eMBB) applications.

The accepted papers focus on several innovative findings coming directly from modern European research in the area, mainly from the 5G-PPP projects 5G-ESSENCE, 5G-DRIVE, 5GCIty, MATILDA, COHERENT, as well as from the Spanish SONAR 5G and 5GRANVIR grants, covering a wide variety of technical and business aspects and promoting options for growth and development. One additional work also comes from the H2020-MCSA-ITN 5G AuRA project.

We would like to thank Dr. Ioannis P. Chochliouros, Research Programs Section, Research and Development Department, Fixed & Mobile, Hellenic Telecommunications Organization (OTE), for his efforts to organize the 5G-PINE scientific event, which was the fifth event in the series. After so many years of continuous presence, this workshop has become a quality and mature event.

Organization

4th Workshop on 5G-Putting Intelligence to the Network Edge (5G-PINE 2019)

Program Chairs

Ioannis P. Chochliouros	Hellenic Telecommunications Organization (OTE), Greece
Uwe Herzog	EURESCOM GmbH, Germany
Oriol Sallent	Universitat Politècnica de Catalunya, Spain
Jordi Pérez-Romero	Universitat Politècnica de Catalunya, Spain
Maria-Rita Spada	Wind Tre S.p.A., Italy
Fidel Liberal	Universidad del Pais Vasco/Euskal Herriko Unibertsitatea, Spain
Athanassios Dardamanis	SmartNet S.A., Greece
Ioannis Neokosmidis	inCITES Consulting SARL, Luxembourg
Tao Chen	VTT Technical Research Center of Finland, Finland
Monique Calisti	Martel Innovate, Switzerland

Program Committee

Latif Ladid	President, IPv6 Forum & SnT/ University of Luxembourg, Luxembourg
Nancy Alonistioti	National and Kapodistrian University of Athens, Greece
George Lyberopoulos	COSMOTE - Mobile Telecommunications S.A., Greece
Begoña Blanco	Universidad del Pais Vasco/Euskal Herriko Unibertsitatea, Spain
Betty Charalampopoulou	Geosystems Hellas S.A., Spain
Pavlos Lazaridis	University of Huddersfield, UK
Anastasios Kourtis	National Centre for Scientific Research Demokritos, Greece
Ioannis Giannoulakis	National Centre for Scientific Research Demokritos, Greece
Alexandros Kostopoulos	Hellenic Telecommunications Organization (OTE), Greece

Michail-Alexandros Kourtis	National Centre for Scientific Research Demokritos, Greece
Daniele Munaretto	Athonet S.R.L, Italy
Konstantinos Patsakis	University of Piraeus, Greece
Juan Sánchez-González	Universitat Politècnica de Catalunya, Spain
Na Yi	University of Surrey, UK
Klaus Moessner	University of Surrey, UK
Vishanth Weerakkody	University of Bradford, UK
Emmanouil Kafetzakis	ORION Innovations Private Company, Greece
Tilemachos Doukoglou	Hellenic Telecommunications Organization (OTE), Greece
Antonino Albanese	Italtel S.p.A., Italy
Paolo-Secondo Crost	Italtel S.p.A., Italy
Claudio Meani	Italtel S.p.A., Italy
Pietro Paglierani	Italtel S.p.A., Italy
Ivana Buntic-Ogor	Smart Mobile Labs AG, Germany
Claus Keuker	Smart Mobile Labs AG, Germany
Leonardo Goratti	TriaGnoSys GmbH, Germany
Tinku Rasheed	TriaGnoSys GmbH, Germany
Elisenda Temprado-Garriga	TriaGnoSys GmbH, Germany
Elisa Jimeno	ATOS Spain S.A., Spain
Vasilios Vassilakis	University of West London, UK
Irene Karapistoli	Cyberlens Ltd., UK
Manos Panaousis	University of Brighton, UK
Alssandro Vincentini	Wind Tre S.p.A., Italy
Jose-Oscar Fajardo	Universidad del Pais Vasco/Euskal Herriko Unibertsitatea, Spain
Pouria Sayyad Khodashenas	Fundació Privada i2CAT, Internet i Innovació Digital a Catalunya, Spain
August Betzler	Fundació Privada i2CAT, Internet i Innovació Digital a Catalunya, Spain
Hicham Khalifé	Thales SIX GTS France SAS, France
Olga Segou	ORION Innovations Private Company, Greece
Juha Jidbeck	VTT Technical Research Center of Finland, Finland
Maria Belesioti	Hellenic Telecommunications Organization (OTE), Greece
Evangelos Sfakianakis	Hellenic Telecommunications Organization (OTE), Greece
Eirini Vasilaki	Hellenic Telecommunications Organization (OTE), Greece
Ioannis Stephanakis	Hellenic Telecommunications Organization (OTE), Greece
Konstantinos Helidonis	Hellenic Telecommunications Organization (OTE), Greece

Christos Mizikakis	Hellenic Telecommunications Organization (OTE), Greece
Anastasia Spiliopoulou	Hellenic Telecommunications Organization (OTE), Greece
Nina Mitsopoulou	Hellenic Telecommunications Organization (OTE), Greece
Ioanna Papafili	Hellenic Telecommunications Organization (OTE), Greece
Mike Iosifidis	Clemic Services S.A., Greece
Michalis Tzifas	Eight Bells Ltd., Cyprus
Jordi Ferrer Riera	Eight Bells Ltd., Cyprus
Elina Theodoropoulou	COSMOTE - Mobile Telecommunications S.A., Greece
Ioanna Mesogiti	COSMOTE - Mobile Telecommunications S.A., Greece
Kostis Kaggelides	Gnomon Informatics S.A., Greece
Dimitrios Tzempelikos	Municipality of Egaleo, Greece
Theodoros Rokkas	inCITES Consulting S.A.R.L., Luxembourg
Dimitrios Xydias	inNCITES Consulting S.A.R.L., Luxembourg
Donal Morris	RedZinc Services, Ireland
Luis Cordeiro	OneSource Consultoria Informatica, LDA, Portugal
Makis Stamatelatos	National and Kapodistrian University of Athens, Greece
Panagiotis Kontopoulos	National and Kapodistrian University of Athens, Greece
Vasilios Vlachos	Technological Educational Institute of Larisa, Greece
Andreas Drakos	Channel VAS, Greece
Srdjan Krčo	DunavNET, Serbia
Nenad Gligoric	DunavNET, Serbia
Luca Bolognini	Italian Institute for Privacy, Italy
Camilla Bistolfi	Italian Institute for Privacy, Italy
Mariana Goldhamer	4GCelleX, Israel
Christos Tsirakis	OTE Academy S.A., Greece
Panagiotis Matzoros	Hellenic Telecommunications Organization (OTE), Greece
Marinos Agapiou	National and Kapodistrian University of Athens, Greece

A Cloud-Based Architecture for Video Services in Crowd Events

Alexandros Kostopoulos[1]([✉]) [iD], Ioannis Chochliouros[1],
Evangelos Sfakianakis[1], Daniele Munaretto[2], and Claus Keuker[3]

[1] Hellenic Telecommunications Organization (OTE) S.A., 99 Kifissias Avenue,
15124 Maroussi, Athens, Greece
alexkosto@oteresearch.gr
[2] Athonet S.R.L., Via Cà del Luogo 6/8, 36050 Bolzano Vicentino, Italy
[3] Smart Mobile Labs AG, Kistlerhofstr. 70, Geb. 88, 81379 Munich, Germany

Abstract. In this paper, we discuss a use case focused on crowd events in the context of the original 5G ESSENCE project [1], emphasizing on the provision of video services to the involved end-users. In particular, we investigate the core architectural components, as well as the cloud testbed for the deployment of our use case.

Keywords: Cloud-enabled Small Cell (CESC) ·
Mobile Edge Computing (MEC) · Network Functions Virtualization (NFV) ·
Radio Resource Management (RRM)

1 Introduction

The 5G ESSENCE project [1] addresses the paradigms of Edge Cloud computing and Small Cell as-a-Service (SCaaS) by fuelling the drivers and removing the barriers in the Small Cell (SC) market, forecasted to grow at an impressive pace up to 2020 and beyond, and to play a "key role" in the 5G ecosystem. 5G ESSENCE provides a highly flexible and scalable platform, able to support new business models and revenue streams by creating a neutral host market and reducing operational costs, by providing new opportunities for ownership, deployment, operation and amortization.

The 5G ESSENCE accommodates a range of use cases, in terms of reduced latency, increased network resilience, and less service creation time. One of its major innovations is the provision of E2E network and cloud infrastructure slices over the same physical infrastructure, so that to fulfil vertical-specific requirements as well as mobile broadband services. In this paper, we investigate the core architectural components, as well as the cloud testbed for the deployment of our use case.

2 Use Case Description

Broadcasters are looking for new ways to cover events, to offer exciting point-of-view perspectives to viewers *on one hand*, and to reduce production and delivery costs *on the other*. At the same time, network operators "target" to increase the usage of their

J. MacIntyre et al. (Eds.): AIAI 2019 Workshops, IFIP AICT 560, pp. 7–18, 2019.
https://doi.org/10.1007/978-3-030-19909-8_1

networks, while stadium owners have a strong interest in making the visitors' experience as pleasant as possible and look for ways to increase side-revenues apart from ticket sales. The reception of live content from cameras located in the playing field, replays and additional contextual information on mobile devices, becomes a strong use case for all the above actors. The main challenges even with 4G networks are the delay in the delivery of such content in the range of milliseconds rather than seconds and the considerable strain imposed on the backhaul network. By deploying a 5G ESSENCE-based network these challenges can be efficiently "addressed".

The 5G ESSENCE delivers benefits to media producers and mobile operators as it enables them to offer a highly interactive fan experience and optimizes operations by deploying "key functionalities" at the edge, i.e., evolved Multimedia Broadcast Multicast Services (eMBMS) or local network services like real-time analytics together with multitenancy support by small cells. By leveraging the benefits of SC virtualization and radio resource abstraction, as well as by optimizing network embedded cloud, it becomes possible to ease the coverage and capacity pressure on the multimedia infrastructure and also to increase security, since content will remain locally. Furthermore, additional benefits for the operators and the venue owners arise such as: (i) lower latency, due to shortening the data transmission path, and; (ii) maintained backhaul capacity, due to playing out the live feeds and replays locally that puts no additional strain on the backhaul network and upstream core network components. Figure 1 depicts the use case "5G edge network acceleration at stadium".

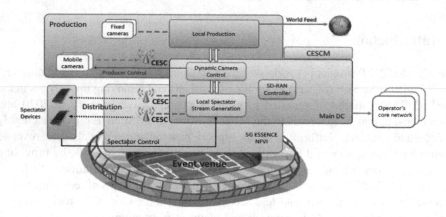

Fig. 1. 5G edge network acceleration at stadium

The scenario provides the logic for distributing the live video feeds received from the local production room to local spectators in a highly efficient manner. Different scale facilities can be used for the validation of the deployment topology. First, a small-scale facility as the municipal open swimming pool with a capacity of 500 spectators; secondly a medium-scale facility like the municipal indoor stadium (which is used for basketball, volleyball and handball games) with a capacity of 2,000 spectators, and; thirdly a large-scale facility as the municipal football stadium "Stavros Mavrothalasitis" which is located at the centre of Egaleo town in Athens and it is an open stadium with capacity of about 8,000 spectators. Considering a proper selection from the aforementioned facilities, the selected facility will be covered with a cluster of eMBMS enabled CESCs (Cloud Enabled SCs) and, together with the Main DC (Data Centre), can be connected to the core networks of multiple telecom operators. The video content from cameras will be sent for processing locally at the Edge (similar to the proposed use case by ETSI MEC [2–9]). Then the video streams will be broadcasted locally using the 3GPP eMBMS functionality. Spectators will be able to dynamically select among different offered broadcast streams. In this and in similar "big event" scenarios, massive data traffic will not affect -nor overload- the backhaul connection as it will be produced, processed and consumed just locally (i.e. a case of a 5G MEC scenario, aligned to the 5G 3GPP specifications [10–17]).

3 Architectural Components

The stadium use case shows a typical MEC configuration that keeps traffic as close as possible to the users to allow them to consume digital media with high quality and low latency. It shows that integrating network functionalities at the edge allows to fully benefit from advanced applications and services, including also broadcast or multicast-based technologies.

Within the 5G ESSENCE infrastructure, the stadium use case will leverage the main DC to realize its services running as VNFs (Virtual Network Functions). The actual distribution of the service across the data centres depends on the actual load required by the system. The Edge Video Orchestrator – Master Orchestrator (EVO-MO) service, eMBMS and EPC (Evolved Packet Core) functionalities actually run as VNFs in the DCs. In case where a cluster of CESCs is to be used to enable larger deployments, the aforementioned architecture can be further extended. The Edge Video Orchestrator (EVO), eMBMS and EPC core services can be deployed on each CESC's light DC, while the EVO instances being managed by an EVO-MO located on a central location. In order to achieve multi-tenancy, the EVO, eMBMS and EPC core services could be instantiated multiple times, depending on whether the services needed are also "multi-tenancy capable". The eMBMS functionality will be triggered by the EVO-MO communicating to a Broadcast Multicast Service Centre (BMSC), which is running locally in the stadium premises. If a camera's stream is to be transmitted via eMBMS (controlled by a management application), then the EVO-MO will request the BMSC to set up an eMBMS channel. Once this is set up, the BMSC acts as a proxy for the data and forwards it to respective eMBMS channels.

All devices use unicast transmissions for connecting to the EVO network service, which subsequently manages data transmission. Camera/Encoders use unicast transmission to transmit video and audio to the EVO service. Clients use eMBMS multicast reception to receive video and audio transmissions. The EVO services can deliver data to the 5G ESSENCE telemetry and analytics systems that can feed, for example the NFV Orchestrator (NFVO). Typical values that can be sent (other than platform related values such as CPU (Central Processing Unit), occupancy, network traffic, etc.) are application specific information used for orchestration like the number of connected users. More information regarding the 5G ESSENCE architecture is provided in [18] and [19].

The solution platform can be deployed in another different context, as it can be **event-specific** (stadium, concert, etc.), **venue-specific** (mall, museum, university, airport, etc.) or **area-specific** (neighborhood, city and region). In the following sections, the main components of the solution architecture are presented.

3.1   Hotspot LTE eMBMS

The EPC and eMBMS VNFs build the so-called hotspot LTE (Long Term Evolution) eMBMS. In practice, the two VNFs, EPC and eMBMS, are the "core" network components allowing the provision of LTE unicast communications and broadcast communications in the stadium. The two VNFs are also a MEC solution to offload traffic in a certain edge area without affecting the national backbone, as the local traffic stays local.

With the advent of the LTE technology, eMBMS has become an "attractive" solution for network operators who desire to increase bandwidth capacity and improve service quality, while maintaining low-cost investments for upgrading the network architecture. The eMBMS is an optimized broadcast/multicast service, which leverages on a point-to-multipoint link to transmit control/data information from the base station (eNB) to a group of users.

One of the key hurdles of eMBMS deployment for business/mission critical applications is that an eMBMS "island" must be integrated within the existing service provider and/or private national mobile network. Our solution solves this problem by providing partial functions of the EPC integrated with the broadcast functions to: *(i)* eliminate dependencies on a national/centralized mobile core network while being able to interface with it via existing interfaces; *(ii)* rapid low latency signalling; *(iii)* optionally eliminate failures due to backhaul scarcity, latency and failures, *and; (iv)* flexibly deploy virtualized functions at the network edge.

The eMBMS solution can be fully integrated with an existing service provider mobile core network. Moreover, depending on the customer's needs, the eMBMS can be deployed centralized or distributed to the edge of the network. The latter represents an important step towards making eMBMS efficient in terms of resource usage and delivery delay, while avoiding impacts on the national core network. The eMBMS can also interoperate with an external EPC. The SGi interface of the network operator (MNO)'s P-GW (Packet Data Network Gateway) is used to deliver a media (provided by the MNO) as IP multicast through the BMSC and MBMS-GW.

3.2   Edge Video Orchestrator and Distributor

According to [20], the EVO solution typically consists of the following components: Master Orchestrator (MO), Distributor, encoder and corresponding applications. Additionally, in case of LTE broadcast distribution, the eMBMS component is necessary. The core part of EVO is represented by the MO. The MO is provided as a virtual machine image using *CentOS Linux* as a base system. The main purpose of MO is to: (i) receive the encoded video streams from one or more connected encoders; (ii) forward the streams to one or more distributors (for unicast distribution); (iii) forward the streams to the eMBMS component (for broadcast distribution), *and*; (iv) encrypt video streams.

In each practical deployment there is always one MO and one or more Distributors. The encoders are always connected to the MO only. For unicast distribution and multicast, the system does not require any extra hardware components. Configuration of the multicast operation can be done by the EVO interface. Once the parameters are configured the EVO can be used to "tell" specific cameras attached to it to deliver their data to the according multicast channel.

Opposite to that, for LTE multicast, an additional eMBMS component provides HTTPS control interface and dynamic UDP (User Datagram Protocol) ports for video and audio data. The HTTPS control interface provides an API (Application Programming Interface) for managing broadcast sessions. This includes creating and starting broadcast sessions, querying the currently active sessions, and stopping a session. Each created session is identified by the Temporary Mobile Group Identifier (TMGI) and it contains one or more streams (e.g. HD (High Definition)/SD (Standard Definition) streams and audio stream). The number and type of the required streams is specified by the MO when the session is created and cannot be changed afterwards. The process is as follows:

1. MO creates a session and specifies the number and type of channels/streams to allocate.
2. The eMBMS component creates the session and returns a pair of UDP ports for each allocated channel and the TMGI of the created session.
3. The MO starts the session on the eMBMS component and starts pushing the associated video and audio streams to the eMBMS component.
4. The eMBMS component broadcasts them to the UEs (User Equipments).

To connect to the session and open the stream on the UE side, the following information is needed: (i) TMGI of the session, (ii) Multicast address which is used to broadcast the data within the session, (iii) UDP ports used for video and audio data, *and*; (iv) Key for decrypting the data.

The application retrieves this information from the MO and Distributor upon startup, using a dedicated unicast connection. This ensures that only authenticated users can receive and decrypt the broadcasted streams. After that, the application uses the Qualcomm Broadcast SDK (Software Development Kit) [21] to enable the session using the TMGI and receives the UDP data afterwards, which it can then decode and display.

When using a multicast delivery means, either eMBMS or Wi-Fi, the packet loss probability increases due to the missing MAC HARQ mechanisms. In order to mitigate this problem, it is possible to add redundancy to the user plane meaning that the same data is repeated in a special way in the user plane. If some data is lost, the original data might still be able to be recovered from the received subset. The mechanism is similar as the well-known FEC (Forward Error Correction) mechanisms employed by 3GPP on the radio link. The benefit of additional redundancy in the data path must be traded against higher data volume on the link. Therefore, it is possible to configure the amount of data plane redundancy provided by the system. Further, the system needs a distributor component in case the EVO service should be offered in multiple locations or if one MO instance cannot handle all the load and the installation must be scaled up to multiple physical machines. Basically, the distributor is the same component as the MO, just with a different configuration.

To be completely functional, the system also needs encoders. They receive the captured video and audio data using HDMI (High-Definition Multimedia Interface) or HD-SDI (High-Definition – Serial Digital Interface) and convert them to one or several IP streams. Thus, MO manages these provided streams. The advantage of such approach is that any professional or consumer camera that provides the necessary signal can be used. The encoders are specially designed and manufactured. Its software is based on *OpenWrt* and extended in such a way that it can directly connect to the MO via the web API.

3.3   Radio Access and Small Cells

The deployment architecture of the stadium use case also includes the small cells that provide the radio interface to support the video transmission to the UE. The small cells will form a zone-based architecture comprised of multiple low power access points coordinated by a localized zone controller, thus enabling the operators to offer high user experience while offloading unwanted data traffic from their macro and core networks. With the deployment of LTE SC technologies, mobile operators (and/or virtual mobile operators) are enabled to service a large number of mobile users, as well as provide users with the bandwidth they need to utilize mobile devices to enhance their productivity. Additionally, since poor 3G coverage remains an issue, mobile operators are enabled to deploy dedicated indoor coverage for voice and data in public indoor and enterprise locations.

Using SCs provides seamless mobility and enhanced user experience in enterprise and public locations by improving the coverage/capacity of the network. Moreover, these SCs provide LTE and Wi-Fi offloading capabilities. The multi-support of both LTE/3G and Wi-Fi access, integrated within a single compact form factor allows for reduced number of boxes and shared services (i.e., power, backhaul, etc.).

3.4   User Equipment

To enable the eMBMS reception in the end devices (UEs), special requirements have to be fulfilled. First, the modem part of the UE hardware and firmware must be eMBMS enabled, meaning the eMBMS technology must be implemented in physical and MAC/L3 layers of the modem chip. To make this functionality usable by an application running under the control of the UE's operating system (*iOS*, *Android*), this eMBMS functionality should be controlled from the UE's application processor (typically different from the modem). Thus, a so-called eMBMS middleware must be present on the phone to form the interface between the application receiving video and audio data and the low-level functions on the modem. Currently, there are a limited set of middleware SW products allowing this, but are not yet recognized and spread in the market. Hence, special UEs have to be used for this use case. A further challenge for the UEs, in order to use low latency video transmission, is that chunk-based transport cannot be used. The edge video orchestration service uses the RTP (Real-Time Transport Protocol) and eMBMS functions such as service announcements are not used. The EVO product uses own control channels to convey the information. Correspondingly, the eMBMS middleware of the UE must allow it to only use a subset of the standardised eMBMS functionality.

As described in [20], the corresponding client application is available for *Android* and *iOS* systems. The client application shows the available cameras. One of the options that can be chosen is eMBMS. If on, then the client will display the video received via eMBMS. Only eMBMS enabled camera feeds can be shown via eMBMS. Users can adjust the number of viewable streams. The client enables up to 9 streams to be shown simultaneously.

3.5   Main Data Center

The 5G ESSENCE platform has been designed to take advantage of MEC concepts to improve user experience, bandwidth efficiency and help mobile operators lighten the service delivery process. The two-tier virtualised execution environment makes a distinction between a very light computational environment, directly attached to the Small Cells (Light DC) – typically used to support the virtualisation of the SC and the execution of "light" service VNFs – and the Main DC, where the most computationally demanding VNFs can run and where implementing all the processes can take advantage of a centralised view of the underlying infrastructure.

Depending on the deployed scenario, the border between Light DC and Main DC can be more or less evident with the possibility, in specific circumstances, to collapse it in a unique physical layer. For small or medium size deployments, the Light DC makes room for the Main DC as the only tier of the Edge DC. The choice of edge architecture is mainly based on the size of covered area and on the number of SCs. In a small deployment scenario, the hardware of the Main DC can vary from one to a few nodes (servers), clustered together through a typical Ethernet infrastructure. In this use case we have no constraints related to physical dimensions or power consumption, so there are many possibilities in the choice of computing resources. If transcoding applications would be needed, the platform could be equipped with one or more GPUs (Graphics Processing Units). This kind of resources could be also useful for applications requiring Machine Learning (ML) algorithms.

Apart from that, this use case does not provide demanding applications in terms of computing resources. On top of the HW Infrastructure there is the virtualization layer that will make use of a standard KVM Hypervisor. This layer will make available the Virtual Machines for hosting the required VNFs (vEPC, eMBMS, EVO-MO).

4   Cloud Testbed

The cloud testbed that will be used for the duration of the 5G ESSENCE, to enable this use case, consists of three different site deployments: (i) The campus of *NCSR "Demokritos" (NCSRD)*, in north-east Athens, is a 150-acre area, combining indoor and outdoor environments, covered by five software-driven 5G wireless nodes and supported by an optical backbone. (ii) The *OTE building (OTE Academy)*, to the north of the city, is a multi-functional complex, combining various indoor and outdoor usage scenarios, *and*; (iii) The *Egaleo Stadium*, in west Athens, is going to be an actual "field" testbed, supporting a wide variety of real-life scenarios, ranging from massive MTC (Machine-Type Communications) to flash crowd events. The interconnected sites are located approximately 10–15 km apart and their interconnection is based on microwave links. All three sites use a common base infrastructure, but each one has different features.

4.1 NCSR "Demokritos" (NCSRD) Campus

The experimental setup at the campus of NCSR "Demokritos" comprises of five main parts: the core network, the backhaul network, the access network, mobile terminals connecting to the access network and distributed cloud deployments with computing, storage and networking resources. Topology and infrastructure are discussed as follows:

Topology: The related infrastructure consists of a macro-cell located at a high mast, covering a wider area, within the campus and three SCs serving focused coverage areas. Both the macro-cell and SCs are purely software-defined, in the sense that: (i) they are driven by fully reconfigurable and open SDR equipment, and; (ii) they also feature edge computing equipment ("light Data Centres") for hosting virtual appliances. All radio access points are connected to a core facility (currently based on LTE EPC) through dedicated fibre links.

Infrastructure: The radio infrastructure for the front-end is as follows:

- For the macro cell: SDR (Software-defined Radio) platform running a full software-based eNodeB implementation, driving a 5 W HPA (High-Power Amplifier) and a sector antenna (outdoor, installed on a 70 m-high mast).
- For the small cells: SDR platform running a full software-based eNodeB implementation, with indoor low-power antennas.

The testbed also features micro-servers integrated in each macro-/small cell, according to the CESC concept, which has been adopted in 5G SESAME project [22] and the 5G ESSENCE project [1] for mobile edge services. These micro-servers create a distributed Network Function Virtualisation Infrastructure (NFVI) based on OpenStack (supporting VMs or Containers) and OpenDaylight. In this manner, CESCs are both edge computing-capable and multitenant, enabling a small cell infrastructure to be shared among multiple tenants. Edge services deployed in the CESCs include several VNFs (vDPI, Security Appliance, Network Monitoring) as well as of virtualized appliances (Transcoder, Video analysis for object recognition).

The core functions (EPC) are also located on site. EPCs from different vendors have been tested. The eNodeBs (SCs and Macro Cell) are connected to the EPC over different types of backhaul links (fibre, RF, copper). UEs of various types have been tested (mobile phones by various vendors, laptops equipped with appropriate dongles, software-defined UEs based on SDN platforms). All types of UEs have embedded USIMs, appropriate for authentication to the EPC.

The testbed also hosts a core Cloud/SDN experimental platform for the experimentation needs of the 5G ESSENCE project. The cloud infrastructure is based on the OpenStack Cloud Operating System, comprising of 18 compute nodes (180 CPU cores, 1.5 TB RAM) and storage system supporting SAS (Serial Attached SCSI) and iSCSI (Internet Small Computer System Interface). NCSRD's testbed also features SDN-enabled network devices that support OpenFlow protocol (i.e., HP 3500yl-24G, Dell PowerConnect 5524), as well as legacy devices including firewalling and routing equipment (i.e., a Cisco 2921 Integrated Router, a Cisco ASA 5510 Firewall). Finally, the NCSRD site connects to the Internet via the national NREN (GRNET), using a dedicated hardware firewall whose rules are fully customizable. VPN access is possible, via SSL (Secure Socket Layer) and IPSec (IP Security) connections (Fig. 2).

Fig. 2. (left) High (70 m) mast within the campus of NCSRD, hosting the macro-cell base station; (right) Cloud/SDN infrastructure in NCSRD

4.2 OTE Testbed

OTE's testbed topology is as illustrated in Fig. 3, below.

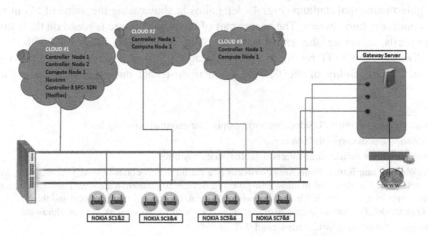

Fig. 3. Topology of the testbed in OTE premises

The OTE's testbed includes the following equipment:

(i)   An OpenStack-based cloud infrastructure (>220 CPU cores, >30 TB HDD, >340 GB RAM), consisting of 1 gateway, 5 controllers, 4 x86 + 2 ARM-*based* compute nodes, a VPN Server, a CISCO PIX FW[1], switches/routers while being interconnected to OTE's Labs thus providing additional capabilities for testing new technologies either for proof-of-concept (PoC) or for field trials.

(ii)   Eight Nokia 4G/4G+/Wi-Fi Small Cells distributed in two floors.

(iii) A flexible and scalable E2E (end-to-end) IoT (Internet of Things) platform, developed from scratch exclusively by OTE, including: (a) A wide range of end-devices/sensors such as, air-quality, temperature, humidity, pressure, activity, luminance, fire as well as power/energy ones, communicate with the backend (cloud) infrastructure over a wide range of short/long range technologies (Ethernet, Wi-Fi, z-wave[2], BLE[3], LoRaWAN[4], NB-IoT[5]); (b) IoT hubs/gateways (local and remote - based on LoRaWAN) for facility automation and energy management/control (based on events/rules) supporting multiple HAN (Home Area Network)/BAN (Body Area Network)/LAN (Local Area Network)/WAN (Wide Area Network) technologies/interfaces; over 150 Techs/protocols are currently supported, and; (c) A (common) backend infrastructure (including storage, monitoring/data visualization, command exchange, etc.).

(iv)   A broadband connection over GRNET[6], serving as backhaul link.

4.3   Egaleo Stadium

The Egaleo municipal stadium "Stavros Mavrothalassitis" is a football ground located in Egaleo, in the west of Athens. The stadium was built in 1966 and totally renovated in 2006 (Fig. 4). The stadium belongs to the Municipality of Egaleo (MoE) and its capacity is 8.217 (seated) spectators. The stadium is used by the football team of Egaleo (Egaleo FC). In addition to the football matches, the stadium is used for various events, such as music concerts. In general, the Egaleo municipal stadium is a modern stadium and has all the appropriate facilities and infrastructures. The infrastructure at the Egaleo municipal stadium (Fig. 4 - left) aims at showcasing the value of 5G in big sports and/or cultural events. The access part of the infrastructure is based on three low-power cells, covering the entire stadium (Fig. 4 - right), integrated with local virtualization-capable IT resources, thus forming CESCs as described in the previous section. The capability of the CESCs to be multi-tenant and to host edge services

---

[1] https://www.cisco.com/en/US/docs/security/pix/pix30/user/guide/pixugcfg.html.

[2] https://en.wikipedia.org/wiki/Z-Wave.

[3] https://www.microtronics.com/en/products/BLE-Gateway.html.

[4] LoRaWAN (Long Range Wide Area Network) is a media access control (MAC) protocol for wide area networks. It is designed to allow low-powered devices to communicate with Internet-connected applications over long-range wireless connections. It can be mapped to the second and third layer of the OSI model. For further details also see: https://www.thethingsnetwork.org/docs/lorawan/.

[5] https://en.wikipedia.org/wiki/Narrowband_IoT.

[6] For more details see: https://grnet.gr/.

enable a new business model, under which the CESC infrastructure is owned by the stadium operator (rather than by MNOs), who, in turn, leases slices to MNOs, MVNOs and enterprise users. The stadium is connected to the main site of the testbed (NCSR "Demokritos"), where the core functions are expected to reside, with a backhaul point-to-point microwave link. A VPN (Virtual Private Network) over the Internet also exists, yet only as a fall-back solution.

Fig. 4. (left) Egaleo municipal stadium; (right) Placement and coverage of radio cells

5 Discussion

5G ESSENCE delivers benefits to media producers and mobile operators as it enables them offering a highly interactive fan experience and optimizes operations by deploying key functionalities at the edge (i.e., eMBMS or local network services like real-time analytics together with multitenancy support by small cells). In this paper, we investigated the core architectural components of the aforementioned use case, as well as the cloud testbed for the respective deployment.

A large-scale facility as the municipal football stadium "Stavros Mavrothalasitis" will be used for the validation of the respective 5G ESSENCE use case. The coverage in this facility will be provided by a cluster of multitenant, eMBMS-enabled SC and a main DC connected to the core networks of multiple telecom operators. The Edge DC will be processing video content from cameras deployed on-site, which will be broadcast locally without affecting the backhaul. Our future work will be focused on validation and testing in order to evaluate the proposed 5G ESSENCE architecture.

Acknowledgements. The paper has been based on the context of the 5G-PPP phase 2 "5G ESSENCE" ("Embedded Network Services for 5G Experiences") Project (GA No. 761592), funded by the European Commission.

References

1. 5G ESSENCE H2020 5G-PPP Project. http://www.5g-essenceh2020.eu
2. White papers from the 5G Infrastructure Association. https://5g-ppp.eu/white-papers/
3. European Telecommunications Standards Institute (ETSI), Multi-access Edge Computing (MEC), at: http://www.etsi.org/technologies-clusters/technologies/multi-access-edge-computing
4. ETSI, Multi-access Edge Computing group releases a first package of APIS. http://www.etsi.org/news-events/news/1204-2017-07-news-etsi-multi-access-edge-computing-group-releases-a-first-package-of-apis
5. ETSI GS MEC 009 V1.1.1(2017-07): Mobile Edge Computing (MEC); General principles for Mobile Edge Service APIs
6. ETSI GS MEC 010-2 V1.1.1 (2017-7): Mobile Edge Computing (MEC); Mobile Edge Management; Part 2: Application lifecycle, rules and requirements management
7. ETSI GS MEC 011 V1.1. (2017-7): Mobile Edge Computing (MEC); Mobile Edge Platform Application Enablement
8. ETSI GS MEC 012 V1.1. (2017-7): Mobile Edge Computing (MEC); Radio Network Information API
9. ETSI GS MEC 013 V1.1. (2017-7): Mobile Edge Computing (MEC); Radio Location API
10. ETSI GS NFV-MAN 001 (2014-12): Network Functions Virtualization (NFV); Management and Orchestration
11. The Third Generation Partnership (3GPP): 3GPP TS 23.501 v15.0.0: "System Architecture for the 5G System; Stage 2 (Release 15)", December 2017
12. The Third Generation Partnership (3GPP): 3GPP TS 23.502 v15.0.0: "Procedures for the 5G System; Stage 2 (Release 15)", December 2017
13. The Third Generation Partnership (3GPP): 3GPP TS 38.300 v15.0.0: "NR and NG-RAN Overall Description; Stage 2 (Release 15)", December 2017
14. The Third Generation Partnership (3GPP): 3GPP TS 38.401 v15.0.0: "NG-RAN; Architecture description; Stage 2 (Release 15)", December 2017
15. The Third Generation Partnership (3GPP): 3GPP TR 38.816 v15.0.0: "Study on CU-DU lower layer split for NR (Release 15)", December 2017
16. The Third Generation Partnership (3GPP): 3GPP TR 38.806 v15.0.0: "Study of separation of NR Control Plane (CP) and User Plane (UP) for split option 2 (Rel.15)", December 2017
17. The Third Generation Partnership (3GPP): 3GPP TS 32.101 v15.0.0: "Telecommunication management; Principles and high level requirements (Rel. 15)", September 2017
18. Chochliouros, I., et al.: Using small cells from enhancing 5G networks. In: Proceedings of IEEE Conference on Network Function Virtualisation and Software-Defined Networks (NFV-SDN 2017), pp. 1–6. IEEE (2017)
19. Kostopoulos, A., Chochliouros, I., Giannoulakis, I., Kourtis, A., Kafetzakis, E.: Small cells-as-a-service in 5G networks. In: Proceedings of the IEEE International Symposium on Broadband Multimedia Systems and Broadcasting (BMSB 2018), pp. 1–4. IEEE (2018)
20. Smart Mobile Labs AG: Edge Video Orchestration EVO – Product description, Release 2.1 2018
21. Qualcomm Technologies, Inc.: LTE Broadcast SDK. https://developer.qualcomm.com/software/lte-broadcast-sdk
22. SESAME H2020 5G-PPP Project. http://www.sesame-h2020-5g-ppp.eu/

A New Self-planning Methodology Based on Signal Quality and User Traffic in Wi-Fi Networks

Juan Sánchez-González[(✉)], Jordi Pérez-Romero, and Oriol Sallent

Universitat Politècnica de Catalunya (UPC), c/Jordi Girona, 1-3,
08034 Barcelona, Spain
juansanchez@tsc.upc.edu

Abstract. Wi-Fi networks have become one of the most popular technologies for the provisioning of multimedia services. Due to the exponential increase in the number of Access Points (AP) in these networks, the automation of the planning, configuration, optimization and management tasks has become of prime importance. The efficiency of these automated processes can be improved with the inclusion of data analytics mechanisms able to process the large amount of data that can be collected from Wi-Fi networks by powerful monitoring systems. This paper presents a new self-planning methodology that collects historical network measurements and extracts knowledge about user signal quality and traffic demands to determine adequate AP relocations. The performance of the proposed AP relocation methodology based on a genetic algorithm is validated in a real Wi-Fi network. The proposed approach can be easily adapted to other contexts such as small cell networks.

Keywords: Self-planning · Wi-Fi · Genetic algorithms · Data analytics

1 Introduction

In the last years, mobile users are increasingly demanding new multimedia services (i.e. high quality video, online multimedia applications, augmented/virtual reality, etc.) that have high bandwidth demands and strict Quality of Service (QoS) requirements. To cope with this demand, network densification through the deployment of small cells operating cellular technologies (e.g. 4G/5G), complemented with Wi-Fi hotspots, which benefit from the unlicensed use of the spectrum, becomes a relevant solution. Indeed, the popularity of Wi-Fi technology among mobile users makes it a competitive option for serving multimedia demands. The amount of traffic of IEEE 802.11 (i.e. Wi-Fi) has suffered a high increase in the last years. It is expected that by 2021, 63% of the global cellular data traffic will be offloaded to Wi-Fi or small cell networks [1]. Globally, there will be nearly 549 million public Wi-Fi hotspots by 2022, up from 124 million in 2017, a fourfold increase. Such a high increase in the amount of traffic volume and the number of Wi-Fi Access Points (AP)/Small Cells makes much more complex the planning, configuration, optimization and management tasks of these networks. For this reason, the automation of these processes is of paramount

J. MacIntyre et al. (Eds.): AIAI 2019 Workshops, IFIP AICT 560, pp. 19–30, 2019.
https://doi.org/10.1007/978-3-030-19909-8_2

importance. Legacy systems such as 2G/3G/4G already started the path towards a higher degree of automation through the introduction of Self-Organizing Network (SON) functionalities [2], namely self-planning, self-optimization and self-healing. However, the lessons learnt from cellular SON cannot be directly applied to Wi-Fi systems. Several works such as [3, 4] identify challenges and use cases to introduce SON paradigms in Wi-Fi networks. Concerning self-planning aspects in Wi-Fi/Small Cells networks, most of the works found in the literature focus on the determination of the most adequate AP location and the frequency channel allocation and AP transmitted power. As an example, [5] presents a framework for automated cell-planning in multi-tenant Small Cells networks that considers actions such as adding/removing channels and Small Cells. Similarly, [6] presents a theoretical model to determine the most adequate AP location by an accurate characterization of impact of the environment (walls, doors, etc.) on the signal propagation. Other works, such as [7], deal with the determination of the most appropriate locations of Wi-Fi extenders.

On the other side, it is envisaged that the efficiency of automated network management processes can be substantially enhanced through the exploitation of powerful data analytics technologies able to process the large amount of data that can be collected from Wi-Fi networks by powerful monitoring systems. In this respect, (big) data monitoring and analytics combined with SON technologies will become fundamental in order to enable full scale automated network deployment and optimization [8]. The monitoring system provides the ability to collect information about the network resources and performance of the services while the analytics system allows extracted knowledge of the collected data in order to support different decision making processes over the network. As an example, [9] presents a framework for data monitoring and analytics for the optimization of Cloud Enabled Small Cells in the context of the 5G ESSENCE project. The data collected by the monitoring system can be valuable for the extraction of knowledge related to user habits, user mobility patterns, spatio/temporal user resource demands, etc. Some examples are presented in [10] that evaluates user mobility models in a University campus, in [11] that makes use of Wi-Fi measurements to analyze mobility patterns in a Hospital or in [12] that assesses the spatio/temporal traffic correlation of Wi-Fi traffic data measurements and presents a supervised learning approach to classify the different campus spaces.

Within this context, this paper presents a new self-planning methodology to determine adequate relocations of APs to improve the provided coverage/quality at those regions of the network with low signal quality and high traffic demands. The methodology makes use of a monitoring system that collects historical network measurements and an analytics system that extracts valuable knowledge from the collected data. This knowledge feeds the AP relocation strategy that is based on a genetic algorithm. The performance of the proposed relocation actions are validated in a real Wi-Fi network. Although the AP relocation methodology considered in this paper focuses on a Wi-Fi network, it could be adapted as well to other contexts, for example exploiting the monitoring and analytics framework for small cell networks defined by the 5G ESSENCE project in [9].

The remaining of the paper is organized as follows. Section 2 presents the different steps of the proposed self-planning methodology, while the details of the AP relocation algorithm are presented in Sect. 3. The performance of the proposed approach is empirically evaluated in Sect. 4, while Sect. 5 summarizes the conclusions.

2 Proposed Self-planning Methodology

The proposed self-planning methodology assumes a Wi-Fi network with monitoring capabilities enabling the collection of a number of measurements reported by the users when connected to the different APs. The collected data is processed by a data analytics module to generate actionable insights to be used by the self-planning process. As a result, the self-planning process will be able to detect those situations in which the network performance is not satisfactory thus requiring relocation of one or several APs to other positions. The network is represented as a group of K Access Points located at specific geographical locations $(x_{AP,k}, y_{AP,k})$. The complete scenario is represented with a set of pixels R, each one associated to a geographical location. According to Fig. 1, the *Network Monitoring* module collects and stores user measurements during a large period of time T_{meas} (i.e. weeks or even months). Each measurement is associated to a particular location s (with $s = 1,...,S$) with coordinates (x_s, y_s), i.e. one of the pixels of the scenario, so that $S \subseteq R$ is the set of locations in the scenario with associated measurements. The location information can be obtained by means of different positioning methodologies which are out of the scope of this work, such as Time of Arrival [13] or fingerprint-based approaches [14]. With these inputs, the *Data Analytics* module generates the following metrics for each location:

1. List of APs where the user was connected to as best server at the s-th location.
2. Average Received Signal Strength Indicator ($RSSI_s$) from the best AP at the s-th location.
3. Average Signal to Noise Ratio (SNR_s) at the s-th location.
4. Normalized traffic volume (V_s) defined as the percentage of traffic transmitted/received at the s-th location with respect to the total amount of traffic volume transmitted/received in all the scenario in the period T_{meas}.
5. The activity factor (T_s) defined as the amount of time in which a user at the s-th location is connected to the network with respect to the measurement period T_{meas}.

These historical measurements are very valuable for the self-planning process in order to decide adequate actions of AP relocation. For example, AP relocations may decide to enhance the performance in certain regions with high traffic demands that experience poor SNR or bit rate by moving APs from regions with lower traffic demands (e.g. stairs and corridors of the building where users do not stay connected too much time and do not transmit large traffic volumes).

The *Data Analytics* module also identifies the regions with relatively high traffic demands by selecting the set $U \subseteq S$ where the normalized traffic volume V_s and activity factor T_s are higher than some specific thresholds Th_v and Th_t, respectively. Then, with the set of samples U, a filtering process is carried out to determine the set of samples $W \subseteq U$ in which the provided coverage and quality are below some specific thresholds Th_RSSI and Th_SNR, respectively. Therefore, the set W represents the most relevant locations of the network where users transmit a high amount of traffic and the network coverage/quality requirements are not guaranteed. The set W is used to trigger the *AP relocation process*. Specifically, if the set W is not empty (i.e. there are some relevant locations with poor coverage/quality), the *AP relocation algorithm* described in Sect. 3 is triggered. Otherwise, if the set W is empty, (i.e. there are no samples with poor coverage/quality) no AP relocation is done and a new period of time T_{meas} starts.

An adequate setting of thresholds Th_v and Th_t is prime important in order to adequately determine the relevant sample locations considered for optimization. A too low value for these thresholds Th_v and Th_t may cause the appearance of false alarms (i.e. wrong activations of the *AP relocation algorithm*) since the existence of non-relevant locations (i.e. low traffic volume and low activity) with bad RSSI and SNR will unnecessarily activate the *AP Relocation algorithm*. On the contrary, a too high value in these thresholds Th_v and Th_t may cause that the *AP Relocation algorithm* may not be activated when needed. Note also that, in case of activation of the *AP Relocation algorithm*, high values of Th_v and Th_t may cause the methodology to miss relevant sample locations (with relatively high traffic volume and activity), which will lead to a sub-optimal AP relocation. As for the thresholds Th_RSSI and Th_SNR, they must be selected in accordance with the RSSI and SNR values that ensure a certain user performance (e.g. a minimum required user bit rate).

By observing the set of measurements W, the *AP Relocation algorithm* will determine a group of M Access Points ($M \leq K$) considered as candidates to be relocated. These M APs are selected as the best serving APs for the samples of the set W. Then, the objective of the *AP Relocation algorithm* is to move one or several of these APs closer to the locations with high traffic demands (i.e. set of samples U) but, at the same time, maintaining enough coverage at all the R pixels of the scenario. Since the APs are usually connected to the wired network and hanged on the walls, the selection of potential AP locations depends on how easily they can be placed. In this respect, an adequate filtering of unfeasible locations will determine the subset $R_C \subseteq R$ that includes only the feasible locations where the APs can be placed. This filtering will reduce the computational complexity of the solution search, which consists in running a metaheuristic algorithm that iteratively proposes and evaluates different candidate solutions until a termination condition is fulfilled.

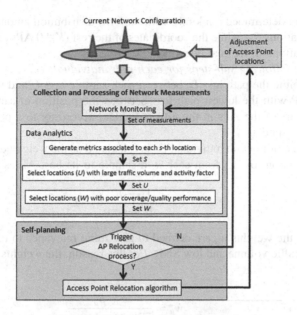

Fig. 1. Self-optimisation methodology.

Different metaheuristic algorithms can be considered (e.g. genetic algorithm [15], simulated annealing [16], etc.). This paper makes use of a genetic algorithm approach which is described in Sect. 3. If the *AP Relocation algorithm* provides a feasible solution, then, the corresponding AP(s) are relocated to the identified position(s).

3   AP Relocation Algorithm

The *AP Relocation Algorithm* makes use of a genetic algorithm optimization that consists on iteratively proposing possible candidate solutions (*individuals*), each one consisting in a combination of AP locations, and evaluate the performance of each individual according to a cost function. The best individuals in an iteration (*generation*) are combined to obtain new individuals that are again evaluated in the subsequent iteration. This process is repeated during multiple generations G. Each individual is represented by a combination of the geographical coordinates of all the K APs in the network. During the execution of the genetic algorithm, only the M APs ($M \leq K$) that are the best serving APs for the samples of the set W are candidates to be relocated, while the rest of APs will remain at the same position. To following steps summarize the operation of the genetic algorithm for relocating the M APs:

(1) *Generate a population of N individuals:* Each n-th individual ($n = 1,...,N$) is represented by a vector v_n with the geographical coordinates of the K APs $v_n = \{x_{AP,1}, y_{AP,1}, ..., x_{AP,k}, y_{AP,k}, ..., x_{AP,K}, y_{AP,K}\}$. Each element of the vector v_n is called a *gene*. For each individual, the coordinates of the M candidate APs to be

relocated are determined randomly with uniform distribution among the subset of feasible locations R_C, while the coordinates of the rest $(K\text{-}M)$ APs are fixed at their current locations in the real network.

(2) *Execute the following sub-steps for each n-th individual:*

  2.1. Determine the path loss L_u between each sample $u \in U$ and its best AP, i.e. the AP with the lowest path loss between the position of sample u and the positions of the APs in the n-th individual according to a predefined propagation model.

  2.2. The cost of the n-th individual C_n is calculated as the weighted average of the propagation loss L_u from each u-th sample to its best AP as follows:

$$C_n = \frac{1}{U} \sum_{u=1}^{U} w_u \cdot L_u \tag{1}$$

where the weights w_u are defined to give more relevance to the regions with high traffic volume and low SNR. For this reason, the weights w_u are defined as:

$$w_u = \frac{\alpha_u \cdot \beta_u}{\sum_{u'=1}^{U} (\alpha_{u'} \cdot \beta_{u'})} \tag{2}$$

where:

$$\alpha_u = \frac{V_u}{\sum_{u'=1}^{U} V_{u'}} \tag{3}$$

$$\beta_u = \frac{1/SNR_u}{\sum_{u'=1}^{U} 1/SNR_{u'}} \tag{4}$$

V_u denotes the normalized traffic volume demanded at the u-th sample and SNR_u is the Signal to Noise Ratio of sample u-th. α_u and β_u are normalized parameters so that $0 \leq w_u \leq 1$ as shown in (3) and (4).

According to Eq. (1), an individual with a lower cost C_n corresponds to a better network layout since it relocates the different APs so that lower values of path loss are observed, especially for samples with high traffic volume or low SNR.

  2.3. Two feasibility conditions are checked. The first condition checks whether the individual guarantees the overall network coverage or not. Then, an individual is not feasible if there is any geographical location in the scenario (i.e. a pixel of the set R) with RSSI lower than $RSSI_{cov}$. The second feasibility condition checks that the proposed individual guarantees that the interference generated from an AP to a neighbor AP that is using the same channel is lower than a threshold Th_RSSI_{neigh}.

(3) *Selection:* This step determines which feasible individuals are selected for the generation of new individuals to be evaluated in the subsequent generation. The cost of each individual C_n is used for the selection process by considering a *roulette wheel* [16] so that the probability of selecting the n-th individual for recombination is:

$$Prob_n = \frac{\frac{1}{C_n}}{\sum_{i=1}^{N} \frac{1}{C_i}} \tag{5}$$

According to this, individuals with lower cost have higher probability to be selected for recombination. Individuals that are not feasible according to the feasibility conditions in step 2.3, are not considered in this selection process.

(4) *Recombination:* This process combines the different genes (i.e. elements of the vectors v_n) of the two individuals selected in the previous step (called *parents*) to generate two new individuals (called *children*). The rationality of this process is to search for new solutions similar to the best individuals of the previous generation by combining their genes. The recombination process considered here is the so-called "1-point crossover" [16]. Considering the genes of the two parents, a crossover point is defined randomly and all the genes beyond this crossover point are swapped between both parents to obtain the children.

(5) *Mutation:* This operator makes small random changes in the genes of the two individuals obtained after recombination. The probability of selecting a gene for mutation is $1/N_{genes}$ where $N_{genes} = 2M$ corresponds to the two coordinates of all the M AP that can be relocated in the individual. As a result, very few genes of an individual are usually modified by this process. When a gene is selected for mutation, the new value, which represents a new AP location, is either an increase or decrease (with equal probability) in one pixel, allowing only changes to locations of the set R_C.

As a result of the selection, recombination and mutation process, a total of two new individuals will be obtained. This process is repeated $N/2$ times until getting the N individuals for the new generation. With the newly generated N individuals, the algorithm executes again the evaluation procedure and computes the associated costs. The process is repeated iteratively until reaching a maximum number of generations G. Then, the final solution of the algorithm is the individual with minimum cost that has been found throughout all the generations.

4 Performance Evaluation

The proposed methodology has been evaluated empirically in a scenario consisting of a building of 40 m × 20 m covered by $K = 3$ APs represented in Fig. 2. A grid with pixel resolution of 1 m is considered. The measurements are made and reported by 241 different users during a period T_{meas} of one month. These reported measurements are collected by the Cisco Prime Infrastructure tool [17]. The locations of the set of $U = 12$ samples in which the demand of traffic is relatively high (i.e. Normalized Traffic

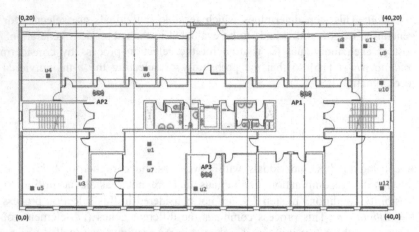

Fig. 2. Considered scenario with the set of $U = 12$ samples.

Table 1. Observed metrics and obtained weight for each sample of the set $U = 12$.

Sample	Location	$SNR_u(dB)$	$V_u(\%)$	α_u	β_u	w_u
u_1	[7, 14]	33.04	1.83	0.006	0.050	0.004
u_2	[22,3]	30.12	1.75	0.012	0.048	0.007
u_3	[7, 4]	17.54	1.68	0.231	0.046	0.118
u_4	[3, 14]	27.24	8.27	0.024	0.227	0.062
u_5	[1, 2]	23.95	1.77	0.052	0.048	0.028
u_6	[13, 15]	29.32	3.56	0.015	0.098	0.017
u_7	[13, 5]	27.13	1.68	0.025	0.046	0.013
u_8	[35, 18]	23.82	1.8	0.054	0.049	0.030
u_9	[39, 18]	22.80	2.34	0.068	0.064	0.049
u_{10}	[39, 14]	22.08	1.78	0.081	0.049	0.044
u_{11}	[37, 18]	33.70	4.96	0.005	0.136	0.008
u_{12}	**[39, 2]**	**14.92**	**4.83**	**0.427**	**0.139**	**0.620**

Volume higher than $Th\_v = 1\%$ and Activity Factor higher than $Th\_t = 1\%$) are represented in Fig. 2. Table 1 presents the average SNR_u, the normalized traffic volume V_u, the normalized parameters α_u and β_u and the weight w_u for the identified $U = 12$ samples. By filtering the U samples, the set W contains one sample with RSSI and SNR below $Th\_RSSI = -81\ dBm$ and $Th\_SNR = 15\ dB$, respectively. This sample corresponds to u_{12} located at coordinates *[39, 2]* as shown in Fig. 2. Although it is just a single sample, it represents a substantial amount of traffic (i.e. 4.83% of normalized traffic volume) and exhibits a very low SNR compared to the rest of samples. At this location, an average bit rate of 14 Mb/s has been observed while the bit rate at other locations inside the building usually varies between 30 and 50 Mb/s. At this location, the users can connect to two different APs, namely AP1 and AP3. Then, the *AP relocation algorithm* will evaluate the relocation of these $M = 2$ APs to improve the performance at the $U = 12$ locations, while maintaining the network coverage (i.e. RSSI of all the R pixels in the scenario is higher than $RSSI_{cov} = -75\ dBm$) and keeping the interference between neighbor APs using the same channel below $RSSI_{neigh} = -70\ dBm$.

The genetic algorithm considers a population of $N = 50$ individuals, each one represented by the location coordinates of the $K = 3$ APs. A total of $G = 5000$ generations have been considered. The propagation model is taken from the ITU-R [18] so that the path loss between the transmitter and the receiver is calculated as:

$$L(dB) = 20log_{10}(f) + N_o log_{10}(d) + P_f(n) - 28 + N_d L_o \qquad (6)$$

where $f = 2.4\ GHz$ is the carrier frequency, $N_o = 30$ for office areas, $P_f(n)$ is the floor attenuation factor considered here 0 dB since all the APs and the users are located at the same floor, N_d is the number of obstacles (i.e. walls and doors) between the transmitter and the receiver and $L_o = 2\ dB$ is the path loss associated to each obstacle. After executing the *AP relocation algorithm*, the best solution found is illustrated in Fig. 3. It consists in moving AP3 to the location *[32, 2]* while keeping AP1 in its current location. This solution has a cost of 75.58 which is considerably better than the cost of 93.6 that was obtained before the execution of the *AP relocation algorithm*.

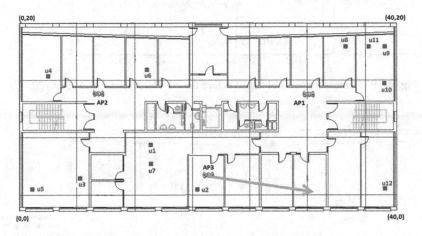

Fig. 3. Solution proposed by the genetic algorithm.

In order to empirically validate the solution proposed by the genetic *AP relocation algorithm*, several RSSI measurements have been done at 47 different locations of the building before and after the AP relocation (i.e. with AP3 located at coordinates *[20, 4]* and *[32, 2]*, respectively). For each location, the RSSI averaged in a period of 2 min is obtained. Figures 4 and 5 present the average RSSI measurements obtained before and after the AP relocation, respectively. After the AP3 relocation, an average $RSSI = -67\ dBm$ has been measured at u_{12} (i.e. coordinates *[39, 2]*) which is considerably better than an average $RSSI = -82\ dBm$ at the same location before the AP3 relocation.

Moreover, the AP relocation guarantees an RSSI higher than the threshold $RSSI_{cov} =$ *−75 dBm* for all the locations of the scenario. Some other validations have been done by moving AP3 to different locations and collecting the new values of the average RSSI measurements. For example, moving AP3 closer to the location of sample u_{12} (e.g. to coordinates *[37, 2]*) is not a feasible solution since it causes some coverage problems at region around *[17, 8]*. Similarly, relocating AP3 to coordinates *[28, 2]* (i.e. not so close to u_{12}) guarantees the coverage RSSI requirements at all the locations of the building but, an average RSSI = −73 dBm is measured at u_{12}, which is not as good as the average RSSI = −67 dBm obtained when implementing the best solution proposed by the genetic *AP relocation algorithm*.

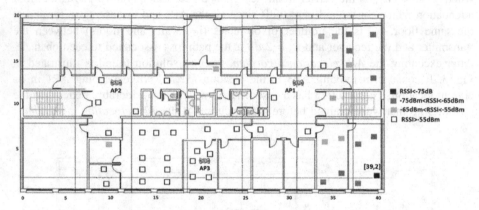

Fig. 4. RSSI measurements obtained before the AP Relocation i.e. AP3 at *[20, 4]*.

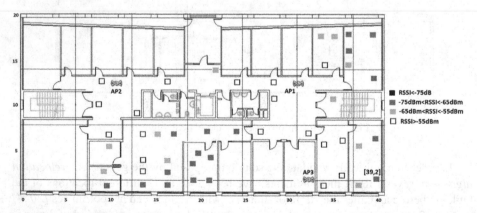

Fig. 5. RSSI measurements obtained after the AP Relocation i.e. AP3 at *[32, 2]*.

5 Conclusions

This paper has presented a new self-planning methodology to determine adequate relocations of APs in a Wi-Fi network based on information about signal quality and user traffic demands extracted from network measurements collected and processed by a monitoring and analytics system. From these measurements, the proposed methodology identifies regions with poor RSSI/SNR and high traffic demand, determines candidate APs to be relocated and applies a genetic algorithm optimization to recommend new locations for these APs. The paper has presented an empirical validation of the algorithm performance, making use of measurements collected from a real Wi-Fi network and comparing the obtained RSSI at different locations before and after the execution of the AP relocation.

Acknowledgements. This work has been supported by the EU funded H2020 5G-PPP project 5G ESSENCE under grant agreement 761592 and by the Spanish Research Council and FEDER funds under SONAR 5G grant (ref. TEC2017-82651-R).

References

1. Cisco Visual Networking Index. "Forecast and Trends, 2017–2022". Cisco white papers, November 2018
2. Ramiro, J., Hamied, K.: Self-Organising Networks. UMTS and LTE. Wiley, London, Self-Planning, Self-Optimization and Self-Healing for GSM (2012)
3. Gacanin, H., Ligata, A.: Wi-Fi self-organizing networks: SON challenges and use cases. IEEE Commun. Mag. **55**(7), 158–164 (2017)
4. Singhal, C., Swades, D.: eM-SON: efficient multimedia service over self-organising Wi-Fi network. IET Networks **7**, 181–189 (2018)
5. Muñoz, P., Sallent, O., Pérez-Romero, J.: Self dimensioning and planning of small cell capacity in multi-tenant 5G networks. IEEE Trans. Veh. Tech. **67**, 4552–4564 (2018)
6. Politi, A., Zamboni, L.C., Pasti, R., de Castro, L.N.: An optimization model for the indoor access point placement problem with different types of obstacles. In: Latin America Congress on Computational Intelligence (LA-CCI) (2015)
7. Atawia, R., Gacanin, H.: Self-deployment of future indoor Wi-Fi networks: an artificial intelligence approach. In: IEEE Global Communications Conference (GLOBECOM) (2017)
8. Chin-Lin, I., Liu, Y., Han, S., Wang, S., Liu, G.: On big data analytics for greener and softer RAN. IEEE Access **3**, 3068–3075 (2015)
9. Perez-Romero, J., et al.: Monitoring and analytics for the optimisation of cloud enabled small cells. IEEE International Workshop on Computer-Aided Modeling Analysis and Design of Communication Links and Networks (CAMAD), September 2018
10. Kim, J., Helmy, A.: Analysing the mobility, predictability and evolution of WLAN users. Int. J. Auton. Adapt. Commun. Syst. **7**, 169–191 (2014)
11. Ruiz-Ruiz, A., Blunck, H., Prentow, T., Stisen, A., Kjaergaard, M.: Analysis methods for extracting knowledge from large-scale wifi monitoring to inform building facility planning. In: IEEE International Conference on Pervasive Computing and Communications, March 2014

12. Redondi, A.E., Cesana, M., Weibel, D.M., Fitzgerald, E.: Understanding the WiFi usage of University Students. In: International Wireless Communications and Mobile Computing Conference (2016)
13. Ciurana, M., Barceló, F.: Indoor tracking in WLAN location with TOA measurements. In: 4th International Workshop on Mobility Management and Wireless Access, Torremolinos, Spain (2006)
14. Wang, X., Gao, L., Mao, S., Pandey, S.: CSI-based fingerprinting for indoor localization: a deep learning approach. IEEE Trans. Veh. Technol. **66**, 763–776 (2017)
15. Aarts, E., Korst, J.: Simulated Annealing and Boltzmann Machines. Wiley, London (1989)
16. Davis, L. (ed.): Handbook of Genetic Algorithms. International Thomson Computer Press, Stamford (1996)
17. Cisco Prime Infrastructure 3.5 Administrator Guide. www.cisco.com
18. Propagation data and prediction methods for the planning of indoor radio communication systems and the radio local area networks in the frequency range 900 MHz to 100 GHz, ITU-R Recommendations, Geneva (2001)

Enhanced Mobile Broadband as Enabler for 5G: Actions from the Framework of the 5G-DRIVE Project

Ioannis P. Chochliouros[1]([⊠]) [iD], Na Yi[2], Anastasia S. Spiliopoulou[1], Alexandros Kostopoulos[1], Nathan Gomes[3], Uwe Herzog[4], Tao Chen[5], Athanassios Dardamanis[6], Olga Segou[7], Philippos Assimakopoulos[3], Klaus Moessner[2], Juha Jidbeck[5], Rahim Tafazolli[2], and Latif Ladid[8]

[1] Hellenic Telecommunications Organization (OTE) S.A., 99 Kifissias Avenue, 15124 Maroussi, Athens, Greece
ichochliouros@oteresearch.gr
[2] University of Surrey, ICS, Stag Hill, Guildford, Surrey GU2 7HX, UK
[3] University of Kent, Jennison Building, Canterbury, Kent CT2 7NZ, UK
[4] EURESCOM GmbH, Wieblinger Weg 19/64, 69123 Heidelberg, Germany
[5] VTT Technical Research Center of Finland, Kaitoväylä 1, 90571 Oulu, Finland
[6] SmartNet S.A., 2 Lakonias Street, 17342 Ilioupolis, Athens, Greece
[7] ORION Innovations PC, 43, Ameinokleous Street, 17444 Athens, Greece
[8] University of Luxembourg, 6, Avenue de la Fonte, 4364 Esch-sur-Alzette, Luxembourg

Abstract. In the new fascinating era of 5G, new communication requirements set diverse challenges upon existing networks, both in terms of technologies and business models. One among the essential categories of the innovative 5G mobile network services is the enhanced Mobile Broadband (eMBB), mainly aiming to fulfill users' demand for an increasingly digital lifestyle and focusing upon facilities that implicate high requirements for bandwidth. In this paper we have discussed eMBB as the first commercial use of the 5G technology. Then, we have focused upon the original context of the 5G-DRIVE research project between the EU and China, and we have identified essential features of the respective eMBB trials, constituting one of the corresponding core activities. In addition, we have discussed proposed scenarios and KPIs for assessing the scheduled experimental work, based on similar findings from other research and/or standardization activities.

Keywords: The Third Generation Partnership Project (3GPP) · 5G · 5G New Radio (5G NR) · enhanced Mobile Broadband (eMBB) · massive Machine Type Communication (mMTC) · Ultra-Reliable and Low-Latency Communication (URLLC)

© IFIP International Federation for Information Processing 2019
Published by Springer Nature Switzerland AG 2019
J. MacIntyre et al. (Eds.): AIAI 2019 Workshops, IFIP AICT 560, pp. 31–45, 2019.
https://doi.org/10.1007/978-3-030-19909-8_3

1   Introduction

Both the European and the global economy have faced multiple challenges for growth due to the immense evolution of the Internet and the expansion of the broader electronic communications sector in a fully converged environment, promoting competition and wider service offerings for the involved market players [1]. Within the forthcoming years it is also expected that the underlying (usually heterogeneous) network infrastructure will be able of "*connecting everything*" according to an extended multiplicity of application-*specific* requirements (thus including users, things, goods, computing centres, content, knowledge, information and processes), in a purely flexible, mobile, and quite powerful way.

In order to "face" these major challenges, such innovative aspects not only necessitate but also imply for the proper establishment and the effective operation and management of a relevant novel kind of infrastructure being able to deliver network attributes and performance characteristics to assure progress and growth in all corresponding domains (i.e., technical, business, financial, regulatory, social, etc.). Major network operators are strongly involved in such processes, whilst creating new opportunities for novelty and investments. These chances are so expected to take place within the forthcoming "fifth generation" -*or 5G*- of telecoms systems, that will be the most critical building block of our "digital society" in the following years [2]; in particular, 5G will not only be an evolution of mobile broadband networks but will "bring" new unique network and service capabilities, creating a sustainable and scalable technology as well as a proper ecosystem for technical and business innovation [3, 4]. 5G has the potential to deliver substantial performance and capacity improvements for personal, public and enterprise communications. It has also the ability to provide a suitable communication solution basis for many vertical applications, as well as to offer new architectural concepts and value chains to efficiently support innovation and future needs [5]. 5G can therefore facilitate connectivity, network access and service security of different vertical sectors and be instrumental to the management and automation of business assets and processes.

The 5G system is expected to be able to deliver optimized support for a diversity of services, traffic loads and end-user communities [6]. To this aim, several industrial approaches [7] have proposed the conceptual framework of a system concurrently supporting various combinations of reliability, latency, throughput, positioning and availability. This sort of growth and development can be realised via the inclusion of modern technologies, both in access and the core network concept, offering flexibility and scalability of involved network resources. However, apart from increased flexibility and optimization, a 5G system has to support strict KPIs (Key Performance Indicators) for latency, reliability, throughput, etc. Furthermore, a modern 5G system is also expected to support innovative business models such as those for IoT (Internet of Things) and enterprise managed networks. Flexible network operations are essential features of the 5G system. Offering the intended degree of flexibility implicates the usage of features such as network slicing, network capability exposure, scalability, and diverse mobility. The 5G system will handle the great variability of all potential scenarios of use in a resource efficient manner. The corresponding use cases introduce new deployment requirements for indoor and outdoor, local area connectivity, high user density, wide area connectivity, and User Equipments (UEs) travelling at high speeds. Other 5G aspects may implicate requirements for various combinations of latency and reliability, as well as higher accuracy for positioning.

The work in the present paper is as follows: Sect. 2 discusses the critical role of the enhanced Mobile Broadband (eMBB) as a promoter of the first phase of the 5G implementation, within the scope of the New Radio (NR) actions, as originally performed by the Third Generation Partnership project (3GPP). Then Sect. 3 emphasizes on context of the specific eMBB trials within the framework of the 5G-DRIVE project; in particular, we identify several scenarios which include indoor hotspot, dense urban deployment and macro cells deployment and we propose related attributes. In order to promote the project actions for the scheduled trials, we also identify and briefly discuss corresponding KPIs, coming from similar research and/or standardization actions. Finally, Sect. 4 provides several concluding remarks.

2   Enhanced Mobile Broadband as Fundamental Enabler of the "First Phase of 5G"

The eMBB is one of three primary 5G New Radio use cases [8] defined by the 3GPP as part of its SMARTER ("Study on New Services and Markets Technology Enablers") project [9, 10]. The 3GPP qualifies ultra-fast mobile broadband as mobile systems capable of delivering speeds of 20 gigabits per second, at least uni-directionally, and without specific latency requirements [11]. The eMBB will initially be an extension to existing 4G services and will be among the first 5G services, which could be commercially available as early as 2019. The objective behind SMARTER [12] was to develop high level use cases and identify what features and functionality 5G would need to deliver to enable them. This specific project began in 2015 and resulted in over 70 use cases, initially grouped into five essential categories which have, *since*, been trimmed to three. They are characterised by the performance attributes the particular use cases will require, although there is some overlap. The three fundamental sets of use cases are as follows:

- *Enhanced Mobile Broadband (eMBB):* This "addresses" the human-centric use cases for access to multi-media content, services and data. Based on the original scope of the SMARTER approach, related requirements have been defined on high data rates, higher traffic or connection density, high user mobility, and those relevant to various deployment and coverage scenarios. The scenarios have addressed different service areas (e.g., indoor/outdoor, urban and rural areas, office and home, local and wide areas connectivity), and special deployments (e.g., massive gatherings, broadcast, residential, and high-speed vehicles). Actual technology trends purely "demonstrate" that the demand for mobile broadband will continue to increase, thus leading to enhanced Mobile Broadband. The enhanced Mobile Broadband usage scenario will come with new application areas and requirements in addition to existing Mobile Broadband applications for improved performance and an increasingly seamless user experience. This usage scenario covers a range of cases, including wide-area coverage and hotspot, which have different requirements. We can distinguish the following: (i) For a hotspot case, that is for an area with high user density, very high traffic capacity is needed, while the requirement for mobility is low and user data rate is higher than that of wide area coverage; (ii) For the wide area coverage case, seamless coverage and medium to high mobility are desired, with much improved user data rate compared to existing data rates. However, the data rate requirement may be relaxed compared to hotspot. The eMBB traffic can be considered to be a direct extension of the 4G broadband service. It is characterized by large payloads and by a device activation pattern that remains stable over an extended time interval. This allows the network to schedule wireless resources to the eMBB devices such that no two eMBB devices access the same resource simultaneously. The objective of the eMBB service is to maximize the data rate, while guaranteeing a moderate reliability, with packet error rate (PER) on the order of 10^{-3}.

- *Ultra-Reliable Low Latency Communications (URLLC):* This set has stringent requirements for capabilities such as throughput, latency and availability. In particular, it implicates for strict requirements on latency and reliability for mission critical communications, such as remote surgery, autonomous vehicles or the Tactile Internet; the latter can be defined by extremely low latency in combination with high availability, reliability and security and it will have a marked impact on business and society, introducing numerous new opportunities for emerging technology markets and the delivery of essential public services. Some other examples include wireless control of industrial manufacturing or production processes, remote medical surgery, distribution automation in a smart grid, transportation safety, etc. URLLC transmissions are also intermittent, but the set of potential URLLC transmitters is much smaller than for mMTC. Supporting intermittent URLLC transmissions requires a combination of scheduling, so as to ensure a certain amount of predictability in the available resources and thus support high reliability; as well as random access, in order to avoid that too many resources being idle due to the intermittent traffic. Due to the low latency requirements, a URLLC transmission should be localized in time. Diversity, which is critical to achieve high reliability, can hence be achieved only using multiple frequency or spatial resources. The rate of a URLLC transmission is relatively low, and the main requirement is ensuring a high reliability level, with a PER typically lower than 10^{-5}, despite the small block-lengths.

- *Massive Machine Type Communications (mMTC):* This set is characterised by a very large number of connected devices typically transmitting a relatively low volume of non-delay-sensitive data. These devices are usually located in a small area, which may only send data sporadically, such as Internet of Things (IoT) use cases. Devices are required to be low cost, and have a very long battery life. The mMTC has been already developed as part of 3GPP Release 13/ Release 14 [13, 14] low power wide area (LPWA) technologies [15], which includes Narrowband Internet of Things (NB-IoT). These are expected to "meet" most 5G mMTC requirements, while others that require more bandwidth with ultra-reliable low latency (full URLLC) will require the 5G Core deployment for full end-to-end latency reduction. Mission critical applications that are especially latency-*sensitive* will also require wide coverage, which is highly unlikely in early 5G deployments, so this development is expected to come later. An mMTC device is active intermittently and uses a fixed, typically low, transmission rate in the uplink. A huge number of mMTC devices may be connected to a given base station (BS), but at a given time only an unknown (random) subset of them become active and attempt to send their data. The large number of potentially active mMTC devices makes it infeasible to allocate a priori resources to individual mMTC devices. Instead, it is necessary to provide resources that can be shared through random access. The size of the active subset of mMTC devices is a random variable, whose average value measures the mMTC traffic arrival rate. The objective in the design of mMTC is to maximize the arrival rate that can be supported in a given radio resource. The targeted PER of an individual mMTC transmission is typically low, e.g., on the order of 10^{-1}.

The grand objective of 5G wireless technology is to support the above three generic services with vastly heterogeneous requirements, that is eMBB, mMTC and URLLC. Service heterogeneity can be accommodated by network slicing, through which each service is allocated resources to provide performance guarantees and isolation from the other services [16]. Under a broader concept, the Mobile Broadband (MBB) enhancements aim to fulfil a number of innovative KPIs. These pertain to high data rates, high user density, high user mobility, highly variable data rates, deployment, and coverage. High data rates are driven by the increasing use of data for services such as streaming (e.g., video, music, and user generated content), interactive services (e.g., Augmented Reality (AR)), and IoT.

More specifically, to support the initial rollout of eMBB services, since March 2017 the 3GPP's RAN (Radio Access Network) Group committed to finalise the Non-Standalone (NSA) 5G NR variant by March 2018. In fact, the standard was approved in December 2017 [17]. The NSA mode considers the current 4G network, as supplemented by 5G NR carriers to boost data rates and decrease latency. The NSA 5G NR will utilize the existing LTE (Long Term Evolution) radio and core network as an "anchor" for mobility management and coverage, while adding a new 5G carrier. This is the configuration that will be the target of early 2019 deployments (in 3GPP terminology, this is NSA 5G NR deployment scenario Option 3). The Standalone (SA) variant was to be completed by September 2018 but was also finished early, in June 2018. The SA 5G NR implies full user and control plane capability for 5G NR, utilizing the 5G next-generation core network architecture (5G NGC) also being done in 3GPP. SA 5G NR technical specifications have been completed in June 2018 as part of 3GPP Release 15. Thus, eMBB can be assessed as "the first phase of 5G", which will be encompassed in the 3GPP Release 15 standard [18]. The 5G Phase 2 will go beyond the eMBB services to more transformational URLLC and mMTC applications and will be included in Release 16, which is due to be completed at the end of 2019. By considering the case of connected cars as a characteristic example, the first phase of eMBB services will include enhanced in-vehicle infotainment, like real-time traffic alerts, high-speed internet access, streaming real-time video or playing games involving 3D 4K video. The second phase would involve autonomous vehicles on a mass scale capable of connecting to and interacting with other vehicles and/or with the nearby road infrastructure [19].

Following to the above context, the eMBB can be seen as a natural development of current 4G networks that will deliver faster data rates and, *consequently*, a better user experience than present mobile broadband services [20]. Nevertheless, it is expected that eMBB will evolve further and assure faster downloads to offer a progressively more seamless user experience that will conceal the quality of service we now experience from fixed broadband technologies. In the long run, it will also allow the provision of 360° video streaming, rightly immersive Virtual Reality (VR) and Augmented Reality applications and a variety of modern solutions. In fact, if we assess the framework of potential eMBB use cases, there are three separate features that 5G has to guarantee: (i) Higher capacity, which implicates that broadband access has to be offered in densely populated areas, both indoors and outdoors (including, for example: city centres, office buildings or public venues such as malls, stadiums, conference centres, concerts sites, etc.); (ii) enhanced connectivity, implicating that broadband access has to be obtainable everywhere with the aim of offering a reliable user experience, and; (iii) higher user mobility that will allow for the provision of mobile broadband services in moving vehicles (including cars, buses, trains and planes). These categories of use cases will implicate for diverse requirements. In fact, as of the case of a "hotspot" scenario where there are many end-users (such as viewers at a sporting event), there will be a prerequisite for very high traffic capacity to satisfy the needs of all the participating end-users, but these will be static -or moving slowly- so the request for mobility will be assessed as low. However, when offering eMBB services/facilities to travellers in a high-speed train this by default necessitates for a high degree of mobility although the traffic capacity shall be lower than if compared to that of a hotspot scenario. Being somewhere between the above two essential use cases, the coverage of a wide area may implicate for a kind of "medium" level of mobility and although data throughput can be higher than the actual experience, it cannot be as high as in a hotspot.

3   eMBB Within the Context of the 5G-DRIVE Project

The 5G-DRIVE project [21] as it is actually funded by the European Commission within the framework of the 5G-PPP Phase 3 [22], aims to perform a "close" collaboration between EU and China to synchronise 5G technologies and spectrum issues before the final roll-out of 5G in order to "address" two most promising 5G deployment scenarios, namely enhanced Mobile Broadband (eMBB) and Vehicle-to-Everything (V2X) communications.

The main scope of the 5G-DRIVE's effort is to conduct 5G trials addressing two specific scenarios of prime importance in modern 5G-oriented applications, as follows: (i) Scenario no 1 - enhanced Mobile Broadband (eMBB) on the 3.5 GHz band, which is a priority band in the two regions for early introduction of very high rate services; *and*; (ii) Scenario no 2 - Internet of Vehicles (IoV) based on LTE-V2X using the 5.9 GHz band for Vehicle-to-Vehicle (V2V) and the 3.5 GHz band for Vehicle-to-Network (V2N). The overall goal is to evaluate in real setup innovative end-to-end 5G systems built on the outcomes of the previous phases of the 5G Research and

Innovation (R&I). Both scenarios shall be implemented in both regions through test-beds with interoperability forming the core of the R&I work.

The underlying trials' testing facilities shall implement the latest mature and broadly commonly agreed 5G systems, network architectures and technologies spanning from the core/transport networks, the radio access, up to the service, orchestration, management and security components. The trial facility shall not be restricted to innovative 5G radio access technology, but should include and enable the evolution of 5G networks innovations in network slicing, virtualisation, cross-domain orchestration, in view of supporting resource control from multiple tenants.

The focus of the testing will be upon the radio interface except for some KPIs, features and use cases selected for eMBB scenarios considered in the 5G-DRIVE, which need to be quantified in an end-to-end configuration, (e.g., various latency measurements, network slicing, etc.). Subject to the availability of trial sites, the non-standalone version or the standalone version of 5G NR will be chosen accordingly. In the NSA architecture, the trials need to consider collocated and non-collocated NR and LTE radio suites to test the dual connectivity between both technologies.

3.1 eMBB Trials Scenarios in the 5G-DRIVE Framework

The collected data of tests will be compared with the targeted requirements and expected performance defined in 3GPP release 15 or release 16 or in the ITU-RM.2410-0 [23], subject to the individual requirement of each trial. The primary aim of building pre-commercial end-to-end testbeds is to test 5G NR with a focus on eMBB using close-to-commercial equipment in realistic settings, which can "reflect" near real-life network performance.

Table 1. Deployment attributes for the eMBB trials scenarios within the 5G-DRIVE framework (i.e.: indoor hotspot, dense urban and urban macro, *accordingly*).

Attributes	Indoor hotspot scenario	Dense urban scenario	Urban macro scenario
Carrier Frequency	Sub 6 GHz (around 3.5 GHz)	Sub 6 GHz (around 3.5 GHz)	Sub 6 GHz (around 3.5 GHz)
Aggregated system bandwidth	100 MHz for sub 6 GHz	100 MHz for sub 6 GHz	100 MHz for sub 6 GHz
Sub-carrier spacing	30 kHz for sub 6 GHz	30 kHz for sub 6 GHz	30 kHz for sub 6 GHz
Carrier prefix (CP) length	2.3 us	2.3 us	2.3 us
Slot length	0.5 ms (14 symbols), 0.25 ms (7 symbols) for sub 6 GHz	0.5 ms (14 symbols), 0.25 ms (7 symbols) for sub6 GHz	0.5 ms (14 symbols), 0.25 ms (7 symbols) for sub6 GHz
Number of layers	1	2	1

(continued)

Table 1. (*continued*)

Attributes	Indoor hotspot scenario	Dense urban scenario	Urban macro scenario
BS antenna elements	Up to 256 Tx and Rx antenna elements (64 or 128 is recommended)	Up to 256 Tx and Rx antenna elements (64 or 128 is recommended)	Up to 256 Tx and Rx antenna elements (64 or 128 is recommended)
UE antenna elements	Up to 8 Tx and Rx antenna elements (4 is recommended) for sub 6 GHz	Up to 8 Tx and Rx antenna elements (4 is recommended) for sub 6 GHz	Up to 8 Tx and Rx antenna elements (4 is recommended) for sub 6 GHz
User location and speed	100% indoor, 3 km/h	100% outdoor, 3 km/h	80% indoor (3 km/h) and 20% outdoor (30 km/h)
Traffic type	Full buffer traffic or non-full buffer traffic depends on the scenario	Full buffer traffic or non-full buffer traffic depends on the scenario	Full buffer traffic or non-full buffer traffic depends on the scenario
Inter site distance	20 m	200 m	500 m

In the 5G-DRIVE project, the collected test data from the two regions (EU and China) will be analysed and compared for interoperability purposes. Therefore, some general trial setup requirements should be listed so that to harmonize the trial development facilities at the various trial sites. The trials planned will cover several deployment scenarios, which include indoor hotspot, dense urban deployment and macro cells deployment. In order to achieve important results, there would have to be enough sites to fulfil the following: (i) Areas with excellent signal to noise ratio (SNR) and negligible interference for peak performance measurements; (ii) areas with poor SNR for minimum performance measurements, and; (iii) areas with low to very high interference for realistic interference measurements. For a dense urban macro deployment, the minimum number of sites would be different to that in an indoor or rural environment in order to achieve the above.

Table 1 illustrates descriptions of the three scenarios, as also provided by NGMN in [24], which will be employed as reference setups for the 5G-DRIVE trial sites, together with the relevant attributes. The indoor hotspot scenario focuses on high user density and high capacity/throughput in indoor small coverage areas. The dense urban scenario focuses on high use density and high traffic loads in city centres with outdoor coverage scenario. Finally, the urban macro scenario focuses on continuous coverage in urban areas.

3.2 KPIs for the Assessment of the eMBB Trials

In the following subsections we list the relevant 5G KPIs related to the radio access network and use as a reference for different trial sites to conduct trials under the same baseline. The sources of the KPI definitions come from various prior works such as: (i) the ITU-R M.2410-0 [23]; (ii) the NGMN 5G Trial and Testing Initiative Pre-commercial Network Trials Framework Definition [24]; (iii) 5G-PPP KPI definitions [25–30], *and*; (iv) the framework proposed by 3GPP in TS 28.554 [31]. Note that the KPIs defined in the above documents are used to provide a throughout performance evaluation of 5G systems, within a broader scope. However, considering the capability and availability of the trial facilities in the 5G-DRIVE project, only a selected set of KPIs will be later evaluated in this project. For this reason, we only list the KPIs relevant to the 5G-DRIVE trials and provide the test procedure. By following the common test procedure, the trial results from different trial sites can be compared. A selected set of KPIs are planned to be measured in both the 5G-DRIVE and the Chinese "twin" project and results will be reported in the joint trial reports. In the following, we first provide the definition of the selected KPIs and describe the test setup, test procedure, evaluation criteria and reporting process of each KPI.

Data rate is the number of bits transmitted through the system per unit of time. There are different terms to represent the data rate. Some documents use the term "data rate", while others use the term "throughput". They have the same meaning in this document. Thus otherwise explicitly mentioned, they are used exchangeable. There are several data rate KPIs related to the performance of 5G systems. In the 5G-DRIVE project, we will "address" peak data rate, user experienced data rate, and cell-edge user data rate. The definitions of these are given below.

Peak data rate in bit/s is the maximum achievable data rate under ideal conditions to a single mobile station, to which all assignable radio resources for the corresponding link direction are assigned, except the radio resources used for PHY (Physical) layer synchronization, reference and pilot signals, guard bands and guard times. In some documents, it is referred to the peak user throughput. The peak data rate can be derived from the simulation and theoretical analysis. In this project, we will measure the data rate through the trials. In this context, it is the maximum DL (Downlink)/UL (Uplink) data rate achievable for a single user located at the best location within a cell. Peak data rate is defined for a single mobile station. In a single band, it is related to the peak spectral efficiency in that band. Let W denote the channel bandwidth and SE_p denote the peak spectral efficiency in that band. Then the user peak data rate R_p is given by:

$$R_P = W \times SE_p \tag{1}$$

Peak spectral efficiency and available bandwidth may have different values in different frequency ranges. In case bandwidth is aggregated across multiple bands, the peak data rate will be summed over the bands. Therefore, if bandwidth is aggregated across Q bands then the total peak data rate is

$$R = \sum_{i=1}^{Q} W_i \times SEp_i \tag{2}$$

where W_i and SEp_i ($i = 1,...Q$) are the component bandwidths and spectral efficiencies respectively. The peak data rate is defined for the purpose of evaluation in the eMBB usage scenario. In [23], the minimum requirements for peak data rate are as follows:

(i) Downlink peak data rate is 20 Gbit/s; (ii) Uplink peak data rate is up to 10 Gbit/s. Note that these requirements make assumptions on the 5G spectrum used in the system. In the project, the measurement results will depend on the availability of the spectrum and the trial setting, which may result in lower peak data rate values.

User experienced data rate is the 5% point of the cumulative distribution function (CDF) of the user throughput. User throughput is defined as the number of correctly received bits, i.e. the number of bits contained in the service data units (SDUs) delivered to Layer 3, over a certain period of time. In case of one frequency band and one layer of transmission reception points (TRxP), the user experienced data rate could be derived from the 5th percentile user spectral efficiency through the following equation. Let W denote the channel bandwidth and SE_{user} denote the 5th percentile user spectral efficiency. Then the user experienced data rate, R_{user} is given by:

$$R_{user} = W \times SE_{user} \qquad (3)$$

In case bandwidth is aggregated across multiple bands (one or more TRxP layers), the user experienced data rate will be summed over the bands. The target values for the user experienced data rate are as follows in the Dense Urban – eMBB test environment: (i) Downlink user experienced data rate is 100 Mbit/s; (ii) Uplink user experienced data rate is 50 Mbit/s. These values are defined assuming supportable bandwidth as described in [23] for each test environment. In the project, the measurement results will depend on the availability of the bandwidth.

Cell-edge user data rate: In 3GPP, the cell edge user data rate is defined as the 5% point of the CDF of user's average data rate. The user's average data rate is linked to the average spectral efficiency, used bandwidth and the number of TRxP used in the system. The average spectral efficiency is the aggregate throughput of all users divided by the channel bandwidth of a specific band divided by the number of TRxPs and is measured in bit/s/Hz/TRxP. In the NGMN trial framework document [24], it refers to cell edge coverage throughput, which is defined as the user data rate at the location of the cell edge with 1–3 dB lower path loss compared to control channel coverage limit (path loss limit).

Latency: As 5G will support ultra-low latency services, the latency is an important parameter to be evaluated in trials. In communications, the latency is the time interval for a bit of data, usually a data packet, to travel across the network from one node or endpoint to another. According to the purpose of evaluation, there are two types of latencies: user plane latency and control plane latency. Depending on which part of user plane is targeted, the user plane latency can be the end-to-end latency, RAN latency and core latency [24]. The control plane latency under the 5G context is tightly related to the radio resource control (RRC) state transitions in the control plane. In this work, we only give the brief definition of these two latencies.

User plane latency: At the application level, the most important latency is the end-to-end latency, which is the maximum tolerable elapsed time from the instant a data packet is generated at the source application to the instant it is received by the desti-nation application. If direct mode is used, this is essentially the maximum tolerable air interface latency. If infrastructure mode is used, this includes the time needed for uplink, any necessary routing in the infrastructure, and downlink. The RAN latency refers to the delay occurring in the RAN. It includes the time it takes to successfully deliver an application layer packet/message from the radio protocol layer 2/3 service data unit ingress point to the radio protocol layer 2/3 SDU egress point via the radio interface in both uplink and downlink directions, where neither device nor base station reception is restricted by discontinuous reception mode (DRX). The core latency refers to the round trip time between gNB and the Application Server. The minimum requirements (recommended by [23]) for the RAN latency are 8 ms for eMBB assuming unloaded conditions (i.e. a single user) for small Internet protocol (IP) packets (e.g. 0 byte payload + IP header), for both downlink and uplink.

Control plane latency refers to the transition time at the UE side from the idle or inactive RRC state to the start of continuous data transfer (e.g. Active state) [32]. The minimum requirement for control plane latency is 20 ms.

Cell capacity is the KPI to evaluate the aggregate capacity of multiple users served by a cell. It can be measured by the cell peak throughput and cell average throughput. In the measurement, multiple UEs are placed in the different locations to represent different propagation environments. The results of cell capacity can be explained as the spectrum efficiency. The cell peak throughput represents the maximum transmission capability of a single cell, without inter-cell interference from other cells. In the measurement of this KPI, all UEs will be placed in the locations with good channel quality. The cell average throughput represents the average transmission capability of a single cell, with the inter-cell interference from neighbouring cells. The tested UEs will be placed in different locations with different level of channel qualities. Among the UEs, the channel qualities to the gNB will be divided to four types: excellent, good, medium, and poor. The average capacity test should consider both UL and DL inter-ference from other cells. In the cell capacity measurement, both single cell and multi-cell should be considered to reflect the cell capacity in different inter-cell interference.

Spectrum efficiency refers to the data rate that can be transmitted over a given bandwidth in a communication system. In the 5G-DRIVE project, it is the data rate per UE at given condition divided by the bandwidth used by UE for corresponding data rate. It is an important performance KPI of 5G system. The spectrum efficiency is also a good indicator to show the performance difference between 4G and 5G systems. Since the spectrum efficiency is obtained from the data rate measurement under a certain bandwidth configuration, the results from user throughput and cell capacity measure-ment can be used to derive the spectrum efficiency. The project will take into account three spectrum efficiency KPIs: (i) Peak spectral efficiency, derived from peak user rate test results; (ii) average spectral efficiency, derived from cell average throughput test results, *and*; (iii) cell edge spectrum efficiency, derived from Cell-edge user data rate test results.

Coverage: The coverage area of a mobile system is the geographic area where the base station and the user device can communicate. The coverage is evaluated by the communication availability, in which the signal strength of a cell needs to exceed a defined minimum threshold and the achieved service quality, in which a minimum data rate in case of mobile data services or a minimum speech quality in case of voice services is required. The coverage depends on several factors, including the environment, buildings, technology and radio frequency and most importantly for two-way telecommunications the sensitivity and transmit efficiency including maximum output power of the base station and the end-user device. To evaluate the coverage of 5G system, the following aspects need to be taken into account: coverage gap between 4G and 5G, beamforming capability of 5G gNB (next generation NodeB) [8], downlink data/control channel coverage difference, and uplink coverage enhancement at UE. Depending on the setting of the trial networks, the following coverage can be evaluated: outdoor single-cell coverage, outdoor multi-cell continued coverage, outdoor to indoor coverage, and indoor coverage. Considering the capability of the trial sites in the project, we will focus on the outdoor single-cell coverage and indoor coverage evaluation.

Mobility is the maximum mobile station speed at which a defined QoS can be achieved (in km/h).The following classes of mobility are defined: (i) Stationary: 0 km/h; (ii) pedestrian: 0 km/h to 10 km/h; (iii) vehicular: 10 km/h to 120 km/h, and; (iv) high speed vehicular: 120 km/h to 500 km/h.

Reliability relates to the capability of transmitting a given amount of traffic within a predetermined time duration with high success probability. Reliability is the success probability of transmitting a layer 2/3 packet within a required maximum time, which is the time it takes to deliver a small data packet from the radio protocol layer 2/3 SDU ingress point to the radio protocol layer 2/3 SDU egress point of the radio interface at a certain channel quality. While the reliability is one of the main KPIs to evaluate URLLC performance, we will evaluate this KPI under eMBB trials. The minimum requirement for the reliability is $1-10^{-5}$ success probability of transmitting a layer 2 PDU (protocol data unit) of 32 bytes within 1 ms in channel quality of coverage edge for the Urban Macro-URLLC test environment, assuming small application data (e.g. 20 bytes application data + protocol overhead). The larger packet sizes, e.g. layer 2 PDU size of up to 100 bytes, may be considered in the trials.

Area traffic capacity is the total traffic throughput served per geographic area (in Mbit/s/m^2). The throughput is the number of correctly received bits, i.e. the number of bits contained in the SDUs delivered to Layer 3, over a certain period of time. This can be derived for a particular use case (or deployment scenario) of one frequency band and one TRxP layer, based on the achievable average spectral efficiency, network deployment (e.g. TRxP (site) density) and bandwidth. Let W denote the channel bandwidth and ρ the TRxP density (TRxP/m^2). The area traffic capacity C_{area} is related to average spectral efficiency SE_{avg} through equation,

$$C_{area} = \rho \times W \times SE_{avg}. \tag{4}$$

In case bandwidth is aggregated across multiple bands, the area traffic capacity will be summed over the bands. The target value for area traffic capacity in downlink is 10 Mbit/s/m^2 in the Indoor Hotspot – eMBB test environment. The conditions for evaluation for the test environment are described in [23].

4   Conclusion

In the present work we have first delineate the importance and the multiple benefits coming from the 5G evolution, affecting both market growth and innovation. In particular, within the context of the effort for the development of the 5G NR, we have identified and discussed the critical role that eMBB has to realize, as a "promoter" of the first phase of the 5G, in parallel with standardization actions coming from the 3GPP. Thus, we have discussed the three fundamental sets of use cases comprising of eMBB, URLLC and mMTC and then we have primarily focused upon the eMBB that can be initially assessed as an extension to existing 4G services and will be among the first 5G services, which could be commercially available as early as 2019. Then we have focused on the specific framework of the actual 5G-DRIVE project funded by the European Commission, which promotes a framework for international research and cooperation between the European Union and China. Among the two core scenarios of this project is the realization of eMBB trials on the 3.5 GHz band for the support of suitable services such as AR/VR. Based on the 5G-DRIVE proposed methodology as well as to approaches proposed by the actual trends and/or bibliography, we have initially distinguished three scenarios which include indoor hotspot, dense urban deployment and macro cells deployment and we have propose corresponding attributes. With the aim of creating a framework for the effective support of the scheduled trials we have then identified and briefly discussed several corresponding KPIs. The 5G-DRIVE trials for the eMBB validation will be aligned to existing practices in order to make results comparable and meaningful.

Acknowledgments. This work has been performed in the scope of the *5G-DRIVE* European Research Project and has been supported by the Commission of the European Communities/ *H2020, Grant Agreement No. 814956.*

References

1. European Commission: Communication of the Commission: "A Digital Single Market Strategy for Europe" [COM(2015) 192 final, 06.05.2015] (2015)
2. European Commission: 5G: Challenges, Research Priorities, and Recommendations – Joint White Paper. European Commission, Strategic Research and Innovation Agenda (2014)
3. Chochliouros, I.P., et al.: Challenges for defining opportunities for growth in the 5G era: the SESAME conceptual model. In: Proceedings of the EuCNC-2016, pp. 1–5 (2016)
4. Andrews, J.G., Buzzi, S., Choi, W., Hanly, S.V., et al.: What will 5G be? IEEE JSAC, Spec. Issue 5G Wirel. Commun. Syst. **32**(6), 1065–1082 (2014)
5. European Commission (2016): Communication of the Commission: "A 5G Action Plan for Europe" [COM(2016) 588 final, 14.09.2016] (2016)
6. The 3rd Generation Partnership Project (3GPP): 3GPP TR 22.864 (V15.0.0) (2016-09): "Technical Specification Group Services and System Aspects; Feasibility Study on New Services and Markets Technology Enablers - Network Operation; Stage 1 (Release 15)" (2016)
7. El Hattachi, R., Erfanian, J.: Next Generation Mobile Networks (NGMN): NGMN 5G White Paper v1.0. Next Generation Mobile Networks Ltd., February 2015

8. The 3rd Generation Partnership Project (3GPP): TR 38.802 (V14.2.0) (2017-09): "Technical Specification Group Radio Access Network: Study on New Radio (NR) Access Technology Physical Layer Aspects (Release 14)" (2017)
9. The 3rd Generation Partnership Project (3GPP): 3GPP TR 22.891 (V14.2.0) (2016-09): "Technical Specification Group Services and System Aspects; Feasibility Study on New Services and Markets Technology Enablers; Stage 1 (Release 14)" (2016)
10. The 3rd Generation Partnership Project (3GPP): 3GPP TR 22.863 (V14.1.0) (2016-09): "Technical Specification Group Services and System Aspects; Feasibility Study on New Services and Markets Technology Enablers - Enhanced Mobile Broadband; Stage 1 (Release 14)" (2016)
11. European Telecommunications Standards Institute (ETSI): TS 122 101 (V8.7.0) (2008-01): Universal Mobile Telecommunications System (UMTS); Service aspects; Service principles (3GPP TS 22.101 version 8.7.0 Release 8)". ETSI (2008)
12. The 3rd Generation Partnership Project (3GPP): TS 22.261 V16.6.0 (2018-12): "Technical Specification Group Services and System Aspects; Service requirements for the 5G system; Stage 1 (Release 16)" (2018)
13. 3GPP: Release 13. http://www.3gpp.org/release-13
14. The 3rd Generation Partnership Project (3GPP): TS 21.914 V14.0.0 (2018-05): "Technical Specification Group Services and System Aspects; Release 14 Description; Summary of Rel-14 Work Items (Release 14)" (2018)
15. GSM Association (GSMA): 3GPP Low Power Wide Area Technologies – GSMA White Paper. GSMA (2016)
16. Popovski, P., Trillingsgaard, K.F., Simeone, O., Durisi, G.: Wireless Network Slicing for eMBB, URLLC, and mMTC: A Communication-Theoretic View. Cornell University, USA, April 2018. https://arxiv.org/abs/1804.05057
17. 3GPP. http://www.3gpp.org/news-events/3gpp-news/1836-5g_nr_workplan
18. The 3rd Generation Partnership Project (3GPP): TR 21.915 (V0.6.0) (2019-02): Technical Specification Group Services and System Aspects; Release 15 Description; Summary of Rel-15 Work Items (Release 15) (2019)
19. The 3rd Generation Partnership Project (3GPP): 3GPP TS 22.186 (V16.1.0) (2018-12): "Technical Specification Group Services and System Aspects; Enhancement of 3GPP support for V2X scenarios; Stage 1 (Release 16)" (2018)
20. Huawei Technologies Co., Ltd.: 5G Network Architecture – A High Level Perspective. Huawei Technologies Co., Ltd. (2016)
21. 5G-DRIVE ("5G harmoniseD Research and trIals for serVice Evolution between EU and China") 5G-PPP Project, Grant Agreement No. 814956. https://5g-drive.eu/
22. 5G Public Private Partnership (5G-PPP) website of Phase 3 projects. https://5g-ppp.eu/5g-ppp-phase-3-projects/
23. International Telecommunication Union – Radiocommunication Sector (ITU-R): ITU-R M2410-0: "Minimum requirements related to technical performance for IMT-2020 radio interface(s)", November 2017
24. Next Generation Mobile Networks (NGMN) Alliance: Definition of the Testing Framework for the NGMN 5G Pre-Commercial Networks Trials – Version 1.0. Next Generation Mobile Networks Ltd., January 2018
25. 5G Public Private Partnership (5G-PPP): KPIs. https://5g-ppp.eu/kpis/
26. Koumaras, H., Tsolkas, D., Gardikis, G., Merino, P.G., Frascolla, V., et al.: 5GENESIS: the genesis of a flexible 5G facility. In: Proceedings of the 2018 IEEE 23rd International Workshop on Computer Aided Modeling and Design of Communication Links and Networks (CAMAD 2018), September 2018, pp. 1–7. IEEE (2018)

27. 5GChampion Project (Grant Agreement No. 723247): Deliverable 2.2: "5GChampion Key Performance Indicator and use-cases defined and specification document written" (2017)
28. 5GCAR Project (Grant Agreement No.761510): Deliverable 2.1: "5GCAR Scenarios, Use Cases, Requirements and KPIs" (2017)
29. ONE5G Project (Grant Agreement No.760809): Deliverable 2.1: "Scenarios, KPIs, use cases and baseline system evaluation" (2017)
30. Cattoni, A.F., Madueno, G.C., Dieudonne, M., Merino, P., et al.: An end-to-end testing ecosystem for 5G the TRIANGLE testing house test bed. J. Green Eng. 6(3), 285–316 (2016)
31. The 3rd Generation Partnership Project (3GPP): 3GPP TS 28.554 (V15.1.0) (2018-12): "Technical Specification Group Services and System Aspects; Management and orchestration; 5G end to end Key Performance Indicators (Release 15)" (2018)
32. The 3rd Generation Partnership Project (3GPP): 3GPP TR 38.913 (V15.0.0) (2018-06): "Technical Specification Group Radio Access Network; Study on Scenarios and Requirements for Next Generation Access Technologies (Release 15)" (2018)

Inclusion of Telemetry and Data Analytics in the Context of the 5G ESSENCE Architectural Approach

Ioannis P. Chochliouros[1(✉)] [ID], Anastasia S. Spiliopoulou[1],
Alexandros Kostopoulos[1], George Agapiou[1], Maria Belesioti[1],
Evangelos Sfakianakis[1], Michail-Alexandros Kourtis[2],
Mike Iosifidis[3], Marinos Agapiou[4], and Pavlos Lazaridis[5]

[1] Hellenic Telecommunications Organization (OTE) S.A.,
99 Kifissias Avenue, 15124 Maroussi, Athens, Greece
ichochliouros@oteresearch.gr
[2] National Centre for Scientific Research "Demokritos",
Patriarchou Gregoriou Street, 15310 Aghia Paraskevi, Athens, Greece
[3] Clemic Services S.A., 55 Salaminos Street, 15124 Maroussi, Athens, Greece
[4] National and Kapodistrian University of Athens, 6 Panepistimiopolis,
15784 Athens, Greece
[5] The University of Huddersfield, Queensgate, HD13DH Huddersfield, UK

Abstract. The 5G will not only be a kind of progress of mobile broadband networks but will also create a set of novel and unique network and service capabilities, structuring a form of a sustainable and scalable technology. Based on the context of the on-going progress of the actual "5G-ESSENCE" EU-*funded* project and, *in particular*, upon its innovative architecture that combines a variety of features from network functions virtualisation (NFV), mobile-edge computing (MEC) and cognitive network management resulting in a pure software-driven environment in nature, we identify the importance of telemetry and analytics. These latter features are expected to play an important role in the 5G ecosystem, especially for the realisation and support of dynamic cognitive management of the 5G ESSENCE network architecture. The Cloud Enabled Small Cell Manager (CESCM) which is a "core" element of the corresponding 5G ESSENCE architectural framework encompasses telemetry and analytics as essential tools for automated and fine grained management of the network infrastructures. To this aim, we have proposed the inclusion of three distinct modules (telemetry, analytics and orchestration) to enhance the original 5G ESSENCE architecture.

Keywords: 5G · Edge Cloud computing · Mobile Edge Computing (MEC) ·
Network functions virtualization (NFV) · Network management ·
Small Cell (SC) · Network softwarisation · Telemetry and analytics ·
Virtual network function (VNF)

© IFIP International Federation for Information Processing 2019
Published by Springer Nature Switzerland AG 2019
J. MacIntyre et al. (Eds.): AIAI 2019 Workshops, IFIP AICT 560, pp. 46–59, 2019.
https://doi.org/10.1007/978-3-030-19909-8_4

1 Introduction

The 5th Generation of Mobile and Wireless Communications (the so called as "5G") represents a complete revolution of mobile networks for accommodating the over-growing demands of users, services and applications. In contrast to previous transitions between mobile networks generations, in 5G there will be a much complex management requirements based on the softwarisation of network resources [1]. This ultimately will lead to a "system" that requires real-time management based on a hierarchy of complex decision-making techniques that analyse historical, temporal and frequency network data. Simultaneously, the softwarisation feature will contribute to automating processes, optimising costs, reducing time-to-market, and providing better quality services.

Modern 5G networks represent a "shift" in networking paradigms, purely implicating to a transition from today's "network of entities" to a sort of "network of functions". Indeed, this "network of (virtual) functions" resulting in some cases in the decomposition of current monolithic network entities can be a pillar for constituting the unit of networking for next generation systems. The above mentioned functions should be able to be composed upon an "on-demand", "on-the-fly" basis. In fact, a research challenge for managing virtual network functions (VNFs) consists in designing solutions, which identify a set of elementary functions -or blocks- to compose network functions, while today they are usually implemented as monolithic. In this framework, uniform management and operations for NVFs are becoming part of the dynamic design of software architectures for 5G. The 5G will not only be a kind of progress of mobile broadband networks but will also create a set of novel and unique network and service capabilities, structuring a form of a sustainable and scalable technology. Consequently, this will support towards establishing a proper ecosystem for technical and business innovation [2]. Among current 5G's priorities is also to incorporate advanced automation, autonomicity and cognitive management features [3] to advance operators' efficiency, having a positive impact on the broader competitiveness of the European ICT industry [4].

During 5G-PPP Phase-1, the SESAME project [5] evolved the Small Cell (SC) concept by integrating processing power (i.e., a low-cost micro-server) and by enabling the execution of applications and network services, in accordance to the Mobile Edge Computing (MEC) paradigm [6]. It also provided network intelligence and applications by leveraging the Network Function Virtualisation (NFV) concept [7]. Within the actual scope of 5G-PPP Phase 2, the ongoing 5G ESSENCE project [8] mainly leverages results from the prior SESAME project as well as from other Phase 1 projects, in order to cover the specific network needs of the vertical sectors and their inter-dependencies. The 5G ESSENCE Project "addresses" the paradigms of Edge Cloud computing and Small Cell as-a-Service (SCaaS) by fueling the drivers and removing the barriers in the Small Cell (SC) market, forecasted to perform play a major role in the 5G ecosystem [6]. Thus, the 5G ESSENCE project provides a highly flexible and scalable platform, able to support new business models and revenue streams by creating a "neutral" host market and reducing operational costs, by providing new opportunities for ownership, deployment, operation and amortisation. The 5G ESSENCE enhances the processing capabilities for data that have immediate value beyond locality; it also addresses the processing-intensive small cell management functions, such as Radio Resource Management (RRM)/Self Organising Network (SON) and, *finally,* it culminates with real-life demonstrations. For all the above, the project suggests clear breakthroughs in the research fields of wireless access, network virtualisation and end-to-end (E2E) service delivery.

The 5G ESSENCE's technical approach exploits the benefits of the centralisation of Small Cell functions as scale grows through an edge cloud environment based on a two-tier architecture, that is: a first distributed tier for providing low latency services and a second centralised tier for providing high processing power for computing-intensive network applications. This allows decoupling the control and user planes of the Radio Access Network (RAN) and achieving the benefits of Cloud-RAN (C-RAN) without the enormous fronthaul latency restrictions [9]. The use of E2E network slicing mechanisms will allow sharing the 5G ESSENCE infrastructure among multiple operators/vertical industries and so customising its capabilities on a *per-tenant* basis. The versatility of the architecture is enhanced by high-performance virtualisation techniques for data isolation, latency reduction and resource efficiency, and by orchestrating lightweight virtual resources enabling efficient Virtualised Network Function placement and live migration.

2 Telemetry and Analytics in the 5G Ecosystem

Among other issues, the modern service-*driven* 5G network architectures intent to deal with and cover a wider set of diversified mobile service requirements, *via a flexible and reliable way.* With Software Defined Networking (SDN) and Network Functions Virtualisation efficiently supporting the underlying physical infrastructure, the related 5G environment can "cloudify" access, transport, and core networks in a very comprehensible and via a quite reliable manner [10, 11]. Cloud adoption allows for better support for diversified 5G services and, *furthermore*, it enables the "key technologies" of end-to-end network slicing, on-demand deployment of service anchors and component-*based* network functions. The extended adoption of SDN, NFV, Cloud and Edge Computing in 5G actual architectures results in environments which are primarily software-*driven* in nature. In turn, this sort of transformation towards "softwarisation" leads to the emergence of a great variety of challenges in *how we can effectively manage and monitor these environments.* The respective challenges are further "amplified" when these software functions need to "run" on infrastructure environments built from standard high-volume servers hosting multi-layer software functions.

On the other hand [12] the intended 5G Network Management is a non-trivial endeavor that faces a host of new challenges beyond 3G and 4G, covering all radio and non-radio segments of the network. Several factors like the number of nodes, the heterogeneity of the access technologies, the conflicting management objectives, the resource usage minimization, and the division between limited physical resources and elastic virtual resources are implicating for a critical change in the respective methodology for realising an efficient network management. In the past frameworks covering previous generations, a distinction was typically made between the control and data plane of the network. Nevertheless, the model of the actual 5G networks can be extended in terms of a "Service and Softwarisation plane", where the management of the network services and the virtualised devices is an integral and indispensable part of the overall network. This approach can be used in order to propose a model for extending the idea of network management to the reliance on an increased overall capacity of computational resources creating a robust solution.

Within the above novel framework, telemetry and analytics are expected to perform a fundamental role in the realisation and management of 5G network architectures [13]. Telemetry is an automated communications process (recording and transmission) by which measurements are made and other data collected at remote or inaccessible points and transmitted to receiving equipment for monitoring. Telemetry data may be relayed by using radio, infrared, ultrasonic, GSM, satellite or cable depending on the application (in fact, telemetry is not only used in software development, but also in meteorology, intelligence, medicine and other fields). Telemetry provides the visibility into what is actually happening in real-time within the compute, network and storage infrastructures and at the service layers. Thus, telemetry can offer insights on which features end-users use most, detection of bugs and issues, and offering better visibility into performance without the need to solicit feedback directly from users [14]. Analytics, *in turn*, provide actionable insights based on the telemetry data collected. Thus, analytics is the discovery and communication of meaningful patterns in data. Being especially valuable in areas rich with recorded information, analytics relies on the simultaneous application of statistics, computer programming and operations research to quantify performance. Analytics often favors data visualisation to communicate insight.

The quality and appropriate exploitation of these insights determines the level of intelligence that exists within a relevant 5G-*like* system architecture, particularly in the ability to automate and to provide fine-grained management of the network infrastructures. Based on actual trends and following to the results of research being in progress, it appears that the 5G architectures will be highly distributed (in particularly with (SC-) small cell-*based* edge deployments), heterogeneous and dynamic in nature [15]. These particular characteristics can have significant implications for the design and use of telemetry and analytics systems. For example, when and where analysis takes place will be constrained by the available bandwidth, processing power, network bandwidth etc. Data analytics (DA) is the process of examining data sets in order to draw conclusions about the information they contain, increasingly with the aid of specialized systems and software. Data analytics will be required to support a wide variety of usage scenarios such as identifying the bandwidth required to deliver a given level of user experience, based on application or user profiles. Analytics will also evolve beyond looking at what has happen historically within the system to provide views on "what will happen in the future", e.g. predictive service KPIs. This type of capability can support smarter and more dynamic capacity planning in order to "size" the infrastructure resources, implicating for more efficient asset utilisation in-line with the needs of the business and customers. Besides, analytics will be required to underpin faster service deployments and more responsive service behaviours based on changes in service context (e.g. bubble loads).

The use of telemetry for infrastructure and network monitoring is a well-established discipline. Yet, until today telemetry solutions have been based on a variety of either open source or proprietary tools such as Internet Protocol Flow Information (IPFix)/ NetFlow [16] or the Simple Network Management Protocol (SNMP) [17] (e.g. traps and pulling), etc. In fact, SNMP is the *de facto* telemetry protocol for collecting data from network devices. Nevertheless, its applicability diminishes significantly in NFV/SDN environments. Here, computer infrastructure type metrics have more significance, however not completely at the expensive of standard network oriented metrics. In the forthcoming 5G environments there will be significant more diversity in the sources of telemetry data which must be consumed due to a large network edge footprint and wider variety of use cases. The situation becomes even more exacerbated in multi-vendor environments, due to the complexity of device heterogeneity in different network segments. The variety and diversity of potential data sources results in different data format, data models, resolution, non-standard interfaces, etc., making it challenging to have a fully correlated and end-to-end view of the infrastructure environment and the services running in the environment. Addressing these challenges requires a telemetry fabric which provides an end-to-end platform for metrics collection and processing. The fabric also needs to have multiple hierarchical analytical and actuation points in order to efficiently exploit the metrics [18].

In 5G the use of approaches such as network slicing, push data strategies, embedded metadata, dimensional reduction, in-situ data processing etc., will be used to provide better level of control over the availability and quality of telemetry data. These capabilities lay the foundation for supporting critical analytics which makes possible to achieve real-time and automated intelligence that can seamlessly travel from the cloud to a large number of distributed end-points [19]. To date, the application of telemetry metrics and analytics has focused primarily on the general health and performance of services and host infrastructures. In the 5G this focus is expected to be extended so that to support the efficient deployment, management and optimisation of services and infrastructures. Thus, the range of expected use cases can include [20], *inter-alia*: (i) Infrastructure, network health; (ii) troubleshooting, forensic system observations, resolution; (iii) SLA (Service Level Agreement) compliance, KPI monitoring, prediction, performance tuning; (iv) dynamic reconfiguration (e.g. scaling, migration, load balancing); (v) security threat identification/remediation; (vi) capacity planning; (vii) resource/feature allocation optimisation, *and*; (viii) deployment model performance, topology confirmation.

While many of these use cases not necessarily knew their operational implementation, this will require different behaviours from the telemetry and analytics systems in order to "meet" the significantly different needs of 5G. First is the need to "address" the big data challenges of volume, variety and velocity. Telemetry will also need to become more software-*defined*. A trend which has already been embraced within the network domain in the form of software-*defined* networking is the ability to dynamically change the behaviour of telemetry systems (i.e. enable/disable metrics, change data resolution, add/remove metadata, etc.) and this will become important. This capability is necessary in order to adapt to dynamic service environments, particularly at the network edge in response to new services, architectural changes, changes in user behaviour or service provider business needs. While, initially, this can primarily be a human-*driven* activity, telemetry systems in concrete with management and orchestrations systems (MANO) are expected to evolve to higher levels of self-autonomy in order to "dynamically adapt", based on analytically driven behaviour evolution [21]. Telemetry systems will also need to become hierarchical in nature, following to the wider 5G evolutionary trends. While there is a trend towards centralisation, this unlikely seems to be scalable particularly in high distributed multi-domain edge networks.

Furthermore, telemetry systems are more likely to be domain specific with first level data centralisation within that domain. Selected data from lower level domains can then be aggregated at higher level domains within a dedicated hierarchical systems architecture, as shown in Fig. 1. The higher level analytics can also provide specific inputs into lower level analytics *-or vice versa-* in order to improve either local or global optimisation requirements. A hierarchical approach also distributes issues such as data normalisation, transport mechanisms data models and timestamps in more manageable blocks.

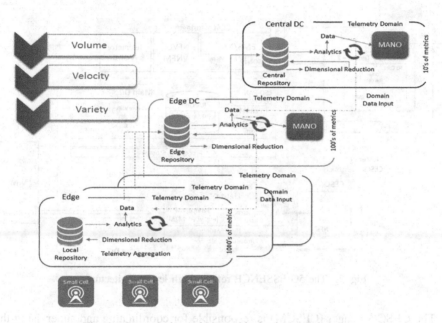

Fig. 1. General view of hierarchical telemetry domains.

3 Telemetry, Analytics and Orchestration Framework in the Revised 5G ESSENCE Architecture

Figure 2 provides a high-level architecture of the 5G ESSENCE according to the two-tier approach explained in detail in [22]. At the network's edge, each CESC is able to host one or more service VNFs, directly applying to the users of a specific operator. Similarly, VNFs can be instantiated inside the Main DC (Data Centre) and be parts of a Service Function Chaining (SFC) procedure. The Light DC can be used to implement different functional splits of the Small Cells as well as to support the mobile edge applications of the end-users. At the same time, the 5G ESSENCE proposes the development of small cell management functions as VNFs, which run in the Main DC and coordinate a fixed pool of shared radio resources, instead of considering that each small cell station has its own set of resources. The CESC (Cloud Enabled Small Cell) offers virtualised computing, storage and radio resources and the CESC cluster is considered as a cloud from the upper layers. This cloud can also be "sliced" to enable multi-tenancy. The execution platform is used to support VNFs that implement the different features of the Small Cells as well as to support for the mobile edge applications of the end-users. The 5G ESSENCE architecture allows multiple network operators (tenants) to provide services to their users through a set of CESCs deployed, owned and managed by a third party.

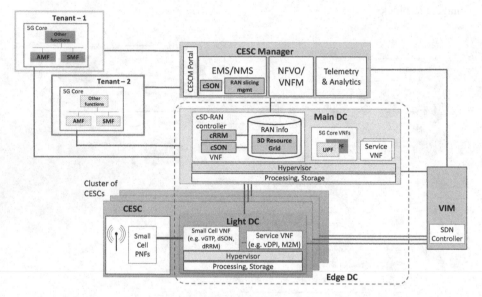

Fig. 2. The 5G ESSENCE refined high level architecture.

The CESC Manager (CESCM) is responsible for coordinating and supervising the use, the performance, and the delivery of both radio resources and services. It controls the interactions between the infrastructure (CESCs, Edge DC) and the network operators. In addition, it handles Service Level Agreements (SLAs) while, *on an architectural basis*, CESCM encompasses telemetry and analytics as fundamental tools for efficiently managing the overall network. The Virtualised Infrastructure Manager (VIM) is responsible for controlling the NFV Infrastructure (NFVI), which includes the computing, storage and network resources of the Edge DC.

It should be mentioned that the 5G ESSENCE does not only propose the development and adaptation of the multitenant CESC platform, the virtualisation infrastructure and the centralisation of the software-*defined* radio resource management described above; it also "addresses" several aspects that affect performance in 5G virtualised environments such as virtual switching, VNF migration, and Machine Learning (ML) algorithms, which allow orchestrating diverse types of lightweight virtual resources. Last but not least, it is worth noting that the abovementioned two-tier architecture of the 5G ESSENCE is well aligned with the current views on 5G architecture described by 5G-PPP in [23], where the infrastructure programmability and the split of control and user planes are identified as two key logical architecture design paradigms for 5G. First, the 5G ESSENCE achieves infrastructure programmability by leveraging the virtualised computation resources available at the Edge DC. These resources will be used for hosting VNFs tailored according to the needs of each tenant, on a per-slice basis. Second, the Main DC allows centralising and softwarising control plane SC functions to enable more efficient utilisation of radio resources coordinated among multiple CESCs. In addition to the abovementioned aspects, the 5G ESSENCE contributes to other 5G architectural concepts identified in [23] such as, *for example*, the realisation of the network slicing concept, which is a fundamental requirement of the 5G ESSENCE for enabling that multiple tenants and vertical industries share the same CESC infrastructure.

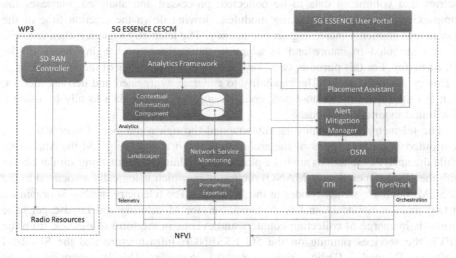

Fig. 3. Components of the telemetry, analytics and orchestration framework in the 5G ESSENCE refined high level architecture.

The 5G ESSENCE system presents a high degree of dynamicity, due to the constantly changing behaviour of services and workloads to be supported by the radio and cloud infrastructure. This perspective implicates for a proper monitoring system, able to adapt to the different supported scenarios. Data collected by this system shall be used for visualisation purposes (for human consumption) and it is also provided to a set of analytics techniques capable of extracting insights from the data and, via feedback loop, enabling the realisation of efficient resource allocation across the infrastructure through the orchestration system. These are the functionalities provided from the 5G ESSENCE CESCM.

In the scope of the revision and extension of the original 5G ESSENCE architecture, below we discuss the proposed components of telemetry, analytics and orchestration that can further enrich the original architectural approach.

3.1 Telemetry Module

One of the challenges for telemetry in the 5G small cell deployments considered in the 5G ESSENCE is the degree of distribution resulting from the distribution of infrastructure functionalities across different nodes of the network going from a centralised location (the Main DC) to the very edge of the network (Light DC) where the small cells are deployed (also see Fig. 2). Then, to achieve a full end-to-end view of both infrastructure and services, the proposed for inclusion telemetry system should be able to instrument and monitor the different devices composing the overall infrastructure as well as to provide a unique and simple-to-access view of the system that can be exposed to both dashboards and analytical techniques. Another challenge is the high complexity which characterises the overall telemetry system as the huge number of metrics and volume of data to be collected, processed and analysed, increases the complexity of the decision-making modules, slowing down the reaction time of the system and implicitly increasing service latency. The telemetry system is then required to be distributed in nature and to adapt to the constantly changing needs of the infrastructure. For this purpose, two "key" desired characteristics of the 5G ESSENCE telemetry platform are: (i) The capability to generate aggregated and derived metrics, *and*; (ii) the capability to store and, *consequently*, access the data locally by using a distributed monitoring approach.

The telemetry functionality is implemented through a number of agents that are distributed in different parts of the architecture, both at the Light and the Main DC, while the analytics functions are to be placed at the Main DC. Something similar occurs with the OSM (Open Source MANO) orchestrator, which is logically associated to the CESCM, but it physically resides at the Main DC. The telemetry module is organised in two main components, that is: Network Service Monitoring and Landscaper. The former is in charge of collecting counters and events, in the form of metrics, from the NFVI, the services running on the 5G ESSENCE infrastructure and the SD-RAN (Software Defined – Radio Access Network) controller. This is supported by the *Prometheus* monitoring tool and a set of exporters, which provide the capability to extract from the system the required information and send that to *Prometheus*. In fact, *Prometheus* natively supports hierarchical federation capabilities that provide to the 5G ESSENCE monitoring system the required flexibility and reliability. Another very important functionality provided by the above fundamental component is the Alerting system, which, *based on the continuous monitoring of metrics*, can identify deviations from normal behaviours of the services and the infrastructure and so to send a signal to the orchestration system. An important aspect of the 5G ESSENCE monitoring framework is the capability of monitoring the RAN, as a difference from most of the existing telemetry platforms, which have typically been used for the collection of measurements related to Information Technology (IT) infrastructure components, e.g., CPU (Central Processing Unit) usage, memory, operating systems, etc. In contrast, the monitoring of the RAN involves collecting radio interface-related measurements from the CESCs.

The 5G ESSENCE considers multi-RAT CESCs that support 4G, 5G and Wi-Fi technologies. The 4G LTE small cells collect a number of measurements at the physical (PHY) layer [24] and at the Layer 2 [25]. These measurements can be collected by the small cell or by the User Equipment (UE) that reports them to the small cell. Similarly, for 5G NR (New Radio) the list of PHY measurements is given in [26], while Wi-Fi measurements are described in [26].

Although the above measurements are available at the small cells, the capability of a telemetry platform -like *Prometheus*- to collect them depends on the actual configuration of measurements that each small cell exposes to an external system, typically through management interfaces defined between the small cell and the EMS (Element Management System) and/or NMS (Network Management System). The interface between the small cells and their EMS is typically vendor specific, but there have been some efforts in defining open standard interfaces such as TR-196 [27] supported by multiple vendors. Similarly, 3GPP has also standardised different Performance Measurement (PM) metrics [28] and Key Performance Indicators combining these metrics [29] to be transferred from the small cells (or their EMS) to the NMS. These PM metrics are provided in the form of XML files following the format of [30] and produced according to a configured reporting interval. Each file can contain one or more granularity periods, which define the time across which measurements are collected and aggregated. In the 5G ESSENCE, the PM files are generated by the cSD-RAN controller. It exposes the relevant metrics to a Representational State Transfer (REST) Application Programming Interface (API) that generates a JavaScript Object Notation (JSON) service that is then translated by a specific exporter, which consumes and translates the data to be understandable by *Prometheus*. Telemetry data obtained from the RAN are then subject to analytics approaches to support the decisions made by different RRM/SON functions for which the cSD-RAN Controller is in charge (and being the core objective of the WP3 of the 5G ESSENCE effort), as seen in Fig. 3. The monitoring framework of the 5G ESSENCE is designed to also collect information about the cloud resources. First the framework requires supporting the identification of available physical resources, which will be allocated to VNF Components and then it requires monitoring the interdependency between virtual and physical resources. In the 5G ESSENCE monitoring framework, this functionality is covered by the Landscaper shown in Fig. 3. The Landscaper is responsible for collecting information related to the resources available in the system. It gathers all the available resources on the NFVI and structures them in the form of a graph, where nodes represent the resources and edges represent relationships between them. Nodes are organised in layers (physical, virtual and service) in order to enable a logical classification of the resources.

3.2 Analytics Module and Orchestration Module

The analytics module in Fig. 3 is envisioned as a collection of tools and approaches to support and execute Analytics/Machine Learning (ML) tools on the telemetry data to generate models to be used for provisioning of insights to the orchestration system (i.e., OSM), and to the cSD-RAN controller of the small cells. The analytics module is characterised by two main components: The Contextual Information component and the Analytics Framework. The Contextual Information component is responsible for the storing of contextual data for services and NFVI and receives its input from the Landscaper (resource mapping), the Network Service Monitoring (telemetry metrics) and the Analytics Framework (models generated over time). This information is exposed to the Analytics Framework where it is processed to generate actionable knowledge, in terms of models, that will support orchestration decisions. This information is sent to the Orchestration system which exploits it for efficient placement and intelligent resource allocation and to the cSD-RAN Controller, which, as mentioned, makes informed and intelligent decisions on radio resource allocation.

The Orchestration module includes the Service Orchestrator (SO) and the Resource Orchestrator (RO) as part of Open Source MANO (OSM), and the Virtual Infrastructure Manager (VIM) as the combination of OpenStack and OpenDaylight (ODL). Moreover, two extra modules are envisioned in the final implementation of the overall orchestration system, which are the Placement Assistant and the Alert Mitigation Manager. The Placement Assistant intercepts the deployment requests sent to the Orchestrator from the 5G ESSENCE User Portal and translates that into an efficient deployment of components based on hints received from the Analytics Framework. The Placement Assistant is responsible for decisions related to the resource allocation for the service components at the deployment time (i.e. where to allocate resource, Main DC vs. Light DC). The Alert Mitigation Manager is instead responsible for managing the service at the runtime, according to anomalous behaviour identified by the Network Service Monitoring. The Network Service Monitoring sends triggers to the Alert Mitigation Manager when something anomalous is measured and the latter decides how to react to the event, on the basis of hints received from the Analytics Framework. The Alert Mitigation Manager is responsible for decisions related to the dynamic adjustment of service configuration and resource allocation.

4 Conclusion

In the present work we have identified the importance of development and inclusion of network softwarisation features within the wider 5G evolutionary scope which, in turn, can lead to more effective network management promoting cognitive features and related behaviors. Based on the specific novel context of the actual 5G ESSENCE research program, being part of the 5G-PPP Phase 2 effort, we have summarised the proposed innovative features of the respective architecture allowing for a dynamic management of the involved network resources as well as for the promotion of a variety of facilities via dedicated VNFs. The wide implementation of SDN, NFV, Cloud and Edge Computing in present 5G architectures, and within the 5G ESSENCE in particular, leads to network operating environments being software-*driven* to a great extent. The transition towards "softwarisation" schemes implicates for greater challenges, regarding management and monitoring of the related infrastructures.

In this framework, both telemetry and analytics are expected to realise a very important role as they can both offer various insights upon a variety of features affecting both network and service performance within the intended 5G architectures. This can be a very important factor towards contributing in the ability to automate and provide fine-grained management of the related 5G network infrastructures.

Within the context of the updated and revised 5G ESSENCE architecture, the CESCM is the central service management and orchestration component. Under a more generalised approach, the CESCM integrates all the traditional network management elements and the novel recommended functional blocks to realise NFV operations and it is responsible for coordinating and supervising the use, performance and delivery of both radio resources and services. In addition, it is also responsible for controlling interactions between the infrastructure and the network operators and it handles SLAs. The CESCM incorporates telemetry and analytics as necessary tools for properly managing the overall network. Aiming to extend and refine the original architectural scope of the 5G ESSENCE, and towards achieving a full end-to-end view of both infrastructure and services, we have proposed for inclusion a suitable telemetry module. The related functionality can be implemented through a number of agents, while the telemetry module is organised in two main components (the Network Service Monitoring and Landscaper), each one serving specific purposes.

In the same approach, we have proposed the inclusion of an analytics module, with the purpose of supporting and performing Analytics/Machine Learning (ML) tools on the telemetry data to produce models for offering of insights to the orchestration system and to the cSD-RAN controller of the small cells. Aiming to "widen" all potentially expected benefits, we have also proposed an orchestration module, for better supporting dynamic adjustment of service configuration and resource allocation. These modules can enhance the original architectural 5G ESSENCE considerations to a more reliable level for a more effective cognitive management of the network resources and of the proposed facilities.

Acknowledgments. This work has been performed in the scope of the *5G ESSENCE* European Research Project and has been supported by the Commission of the European Communities (5G-PPP/H2020, *Grant Agreement No. 761592*).

References

1. Andrews, J.G., et al.: What will 5G be. IEEE JSAC Spec. Issue 5G Wirel. Commun. Syst. **32** (6), 1065–1082 (2014)
2. European Commission: 5G: Challenges, Research Priorities, and Recommendations – Joint White Paper. European Commission, Strategic Research and Innovation Agenda (2014)
3. Blanco, B., Fajardo, J.O., Liberal, F.: Design of cognitive cycles in 5G networks. In: Iliadis, L., Maglogiannis, I. (eds.) AIAI 2016. IAICT, vol. 475, pp. 697–708. Springer, Cham (2016). https://doi.org/10.1007/978-3-319-44944-9_62
4. Chochliouros, I.P., Spiliopoulou, A.S., Kostopoulos, A., Belesioti, M., Sfakianakis, E., et al.: Challenges for defining opportunities for growth in the 5G era: the SESAME conceptual model. In: Proceedings of the EuCNC-2016, Athens, Greece, pp. 1–5 (2016)
5. SESAME ("Small cEllS coordinAtion for Multitenancy and Edge services") 5G-PPP Project, Grant Agreement No. 671596. http://www.sesame-h2020-5g-ppp.eu/

6. Chochliouros, I.P., et al.: A model for an innovative 5G-oriented architecture, based on small cells coordination for multi-tenancy and edge services. In: Iliadis, L., Maglogiannis, I. (eds.) AIAI 2016. IAICT, vol. 475, pp. 666–675. Springer, Cham (2016). https://doi.org/10.1007/978-3-319-44944-9_59

7. Chochliouros, I.P., et al.: Putting intelligence in the network edge through NFV and cloud computing: the SESAME approach. In: Boracchi, G., Iliadis, L., Jayne, C., Likas, A. (eds.) EANN 2017. CCIS, vol. 744, pp. 704–715. Springer, Cham (2017). https://doi.org/10.1007/978-3-319-65172-9_59

8. 5G ESSENCE ("Embedded Network Services for 5G Experiences") 5G-PPP Project, Grant Agreement (GA) No. 761592. http://www.5g-essence-h2020.eu

9. Fujitsu Network Communications Inc.: The Benefits of Cloud-RAN Architecture in Mobile Network Expansion, Richardson, Texas, US (2014)

10. Chochliouros, I.P., Giannoulakis, I. Spiliopoulou, A.S., Belesioti, M., Kostopoulos, A., et al.: A novel architectural concept for enhanced 5G network facilities. In: MATEC Web of Conferences, CSCC-2017, vol. 125, no. 03012, pp. 1–7 (2017)

11. van Lingen, F., Yannuzzi, M., Jain, A., Irons-Mclean, R., Luch, O., Carrera, D., et al.: The unavoidable convergence of NFV, 5G, and fog: a model-driven approach to bridge cloud and edge. IEEE Commun. Mag. **55**(8), 28–35 (2017)

12. Mullins, R., Barros, M.: Cognitive network management for 5G. 5G-PPP Network Management and Quality of Service Working Group, October 2016

13. Santhosh, S., Vaden, M.: Telemetry and analytics best practices and lessons learned. In: Seif, E.-N.M., Drachen, A., Canossa, A. (eds.) Game Analytics, pp. 85–109. Springer, London (2013). https://doi.org/10.1007/978-1-4471-4769-5_6

14. Pérez-Romero, J., et al.: Monitoring and analytics for the optimisation of cloud enabled small cells. In: Proceedings of the IEEE 23rd International Workshop on Computer Aided Modeling and Design of Communication Links and Networks (CAMAD), pp. 1–6. IEEE (2018)

15. Chochliouros, I.P., et al.: Using small cells for enhancing 5G networks. In: Proceedings of IEEE Conference on Network Function Virtualisation and Software-Defined Networks (NFV-SDN 2017), pp. 1–6. IEEE (2017)

16. Ranjbar, A.: Using specialized maintenance and troubleshooting tool in troubleshooting and maintaining cisco IP networks (TSHOOT). Cisco Press, Indianapolis, USA (2015)

17. Javvin Technologies Inc.: SNMP: Simple Network Management Protocol in Network Protocol Handbook, 2nd edn., Saratoga, CA, USA, pp. 37–43 (2005)

18. McGrath, M.-J., Bayon-Molino, V.: Evolving end to end telemetry systems to meet the challenges of softwarized environments. IEEE Softw. (2017). https://sdn.ieee.org/newsletter/may-2017/evolving-end-to-end-telemetry-systems-to-meet-the-challenges-of-softwarized-environments

19. Barrett, J.: Building 5G: data analytics and artificial intelligence. Global Mobile Suppliers Association (GSA) (2016)

20. Mande, A.: SDN-NFV for Telco DC. Cisco (2017)

21. European Telecommunications Standards Institute (ETSI): NFV Management and Orchestration - An Overview, GS NFV-MAN 001 v1.1.1. ETSI (2014)

22. Chochliouros, I.P., et al.: Enhancing network management via NFV, MEC, cloud computing and cognitive features: the "5G ESSENCE" modern architectural approach. In: Iliadis, L., Maglogiannis, I., Plagianakos, V. (eds.) AIAI 2018. IAICT, vol. 520, pp. 50–61. Springer, Cham (2018). https://doi.org/10.1007/978-3-319-92016-0_5

23. Redana, S., et al.: Views on 5G Architecture, White Paper of the 5G-PPP Architecture WG, July 2016. 5G-PPP, July 2016

24. The 3rd Generation Partnership Project: 3GPP TS 36.214 v15.1.0: Evolved Universal Terrestrial Radio Access (E-UTRA); Physical layer; Measurements (Release 15) (2018)

25. The 3rd Generation Partnership Project: 3GPP TS 36.314 v15.0.0: Evolved Universal Terrestrial Radio Access (E-UTRA); Layer 2 - Measurements (Release 15). 3GPP (2018)

26. The 3rd Generation Partnership Project: 3GPP TS 38.215 v15.1.0: NR; Physical layer measurements (Release 15) (2018)

27. Broadband Forum: TR-196: FAP Service: 2.0 Femto Access Point Service Data Model (2018). https://cwmp-data-models.broadband-forum.org/tr-196-2-0-0.html

28. The 3rd Generation Partnership Project: 3GPP TS 32.425 v15.0.0: Performance Management (PM); Performance measurements Evolved Universal Terrestrial Radio Access Network (E-UTRAN) (Release 15) (2018)

29. The 3rd Generation Partnership Project: 3GPP TS 32.450 v14.0.0: Key Performance Indicators (KPI) for Evolved Universal Terrestrial Radio Access Network (E-UTRAN): Definitions (Release 14) (2017)

30. The 3rd Generation Partnership Project: 3GPP TS 32.435 v14.0.0: Performance measurement; eXtensible Markup Language (XML) file format definition (Release 14) (2017)

A Framework to Support the Role of Telecommunication Service Providers in Evolving 5G Business Models

Ioanna Mesogiti[1(✉)] , Eleni Theodoropoulou[1],
George Lyberopoulos[1], Fotini Setaki[1], Aurora Ramos[2],
Panagiotis Gouvas[3], Anastasios Zafeiropoulos[3], and Roberto Bruschi[4]

[1] COSMOTE Mobile Telecommunications S.A.,
99 Kifissias Avenue, 15124 Maroussi, Athens, Greece
imesogiti@cosmote.gr
[2] ATOS Spain S.A., Valladolid, Spain
[3] UBITECH S.A., Network Softwarization and IoT Group, Athens, Greece
[4] CNIT, Consorzio Nazionale Interuniversitario per le Telecomunicazioni,
Genoa, Italy

Abstract. 5G networks will constitute a complete transformation in the ICT domain by enabling the deployment of vertical services within the network infrastructures, based on extensive use of network softwarization and programmability. This shift will trigger and facilitate the transformation of existing stakeholders' roles, as well as the interactions between multiple stakeholders from the traditionally separated markets. The 5G-PPP project MATILDA aims at delivering a holistic 5G end-to-end services operational framework, including 5G-ready applications lifecycle management from development to deployment over 5G network infrastructures. This paper aims at providing a refined and extended vision of the 5G business roles and their interactions and based on these at defining business applicability of the MATILDA project, with special focus on the project's value proposition addressing the Telecommunication Service Providers.

Keywords: 5G business roles · Verticals · Value proposition ·
Telecommunication Service Provider

1 Introduction

5G networks will go beyond performance enhancements of the existing telecommunication services, to a complete transformation of the ICT domain towards enabling the deployment of various vertical services (industry 4.0, automotive, multimedia, smart cities, eHealth, etc.) over the 5G infrastructures [1]. This shift will be based on extensive use of network softwarization and programmability to provide an integrated logical infrastructure over multiple disaggregated physical resources (in practice telecommunication networks and compute facilities), making use of convergent

© IFIP International Federation for Information Processing 2019
Published by Springer Nature Switzerland AG 2019
J. MacIntyre et al. (Eds.): AIAI 2019 Workshops, IFIP AICT 560, pp. 60–69, 2019.
https://doi.org/10.1007/978-3-030-19909-8_5

technologies for both mobile and fixed access [2, 3]. These technology advancements will trigger and facilitate the emergence of new business models involving a transformation of existing stakeholders' roles, as well as the interactions between multiple stakeholders from the traditionally separated markets.

To this end, a number of projects (EU, national funded, equipment vendor supported, etc.) are focusing on the technical realization of the aforementioned concepts, with MATILDA 5G-PPP project [4] aiming at designing and implementing a novel holistic 5G end-to-end services operational framework tackling the overall lifecycle of design, development and orchestration of 5G-ready applications from multiple vertical sectors, and 5G network services over programmable infrastructure, including intelligent mechanisms to increase automation in most of those processes. However, it is not always clearly defined how the various 5G-related projects and solutions can support the interaction between the stakeholders, and whom they address. This paper aims at defining the business applicability of the MATILDA project with respect to the related business roles (and involved stakeholders) and their interactions, with special focus on the value proposition that is addressing the Telecommunication Service Provider.

The paper is organized as follows: To start with the various business roles in the value chain of the 5G ecosystem are identified. In the next section, the MATILDA solution is briefly presented, to be followed by the description of the MATILDA framework including capabilities and functionalities to the benefit of the basic stakeholders along with the interactions among them. Based on this framework, the following section provides an analysis on the value proposition of MATILDA for the Telecommunication Service Provider that is the main customer targeted by MATILDA solution, while conclusions are drawn at the end.

2 Business Roles in the 5G Ecosystem

In general, the business roles that usually appear in the value chain of the future 5G business ecosystem have been drafted in a number of industry white papers [1, 2, 5], which however mainly adhere to existing business roles and stakeholders. Leveraging these initial definitions, MATILDA focuses on the refinement and extension on these business roles [6], which can be generalized for any 5G business ecosystem, irrespectively of the adoption of the MATILDA technical solution. These business roles definitions are described in this section.

At first, a principal role in the 5G ecosystem is that of the Telecommunication Service Provider (TSP)- (undertaken by Mobile and/or Fixed-network infrastructure providers), operating a programmable (5G) network infrastructure spanning from the radio and/or fixed access to the edge, transport and core network. The network infrastructure can be either owned by the TSP or network resources can be leased (partly or completely) as a Network Service (NaaS) from an Infrastructure Provider.

The latter reveals another significant role, that of the Infrastructure Providers (IPs), putting infrastructure resources (network resources, storage space, compute resources) in place for the 5G-ready applications deployment. Depending on the nature of the required infrastructure resources and the assets of the stakeholders, this role can be split to further roles, performed by one or more stakeholders; namely:

- Network Infrastructure Providers (NPs) operating telecommunication infrastructures and offering network resources and services to end-users, verticals and/or (other) TSPs;
- Cloud Infrastructure Providers (CPs), operating centralized or distributed (in more than one location) cloud/edge deployments and offering compute and storage resources in a programmable way.

The Equipment Vendors' role traditionally providing hardware equipment, now is moving to providing software telecom equipment (i.e. VNFs), thus practically implementing programmable network layer functions and delivering these components/ functions to the stakeholders in charge of their operation.

At this point, we can distinguish the Operation/Business Support System (OSS/BSS) providers' role which consists in designing and developing 5G OSS/BSS systems, towards supporting the multiple, new interactions among the various stakeholders (e.g. TSPs and the Service Providers). Although OSS/BSS providers' role can be undertaken by traditional equipment vendors, there is plenty of room for new businesses to undertake this role.

System integrators undertake the role of supporting the design and development of end-to-end orchestration platforms, at network and application level.

The role of software developers is key in the 5G ecosystem, and includes:

- VNF developers, designing and developing Virtual Network Functions.
- Cloud application developers, designing and developing cloud-applications (e.g. micro services-based applications based on cloud-native principles)
- (Vertical) application developers, designing and developing any type of application combining cloud and network concepts (e.g. Mobile Edge Computing-oriented functionalities).

(Vertical) Application/Service Providers (AP/SP) provide applications/services to end users and aim at enhancing their portfolio and optimising service provisioning.

Finally, Service Consumers/End Users are the individuals or corporate users to consume the 5G applications/services while being static and/or on the move. Vertical industries fall into this category.

The described 5G value chain composed of the aforementioned large number of business roles is depicted in Fig. 1, where the stakeholders primarily addressed by MATILDA are marked in purple.

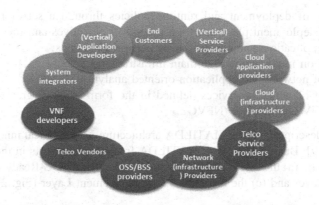

Fig. 1. 5G Ecosystem and Stakeholders addressed by MATILDA (Color figure online)

In a real 5G business environment (especially one adopting the MATILDA concepts) a stakeholder may undertake more than one role, or a stakeholder's role may be assigned to more than one stakeholder depending on the nature of the 5G application/service and the resources that it requires. For instance:

- The NPs may also undertake the role of the CPs depending on their infrastructure assets, or in some cases even the role of the AP/SP
- The Application Developers' and AP/SP's roles could be played by the same stakeholder
- The SP role can be undertaken by a vertical or by a software house providing, while
- Many stakeholders can be considered as Service Consumers, depending on the nature of the applications, e.g. customers of the verticals or the verticals themselves can be Service Consumers, and so on.

3 MATILDA Framework and Users

3.1 MATILDA Solution

The vision of MATILDA [7] is to design and implement a novel holistic 5G end-to-end services operational framework tackling the overall lifecycle of design, development and orchestration of 5G-ready applications and 5G network services over programmable infrastructure. For this purpose MATILDA devises a unified programmability model and a set of control abstractions serving as interface between the 5G applications/services and the 5G infrastructure layers, while incorporating intelligent and unified orchestration mechanisms for the automated placement of the 5G-ready applications and the creation and maintenance of the required network slices. A non-exhaustive list of MATILDA solution capabilities include:

- Enforcement of deployment and runtime policies through a set of mechanisms establishing deployment plans based on high-level objectives and runtime adaptation of the application components and/or network functions;
- Deployment on multi-site/multi-domain infrastructures;
- Extraction of network and application-oriented analytics;
- Management of network services defined in the form of VNF graphs through a multi-site NFV Orchestrator (NFVO).

A detailed description of the MATILDA architecture and technical innovations are provided in [7–9]. Businesswise, the MATILDA framework consists in the following three major layers: (a) the 5G-Ready Application Layer, (b) the 5G-Ready Application Orchestration Layer and (c) the Network Slice Management Layer (Fig. 2).

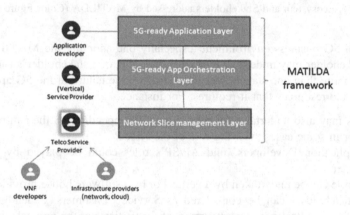

Fig. 2. MATILDA direct users/roles and interactions

3.2   MATILDA Framework Users and Interactions

The interactions that can be realized between the MATILDA stakeholders and the MATILDA framework layers are defined as follows [6]:

(a) The MATILDA 5G-ready Applications Layer is primarily oriented to software developers, to support the design and development of 5G-ready applications, that are distributed-by-nature, consisting of cloud native components relying on a service mesh as a means of network abstraction. This layer also enables the definition of the critical configuration parameters for application components' initial deployment and runtime, their chainable interfaces among them (for the creation of a service graph), quantitative metrics with regard to the required QoS, in terms of compute and network performance functionalities, soft or hard constraints that have to be fulfilled, and so on. The latter is based on the conceptualization of a metamodel (application graph metamodel), to declare information and requirements.

(b) The 5G-Ready Applications' Orchestration Layer is oriented to (vertical) AP/SPs, to support the life-cycle management (deployment and runtime management) of the 5G-ready applications across the available multi-site programmable infrastructure, using a set of optimisation schemes and intelligent algorithms to provide the needed resources. Through their interaction with this MATILDA layer, AP/SPs are also able to specify policies and configuration options on a per application deployment (instance) basis; in other words to formulate the slice intent for the creation of the appropriate application-aware network slice that has to be provided by the TSP. Considering the business landscape, the role of the (vertical) AP/SP can be undertaken by the TSP.

(c) The Network and Computing Slice Management Layer is oriented to TSPs, to support the 5G application-aware network slice instantiation and management during the overall lifecycle of the application, after having got the application deployment request by the 5G-Ready Application Orchestrator. It includes functionalities such as: compute and network slice instantiation and management, network services and mechanisms activation and orchestration, as well as monitoring streams management and runtime policies enforcement. This layer includes an OSS/BSS system, a NFVO and a resources manager to handle the network and compute resources deployment.

It becomes obvious that although the business roles in the value chain benefiting from MATILDA are many, three of them only will be directly interacting with the MATILDA technical layers, namely the 5G-Ready application developers, the (Vertical) AP/SPs and the TSPs.

In the end, the technical benefits that the MATILDA framework users can anticipate are: flexibility for application/VNF developers in the design, development and distribution of 5G-ready applications and VNFs by easy-to-access tools, capability for the vertical SPs of putting policy-based configurable network-agnostic slice requests, capability of full lifecycle management for application-aware network slices over multi-site programmable infrastructure for the TSPs.

4 MATILDA Value Proposition Analysis for Telecommunication Service Providers

The main customer segment targeted by MATILDA is the TSP that by acquiring, operating and maintaining the MATILDA solution will be able to improve its business offerings towards vertical customers and software developers. The value proposition of MATILDA to TSPs "bridging the existing gap in end-to-end orchestration solutions and delivering an easy and flexible environment for integration of vertical applications into a 5G ecosystem" has been analysed on the basis of the Value Proposition Canvas [10] (Fig. 3); the latter identifying how the "pains" of a specific Customer can be relieved and how the "gains" expected by the solution can create revenues and added value for the Customer.

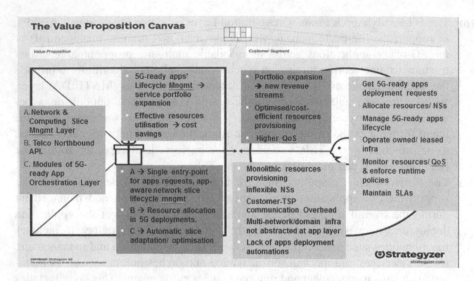

Fig. 3. Overview of MATILDA Value Proposition to TSPs

Considering the Customer Profile, that is the TSPs profile, the "jobs" of the TSPs with regard to the provisioning of 5G-ready applications, include the following processes:

- Receiving customers' requests for advanced telecom services to support 5G-ready applications and manage the lifecycle of the microservices' graph they consist of.
- Analysing/Resolving customers' requests (service graphs along with other data) in terms of identifying infrastructure resources' availability for the provisioning of these services and suitable network functions.
- Allocation of infrastructure resources in a dynamic/flexible/efficient way, so as to optimise their utilisation and fulfil the requested QoS.
- Acquiring infrastructure resources (either own or obtained as a Service from 3rd party Infrastructure Providers) and network functions and providing them to the requested 5G-ready applications (customers). In 5G this process corresponds to efficient slicing of infrastructure resources.
- Continuous monitoring of infrastructure, resources and QoS, and adjusting to runtime policies adherent to each 5G-ready application(s) deployment, following a continuous match-resolve-act approach.
- SLAs' Maintenance.

Existing application deployment frameworks cannot sufficiently support the deployment of 5G-ready applications, because application deployment procedures are detached from underlying network systems and resources. In particular, TSPs have to face a number of challenges, which constitute their main "pains" in the 5G-ready application deployment procedure, the most critical ones being the following:

- Currently, the provision of network resources cannot be modified at runtime because it is performed in a monolithic way, that is on a per-connection and per-technology (fixed or mobile) basis with fixed QoS attributes.
- Network services (NSs) are fixed and at a certain level pre-defined on a per-network technology basis.
- Currently, no automated infrastructure optimisation framework exists with regard to applications/application components' placement; especially in multi-network/multi-domain/multi-Point of Presence (PoP) infrastructure deployments.
- Multi-network/multi-domain/multi-PoP infrastructure deployments are not easily abstracted at application/service layer, and resource provisioning is handled on a per customer case.
- For advanced infrastructure services, direct communication between the customer and the TSP personnel is required.

These "pains" result in significant human and infrastructure resources and cost overheads as well as lack of deployments' flexibility. To relieve part of these "pains" for the TSPs in the deployment of the 5G applications, MATILDA builds a value proposition around an advanced holistic framework [7] consisting of the following products and services:

- The Network and Computing Slice Management Layer (especially the OSS/BSS, the Slice Manager and the NFVO parts).
- The Telco Northbound API, facilitating the translation of slice intent requests to application-aware slice creation and management.
- Modules of the 5G-ready Application Orchestration Layer, including Execution Manager, Policy Engine and Optimisation Engine components.

More specifically, the MATILDA products and services are considered as "pain relievers" in the following ways:

- The MATILDA Northbound API, Vertical Application Orchestrator (VAO), OSS/BSS and NFVO support simplicity, homogeneity, flexibility by providing: (a) a single point/interface for receiving requests from various customers for various 5G-ready and common applications, (b) the means to interpret the advanced resource requirements of the 5G-ready applications' in the service graph in a homogeneous and automatic way without requiring direct communication between the customer and the TSP, as well as (c) the functionality to set up and manage the 5G-ready application deployment and operation over an application-aware network slice (that can abstract technologies/domains/PoPs), thus going beyond the existing monolithic way of services/resources provisioning.
- The MATILDA VAO and Mobile Edge Orchestrator (MEO) include functionalities that offer optimised infrastructure resource allocation in multi-network/multi-domain/multi-PoP infrastructure deployments.
- The Execution Manager, the Policy Engine and Optimisation Engine modules of the 5G-ready Application Orchestration layer, along with the solution monitoring mechanisms, provide the required continuous monitoring functionality of infrastructure, resources and QoS, and enable the adjustment of resources to runtime policies adherent to each 5G-ready application(s) deployment, following a

continuous match-resolve-act approach. They consist of components that are supporting vertical applications and services management, however in continuous interaction with the telco network management mechanisms.

At the same time, the following capabilities of the MATILDA products and services comprise "gain creators" for the TSPs:

- Capability of setting up and managing 5G-ready application deployments and operation over an application-aware network slice; necessary for the fast expansion of the TSP's service portfolio in various vertical markets;
- Effective utilisation of network resources and optimisation of resource allocation and application components' placement also leading to cost savings.

As a result, the "gains" for the TSPs from the MATILDA framework in 5G services deployment are the following:

- Fast and cost efficient expansion of their service portfolio in various vertical industries for the generation of new revenue streams.
- Optimisation of 5G network resources provisioning leveraging the latest technological advancements in telecommunications and computing domains, well before or aligned with the competition.
- Cost-efficient utilisation of infrastructure resources (either own ones and/or obtained as a Service), while maintaining high QoS for advanced services.

5   Discussion

This paper deals with the refinement and extension of the commonly identified business roles in the 5G ecosystem, to be driven by the foreseen transformation in the ICT domain in the forthcoming 5G era. It also discusses the roles/stakeholders interactions on the basis of the business framework to be supported by the 5G-PPP project MATILDA solution. The role of the Telecommunication Service Provider (TSP) in the 5G ecosystem is analysed with respect to the "pains" that are foreseen in the process of delivering 5G services, especially in terms of integrating vertical applications within the 5G (in general programmable) infrastructure, and the "gains" that are expected by these activities. The ways in which these "pains" can be relieved and the expected "gains" can be achieved is analysed in the context of MATILDA's value proposition to TSPs which consists in bridging the existing gap in end-to-end orchestration solutions and delivering an easy and flexible environment for integration of vertical applications into a 5G ecosystem.

Acknowledgements. The research leading to these results has received funding from the European Union's Framework Programme Horizon 2020 under grant agreements (1) No. 761898 and project name "MATILDA: A Holistic Innovative Framework for the Design, Development and Orchestration of 5G-Ready Applications and Network Services over Sliced Programmable Infrastructure".

References

1. 5G-PPP, 5G empowering vertical industries. White Paper (2016). http://ec.europa.eu/newsroom/dae/document.cfm?doc_id=14322
2. NGMN Alliance: NGMN 5G White Paper. https://www.ngmn.org/fileadmin/ngmn/content/images/news/ngmn_news/NGMN_5G_White_Paper_V1_0.pdf
3. 5G-PPP View on 5G Architecture, V2.0 (2017). https://5g-ppp.eu/wp-content/uploads/2018/01/5G-PPP-5G-Architecture-White-Paper-Jan-2018-v2.0.pdf
4. 5G-PPP Project MATILDA. http://www.matilda-5g.eu/
5. IEEE 5G Initiative: 5G an Beyond Technology Roadmap. White Paper (2017). https://futurenetworks.ieee.org/images/files/pdf/ieee-5g-roadmap-white-paper.pdf
6. MATILDA, Deliverable D7.4: Market Analysis, Business Plan, Sustainability Model & Innovation Management, September 2018
7. MATILDA, Deliverable D1.1: MATILDA Framework and Reference Architecture, December 2017
8. Gouvas, P., et al.: Design, development and orchestration of 5G-ready applications oversliced programmable infrastructure. In: First International Workshop on Softwarized Infrastructures for 5G and Fog Computing (Soft5 2017), co-located with the 2017 29th International Teletraffic Congress (ITC 29), Genoa, Italy, pp. 13–18 (2017)
9. Gouvas, P., et al.: Separation of concerns among application and network services orchestration in a 5G ecosystem. In: EuCNC Workshop on "From Cloud Ready to Cloud Native Transformation: What it Means and Why it Matters", Ljubljana, Slovenia (2018)
10. Value Proposition canvas template. https://strategyzer.com/canvas/value-proposition-canvas

Orchestration of Mission-Critical Services over an NFV Architecture

Aitor Sanchoyerto[1], Ruben Solozabal[1], Bego Blanco[1(✉)],
Elisa Jimeno[2], Endika Aldecoa[1], Estrella Basurto[1], and Fidel Liberal[1]

[1] University of the Basque Country, Bilbao, Spain
{aitor.sanchoyerto,ruben.solozabal,bego.blanco,
endika.aldecoa,estrella.basurto,fidel.liberal}@ehu.eus
[2] Atos Spain SA, Madrid, Spain
elisa.jimeno@atos.net

Abstract. In the race towards 5G, NFV (Network Functions Virtualization) arises as one of the enabler technologies. The intelligent orchestration of the network becomes a key element to achieve the demanded network slicing for an efficient allocation of the available shared virtualised resources.

In this paper we propose an intelligent orchestration process of mission critical services over an NFV architecture. Mission critical services have tight requirements in terms of latency and high-availability that must be met in an end-to-end basis. Our proposal includes a monitoring system that collects performance data from the VNF (Virtual Network Function) instances in order to feed the decision-making process of the orchestrator and then elastically assign resources to the network service.

The software components that compose our deployment are presented as well as the validation scenario in which the features of the test-bed are exposed.

Keywords: NFV · Management and orchestration · MC

1 Introduction

In the recent years, the Public Safety (PS) field has shown an increasing interest towards different forms of network sharing models in contrast to building out dedicated legacy PS networks. This interest has led 3GPP to include, from Release 11 onwards, the requirements of Mission Critical (MC) communications as a central topic to address the key requirements of the next generation broadband PS networks.

In order to support the demanding set of requirements of the PS vertical, NFV offers a new way to design, deploy and manage networking services. As a key technology for the development of the 5G ecosystem, NFV decouples the network functions from proprietary hardware appliances in order to be run in a virtualized infrastructure. This architecture drives the rapid development of new network services with elastic scale and automation. Additionally, the use of end-to-end network slicing mechanisms will allow sharing the infrastructure among other vertical industries or services and customising its capabilities on a per-tenant basis.

© IFIP International Federation for Information Processing 2019
Published by Springer Nature Switzerland AG 2019
J. MacIntyre et al. (Eds.): AIAI 2019 Workshops, IFIP AICT 560, pp. 70–77, 2019.
https://doi.org/10.1007/978-3-030-19909-8_6

This paper presents the intelligent orchestration process of a Mission Critical Push-To-Talk (MCPTT) service over an NFV architecture. MCPTT compels tight requirements that include, among others, high availability and reliability, very low latency, support for one-to-one and group calls, talker identification and high audio quality for clear interchange of information. In this context, the network orchestrator must provide the tools to share edge computing capabilities between mission critical and commercial users.

MCPTT is a PS mission-critical voice communication type, aimed at the coordination of emergency teams that are organized in groups [1]. It provides an arbitrated method by which two -or more- users may engage in communication. Users may request permission to transmit (e.g., traditionally by means of a press of a button) and the MCPTT service provides a deterministic mechanism to arbitrate between requests that are in competition (i.e., Floor control). When multiple requests occur, the determination of which user's request is accepted, and which users' requests are rejected -or queued- is based upon a number of characteristics (including the respective priorities of the users in contention).

The challenge consists on transparently and elastically allocating the available resources to the variety of actors requiring different services with different priorities in space and time. To that aim, the network slicing based on virtualization techniques must be used to modify the network behaviour by changing functions or reconfiguring parameters. At this point, the intelligent orchestration process of the network slices, including commercial and MCPTT users, involves the collection of performance data through a monitoring system that processes them and generates the corresponding alerts.

This paper is organized as follows. Next section provides a brief overview on the current state of network management and orchestration towards the definition of service slices. Then, Sect. 3 describes the deployment of an MCPTT service over NFV architecture, including the technical specifications of the platform that will host the service. Section 4 describes the validation scenario to later, in Sect. 5, propose an intelligent orchestration process that includes a monitoring module to feed the decision-making engine. Finally, Sect. 6 summarizes the main contributions and poses new research challenges that will be addressed in the future.

2 Related Work

The previous section remarks the importance of network slicing in NFV architectures to simultaneously provide a multitude of diverse services over a common underlying physical infrastructure. The concept of slicing in 5G and next-to-5G environments has been widely discussed in the recent years.

Authors in [2] define the concept of *slicing* as the separation of a single physical network into multiple isolated logical networks. Another definition in [3] states that a network slice instance is formed by a set of network functions and logical resources enabling the deployment of a complete logical network infrastructure capable of accommodating the requirements for a specific service. Then, the network slicing in an

NFV architecture includes the allocation of the common virtualised resources among the existing services.

Work in [4] shows an example of a network slicing use case over NFV with two tenants, each of them operating several service slices. The authors describe the multiple challenges to be addressed in order to make the slicing process possible. These challenges include the design of adequate resource management mechanisms that enable resource sharing among slices when necessary, without violating their required performance levels. The work in [5] proposes an orchestration system that realises application-aware end-to-end slices on demand, each of which contains not only guaranteed end-to-end bandwidth resources (i.e., in the forms of virtual links, virtual switches, and virtual access points) but also isolated Information Technology (IT) resources (i.e., in the form of virtual network functions) to carry specific applications with quality of service (QoS) guarantees. These examples reflect the interest on network slicing, but the challenge of the elastic resource allocation that dynamically distributes the available virtualized resources among the existing slices instances still remains unsolved, especially when related to the dynamic prioritization of services.

One fundamental issue when addressing the dynamic allocation of resources for network slicing in NFV is related to the possibility of scaling the VNFs. There are many algorithms that employ machine learning or other Artificial Intelligence (AI) methods to decide the optimal number of instances of a VNF needed to provide the requested service. The study in [6] targets the dynamic provisioning of network services expressed as one or multiple service chains in cloud datacentres and designs efficient online algorithms without requiring any information about future traffic rates. Authors in [7] seek a proactive approach to provision new instances for overloaded VNFs ahead of time based on the estimated flow rates. The authors formulate the VNF provisioning problem in order that the cost incurred by inaccurate prediction and VNF deployment is minimized. The work in [8] addresses a dynamic VNF service chain deployment and scaling by a novel combination of an online provisioning algorithm and a multi-armed bandwidth optimization framework, which exploits online learning of the available bandwidths to enable the optimal deployment of a scaled service chain. This kind or methods solve the analytical problem of deciding when and how to scale a VNF, but must jet be introduced into a complete orchestration system in order to be integrated with the management and orchestration (MANO) operation.

The existing literature shows that, although network slicing has gained a great interest, the proposed solutions are still in process of being fully developed. Among the many challenges that arise, one fundamental issue is the automation of the resource allocation for the elastic dimensioning of the slice. The following sections of this paper introduce the concept of service monitoring, that involves the collection and processing of performance data from the NFV architecture. The monitoring system is an intelligent decision-making module that generates the necessary alerts to trigger the orchestration processes, such as VNF scaling, in order to perform the re-allocation of resources as needed.

3 Deployment of Mission Critical Push-to-Talk over an NFV Architecture

To evolve the MCPTT into an NFV-ready service it must be defined as a Network Service and, as such, be described by a Network Service Descriptor (NSD). Each VNF that composes the service chain, for its side, is defined by a VNF Descriptor (VNFD) plus the image that implements its correspondent functionality. When a MC service is instantiated, the orchestrator must create the network slice that accommodates critical services ensuring the high availability, reliability, and low latency expected for these communications. This implies not only the allocation of the necessary resources to instantiate and run the VNF chain, but also the monitoring and scaling of the service in order to meet the elastic demand. The MC slice must have a prioritized access to resources in the cloud infrastructure, which may result in a low-priority service deal-location, if required, in order to meet the service level agreements (SLAs).

The specifications of the platform and the virtualized service are described in the following sections.

3.1 Platform Specifications

The platform selected to perform the testbed complies the ETSI NFV standard [9]. The orchestrator selected is Open Source MANO (OSM) [10], an ETSI-hosted initiative for the development of open-source NFV Management and Orchestration software stacks that is aligned with the ETSI reference architecture. OSM works in conjunction with Canonical's Juju to configure the VNFs. The Virtual Infrastructure Manager (VIM) used in the project is OpenStack.

3.2 Service Specifications

Presenting the service as a single VNF provides little flexibility for scaling possibilities. The service must be separated into functional blocks that belong to different VNFs composing the whole network service. This allows an efficient orchestration of the service according to the demand and at the same time it enables the provision of redundancy to the service.

Key to define the VNFs that compose the service is to detect which ones belong to the signalling plane and which ones to the data plane. Bear in mind that data plane is susceptible to scale up proportionally to the number of users while the control play may follow a different scaling ratio. Being able to separate these planes, enables us to replicate the data plane near the end-user easily, following the demand in specific locations.

Figure 1 shows how MCPTT service has been divided in several VNFs following the user/control plane separation criteria, as well as considering the most efficient way to scale the service. The first elements being isolated are control elements as the DNS (Domain Name System) server, the HSS (Home Subscriber Server) and the controlling CSC (Common Services Core) servers. The CSC is composed by the services: IDMS (Identification Management System), KMS (Key Management System), CMS (Configuration Management System) and GMS (Group Management System). This enables the redundancy of these critical control components. The MCPTT application server is also separated into a functional block that manages the Floor Control responsible for the arbitration of talk turns, and the Media Distribution VNF, in charge of processing the media encryption, recording and media multiplexing tasks. This way the system achieves a complete Control and User Plane Separation. The service descriptors are defined in OSM following the Yang information model.

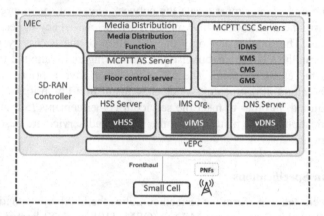

Fig. 1. MCPTT network service

4 Validation Scenario

To demonstrate that this architecture provides a solution for deploying efficient and elastic MC services over a network slice, we will describe a validation scenario [11]. It is composed by three stages with an increasing emergency level, that are described next. The objective of this validation scenario is how the MCPPT service behaves with the increase in each scenario of the number of PS users that will use the MCPTT service when increasing the alarm level. Monitoring and orchestration will ensure continuity and quality of service.

Stage 1: Under normal circumstances, the platform provides different network slices. Some slices correspond to PS organizations running respectively a MC service and while other slices correspond to legacy end users that have subscribed to the classical communications. Each network slice is composed of an allocation of cloud resources. In addition to the QoS guarantees for each tenant, the deployment owner has to assure the required levels of isolation in the provisioning of the network slices.

Stage 2: In case of emergency, the MANO will be able to react to the new service requirements. For instance, the MCPTT communications provider may require additional service in order to cope with an increased number of first responders. Based on service scaling policies, the MANO will implement new elastic resource allocation schemes, giving priority access to first responders and taking into cloud resources (for deploying more resource-consuming cloud services). In this situation, the commercial slices may suffer a service degradation in favor of the PS slices in order to guarantee the quality of service of mission-critical applications.

Stage 3: In case that ICT infrastructure is damaged during a natural disaster or a terrorist attack, the infrastructure should be able to be operative to dynamically instantiate required services to ensure local service continuity until the infrastructure is restored.

5 Monitoring and Orchestration

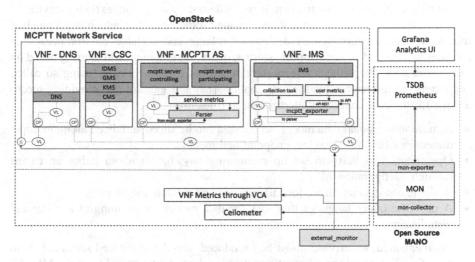

Fig. 2. Service monitoring and orchestration

Telemetry is the automated process of collecting measurements from remote or inaccessible equipment and transmit them to receivers. Monitoring is a continuous assessment that is in charge of the analysis of the data extracted from telemetry and use it to manage the service. The telemetry and monitoring in an NFV system are mainly in charge of managing information that the hypervisor or the VNFs itself expose during execution. These systems are expected to enable additional non-functional requirements such as: scalability, non-intrusiveness and service continuity.

In order to guarantee the quality of the service, the monitoring system must be continuously analyzing the metrics received. These metrics can be oriented towards resources or service performance indicators. With the first ones the system extracts information of the hardware infrastructure on which the services are deployed. And with the second, it ensures that it complies with the agreed SLAs.

Each service requires a specific capacity to perform efficiently, minimizing processing times and delays. The quality of the services offered to customers must comply with the service level contracted, for this reason, the monitoring system must be provided with intelligence. So that depending on the metrics received by telemetry, it can predict the degradation of the quality of service and notify the system orchestrator to perform the most appropriate decision.

Figure 2 represents how the resource metrics are collected using the Open-Stack Monitoring Frameworks [12]. Ceilometer [13] is focused on collecting data from physical and virtual resources available to the cloud deployment. These data can be stored by a Gnochi [14] database, and actions or alarms can be triggered according to predefined conditions set by the user on Aodh [15].

On the other hand, service metrics are exported using Juju's charms, preconfigured with the VCA (VNF Configuration and Abstraction) on the orchestration phase. With this procedure, the VNF can be accessed to gather any information from the running services, in this case scenario these metrics are being collected by the mcptt_exporter service.

Then, the service metrics are collected using Prometheus [16], which is a white box monitoring and alerting system designed for large and scalable environments that includes built-in and active scraping, storing, querying, graphing, and alerting based on time series data. Prometheus covers the domains of instrumentation (using so called "exporters" to instrument platform or applications) and monitoring (providing mechanisms for the data collection, alerting, etc.). It features:

- A multi-dimensional data model, where data can be sliced and diced along multiple dimensions like host, service, endpoint and method.
- Operational simplicity to set up monitoring anywhere without being an expert through configuration files.
- Scalable and decentralized, for independent and reliable monitoring.
- A powerful query language that uses the data model for meaningful alerting and visualisation.

As mentioned, an exporter must be introduced into the monitored service. It is in charge of publishing all the information related to the users, calls and from the MCPTT Server itself. These service metrics are collected and stored by Prometheus, while Grafana is used for graphic visualization.

The data collected during monitoring can be used to trigger events for automated resource re-provisioning, in cooperation with the orchestrator OSM. One of the main methods to guarantee the fulfillment of the SLAs is autoscaling. This solution needs the allocation of a load balancer to monitor and distribute the loads across all the VMs on the scaling group. Hence, autoscaling can increase, decrease, and replace instances without manual intervention even across thousands of instances. This should not be confused with scale-in and scale-out of the Network Service; NS scaling refers to the addition or removal of VNFs. OSM supports scale-out and scale-in operations on running services.

6 Conclusions and Future Work

This paper presents an NFV architecture that deals with the tight requirements of a Mission-Critical service. It is capable of maintaining the high availability and reliability required for the service, while sharing the infrastructure in an elastic manner between mission critical and commercial users thanks to the supervision of a network orchestrator. To that aim, the network slicing based on virtualization techniques is key to maintain isolation between clients.

The intelligent orchestration process of the network slices involves the collection of performance data through a monitoring system that processes them and generates the corresponding action on the infrastructure. Being the most significant the scaling of the service VNFs. There are many algorithms that employ machine learning or other AI methods to decide the optimal number of instances of a VNF needed to provide the requested service. This paper is focused on presenting the architecture, foreseen for the future the definition of the metrics or the development of an intelligent decision-making system that cooperates with the orchestrator.

Acknowledgements. This work has been partly funded by the EU funded H2020 5G-PPP project ESSENCE (Grant Agreement No. 761592) and the Spanish Government's MINECO project 5GRANVIR (TEC2016-80090-C2-2-R).

References

1. Technical Specification Group Services and SystemAspects; Mission Critical Push to Talk (MCPTT) over LTE, 3GPP TS 22.179 v16.1.0 Stage 1(Release 14), April 2018
2. Foukas, X., Elmokashfi, A., Patounas, G., Marina, M.K.: Network slicing in 5G: survey and challenges. IEEE Commun. Mag. **55**(5), 94–100 (2017). https://doi.org/10.1109/MCOM. 2017.1600951
3. Martínez, R., et al.: Network slicing resource allocation and monitoring over multiple clouds and networks. In: Proceedings Optical Fiber Communications Conference and Exposition (OFC), pp. 1–3. IEEE (2018)
4. Ordoñez-Lucena, J., Ameigeiras, P., Lopez, D., Ramos-Munoz, J.J., Lorca, J., Folgueira, J.: Network slicing for 5G with SDN/NFV: concepts, architectures and challenges. IEEE Commun. Mag. **55**(5), 80–87 (2017). https://doi.org/10.1109/MCOM.2017.1600935
5. Han, K., et al.: Application-driven end-to-end slicing: when wireless network virtualization orchestrates with NFV-based mobile edge computing. IEEE Access **6**, 26567–26577 (2018). https://doi.org/10.1109/ACCESS.2018.2834623
6. Wang, X., Wu, C., Le, F., Liu, A., Li, Z., Lau, F.: Online VNF scaling in datacenters. In: IEEE 9th International Conference on Cloud Computing (CLOUD), San Francisco, CA, pp. 140–147 (2016). https://doi.org/10.1109/cloud.2016.0028
7. Fei, X., Liu, F., Xu, H., Jin, H.: Adaptive VNF scaling and flow routing with proactive demand prediction. In: IEEE Conference on Computer Communications, Honolulu, HI, pp. 486–494 (2018). https://doi.org/10.1109/infocom.2018.8486320
8. Wang, X., Wu, C., Le, F., Lau, F.C.M.: Online learning-assisted VNF service chain scaling with network uncertainties. In: IEEE 10th International Conference on Cloud Computing (CLOUD), Honolulu, CA, pp. 205–213 (2017). https://doi.org/10.1109/cloud.2017.34
9. ETSI Industry Specification Group. Network Functions Virtualization (NFV); Virtual Network Functions Architecture. Etsi GS NFV-SWA 001 (2014)
10. Open Source Mano: https://osm.etsi.org/
11. 5G ESSENCE Deliverable D2.2. Overall System Architecture and Specifications, June 2018
12. OpenStack Telemetry: https://wiki.openstack.org/wiki/Telemetry
13. OpenStack Celiometer: https://docs.openstack.org/ceilometer/
14. OpenStack Gnocchi: https://wiki.openstack.org/wiki/Gnocchi
15. OpenStack Aodh: https://docs.openstack.org/aodh/
16. Prometheus: https://prometheus.io/

Testbeds for the Implementation of 5G in the European Union: The Innovative Case of the 5G-DRIVE Project

Ioannis P. Chochliouros[1]([⊠]) [iD], Anastasia S. Spiliopoulou[1],
Alexandros Kostopoulos[1], Eirini Vasilaki[1], Uwe Herzog[2],
Athanassios Dardamanis[3], Tao Chen[4], Latif Ladid[5],
and Marinos Agapiou[6]

[1] Hellenic Telecommunications Organization (OTE) S.A.,
99 Kifissias Avenue, 15124 Maroussi, Athens, Greece
ichochliouros@oteresearch.gr
[2] EURESCOM GmbH, Wieblinger Weg 19/64, 69123 Heidelberg, Germany
[3] SmartNet S.A., 2 Lakonias Street, 17342 Ilioupolis, Athens, Greece
[4] VTT Technical Research Center of Finland,
Kaitoväylä 1, 90571 Oulu, Finland
[5] University of Luxembourg, 6 Avenue de la Fonte,
4364 Esch-sur-Alzette, Luxembourg
[6] National and Kapodistrian University of Athens,
6 Panepistimiopolis, 15784 Ilissia, Greece

Abstract. An essential part of the actual EU policy towards promoting and validating 5G applications and of related solutions is via the establishment of an explicit plan and of a detailed roadmap for trials, tests and experimental activities though dedicated testbeds, in parallel with the current research and development activities coming from the 5G-PPP framework. The present paper discusses the fundamental role of the proposed trials' initiatives within the broader European framework for the establishment and the promotion of 5G and also analyses the corresponding streams as indispensable parts of the 5G-PPP context, aiming to support innovation and growth. In addition, as part of the broader initiative for trial actions we identify the case of the 5G-DRIVE project that aims to realise 5G deployment scenarios (i.e., enhanced Mobile Broadband and Vehicle-to-Everything communications), between the EU and China, by discussing the fundamental features of the respective trials sites.

Keywords: 5G · 5G Action Plan (5GAP) ·
5G Public Private Partnership (5G-PPP) · Horizon 2020 ·
Enhanced Mobile Broadband (eMBB) · Experimental platforms ·
Mobile edge computing (MEC) · Network slicing · Pilot trials ·
Testing and validation facilities · Vehicle-to-Everything (V2X)

© IFIP International Federation for Information Processing 2019
Published by Springer Nature Switzerland AG 2019
J. MacIntyre et al. (Eds.): AIAI 2019 Workshops, IFIP AICT 560, pp. 78–92, 2019.
https://doi.org/10.1007/978-3-030-19909-8_7

1   Introduction

Over the last decade the European Union's (EU) electronic communications policy has been effective in delivering more competition, lower prices and more choices for businesses and consumers [1]. However, the full economic and social benefits of this sort of broader digital transformation will only be achieved if Europe can ensure extensive deployment and reception of very high capacity networks, in rural as well as urban areas and across all of society that will be able to offer innovative facilities and related services in a broad thematic range. One of the central aims of the European Commission's (EC) Digital Single Market Strategy [2] was, *therefore*, to generate the precise environment and conditions for the deployment of advanced digital-very high-capacity-networks.

While "basic broadband" (i.e., of a speed of at least 2 Mbps) is available to every European, mainly enabled by legacy infrastructures, this is no longer good enough for the ongoing digital transformation, strongly promoted by the actual European policies and being aligned to relevant international trends affecting both market and society. Transformative solutions based on Internet connectivity (such as cloud computing, Internet of Things, high performance computing, big data analytics etc.) are expected to modify business processes as well as to influence social interactions. New digital applications -*like virtual and augmented reality (VR/AR), increasingly connected and automated driving, artificial intelligence*- will necessitate the speed, quality and responsiveness that can only be delivered by very high-capacity broadband networks.

Digital technologies support innovation and competitiveness across private and public sectors and enable scientific progress in all disciplines. The proposed Horizon 2020 (H2020) Work Program (WP) 2018–2020 [3] covers a great variety of modern Information and Communication Technologies (ICT) thus aiming to modify multiple domains, with particular emphasis given among others, to the development of the 5th Generation of Mobile Communications (the so called as "5G") ([4, 5]). By properly pursuing the change initiated under the previous EU WPs, it is expected that related research activities will continue to promote more innovation-orientation to ensure that the EU industry remains strong in the core technologies, being at the roots of future value chains.

However, a suitable strategic approach is essential for the EU so as to realise a clear and leading position in the international "arena" and to obtain any relevant (early) advantage of the new market opportunities promoted and enhanced by 5G, via appropriate validation of the related 5G services and facilities, for the benefit of the "whole" economy and society.

2   Actions for Tests-Trials at EU Level Towards the 5G Promotion

The promotion of the digitisation process in some "key" industrial sectors based on 5G connectivity, as well as the dawn of modern business models, clearly implicate for closer partnerships between the concerned sectors and the telecommunication sector.

While a few markets will naturally lead innovation and attract most of the initial investments, a number of sectors recognise the need to "run" pilot trials to increase predictability, reduce investment risks and validate both the technologies and the concerned business models. Experiments are also needed to "provide input" for the standardisation effort towards establishing validated norms and recommendations.

Among the actual priorities of the EC, working interactively with Member States (MSs) and industrial stakeholders/market actors is the voluntary establishment of a common timetable for the launch of early 5G networks (initially scheduled to be operational by the end of 2018) and followed by the launch of fully commercial 5G services in Europe by the end of 2020. According to the 5G Action Plan (5GAP) [6], the relevant EU timetable is actually driven by the following key objectives: (i) Promoting preliminary trials, under the 5G-PPP arrangement [7], to take place from 2017 onwards, and pre-commercial trials with a clear EU cross-border dimension from 2018; (ii) supporting commercial launch of 5G services in at least one major city in all MSs in 2020, *and*; (ii) encouraging MSs to develop national 5G deployment roadmaps as part of the national broadband plans, with uninterrupted coverage in all urban areas and along main transport paths in 2025.

Many EU cities are already strongly engaged in 5G development, trials and pilots and first commercial deployment will already start in specific EU cities in 2019. The EC EU 5G Observatory website/online platform [8] has been officially launched on late of September 2018 and provides independent monitoring information concerning the main actual and likely market developments, 5G trials and other actions taken by MSs, as well as industry stakeholders regarding 5G market introduction in EU and in a global context. This allows assessing the progress of the EU 5GAP and to take actions to fully implement it. The Observatory focuses primarily on developments in EU, along with major international developments that could impact the EU market.

Most of the actual roadmap implementation is both driven and supported by the industry sector, on a private basis. In fact, the core part of the 5G trials and pilots is - and will be achieved- through private trials (commercial and pre-commercial) between network operators and manufacturers/vendors and is increasingly involving vertical stakeholders. Through the present 5GAP, the EC supports the creation of suitable requirements for the intended 5G deployment in Europe, particularly the identification of the related harmonised spectrum and of the regulatory conditions, while supplementary support for trials and pilots is made available from the EC H2020 program in support of the 5G-PPP implementation, specific national programs of MSs as well as from specific programs (such as the European Space Agency (ESA) Satellite for 5G Initiative).

The EC strongly supports pilots and experiments in the course of the 5G growth, though the coordination of the 5G-PPP, via selected 5G trials. The EC counts on the trial results to be able to identify and address specific sectorial policy issues and seek the active support of MSs to resolve them whenever they constitute a major obstacle to high value applications relying on 5G. Furthermore, there is requirement need to guarantee that hardware, terminals (here the term implicates not only for smart phones but also a full range of Internet of Things (IoT) and connected devices (cars, drones, urban furniture, etc.)) and devices based on 5G connectivity are available in due time before 2020, to encourage uptake and demand.

Experimental platforms for 4G/5G in Europe are the results of private and public efforts at national and European level. Accelerating trial capabilities and other pilots, the platforms remain subject to continuous efforts targeting the full 5G picture and future evolutions. As such, actual 5G infrastructure deployment roadmap is highly dependent on the capability to deliver relevant and comprehensive set of platforms addressing remaining gaps & challenges. Thus, one should also consider such platforms as valuable and demonstrated set of 5G enablers, beyond the trial objectives. However, complementarity and efficiency of the efforts deserve coordination among the diversity in the documentation of the existing platforms. As a consequence, it is of tremendous importance to describe the matching elements of each platform compared to the complete 5G landscape. For this, a common classification and documentation for 5G platforms addressing different target groups is mandatory. Consistent data structures and unified meta-information like name of the platform, countries where the platform is deployed and additional information on features and capabilities is fundamental. Collections of data provided by platforms have to support answers of diverse stakeholders' research, public sector or industry.

From a high-level perspective, one way to "view" the 5G ecosystem can be in terms of platforms (hardware (HW) and software (SW), services and use cases). For new platforms and services to be created, key decisions need to be taken, both business-wise and technically. Business cases have so to be developed, while tests, trials and evaluations conducted to satisfy the various stakeholders that expected outcomes need to be achieved. Considering vertical sectors, these will make use of such innovations and generate use cases for their particular sector(s). Investment and development will be required (implicating that new processes or ways of doing business may need to be considered), key decisions are to be made, business cases are to be developed and evaluations are to be conducted. Usually, some use cases may be more demanding than others and will "drive" the platform and services design and implementation. Some vertical sectors can be earlier/early adopters for the new technology/services and others will follow and make use of it, once it is proven.

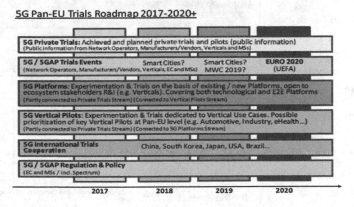

Fig. 1. Pan-European Trials Roadmap 2017–2020 - strategy and streams [9].

Within the 5G-PPP context, the Trials Working Group (WG) is elaborating a solid and comprehensive strategy to develop the Pan-EU coordinated trials [9] as well as international trials with the participation of non-EU countries. The 5G Pan-EU Trials Roadmap is addressing several of the 5G Action Plan (5GAP) key elements and targets to develop the necessary synergies between these elements. The main objectives of the Roadmap are to: (i) Affirm global European leadership on 5G technology, 5G networks deployment and profitable 5G business models; (ii) demonstrate benefits of 5G to vertical sectors, public sector, businesses and consumers; (iii) show a clear path to successful and timely 5G deployment; (iv) provide robust response to the EC 5GAP, *and*; (v) complement commercial trials and demonstrations as well as national initiatives [10].

This roadmap includes several inter-related streams, as depicted in detail in Fig. 1, and these comprise of: (i) Private experimentation and trials; (ii) large-scale 5G events and showcases, including national and pan-EU events; (iii) development and use of Research & Innovation (R&I) platforms for 5G experimentation and trials; (iv) R&I experimentation and trials in the context of vertical applications and use cases; (v) 5G international trials cooperation, *and*; (vi) 5G and 5GAP Regulation and Policy ensuring acceleration of 5G adoption and deployment (including spectrum, network neutrality, EU de-fragmentation, etc.).

In a "similar" *-or somehow "equivalent"-* approach, the EC in cooperation with the 5G Infrastructure Association (5G IA) has also identified [9] the following distinct steps (covering the broader period 2014–2024) as depicted in Fig. 2, below. This figure also incorporates relevance of intended trials to major events, so that to support 5G innovation for the benefit of the involved end-users. In addition, Fig. 2 summarises the overall 5G Pan-EU Trials Roadmap time plan and relevant standardisation, regulatory and ecosystems time plan(s).

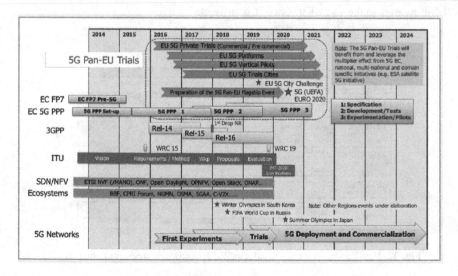

Fig. 2. Overall 5G Pan-European Trials Roadmap 2014–2024 [9].

Before 2018 (i.e., before the first 5G standard release by the 3rd Generation Partnership Project (3GPP) in Release 15, Stage 3) [11] it has been envisaged to have technical trials run by independent trial consortia in various countries, independent of the status of standardisation, to demonstrate and validate the new 5G capabilities as well as foster an ecosystem around the new 5G capabilities. Vertical industries have been involved in this trials' phase, while these trials have demonstrated several key 5G functionalities and technical/technological enablers. During and after 2018 European stakeholders moved to agree on trial specifications (e.g., use-cases, scenarios, interfaces, agreement to transfer use-cases across trial networks) valid for Pan-European trials, based as much as possible on standard-compliant systems. These trials, as performed in a more "extended" framework, aim to demonstrate wider interoperability and support for vertical use-cases in order to claim global public attention. In the following subsections we briefly discuss the various conceptual streams, as appearing in Fig. 1.

5G Private Trials Stream: This has been the case of the early stages when trials have been realised by specific initiatives promoted by some market actors for their own needs and priorities or, *exceptionally*, within the "limited" framework of some collaborative actions or projects.

5G/5GAP Trials Events Stream: There are and will be an increasing number of 5G private experimentations and trials done on bilateral (Network Operator (NO) and Manufacturer/Vendor), trilateral (NO, Manufacturer/Vendor and Vertical stakeholder) and multilateral (NO, Manufacturer/Vendor and different stakeholders) basis. Such experimentations and trials shall be considered upon private basis, while information will be either available *a posteriori* (achieved) or *a priori* (pre-announcement). The 5G-PPP Trials WG is responsible to collect the major public information related to announced and pre-announced experimentation and trials. Specific added value analysis will be achieved through different perspectives, such as: (i) Industrial stakeholders; (ii) countries, (iii) 5G pillars (eMBB, URLLC (Ultra-Reliable and Low-Latency Communication) and mMTC (massive Machine Type Communication)) and KPIs (e.g., data rate, mobility, latency, density, reliability, positioning accuracy, coverage, etc.); (iv) timing (2018, 2019, 2020 and onwards) *and*; (v) standardisation phases and releases (e.g.: 3GPP Release15 [11], Release16 [12] and onwards).

5G Platforms Stream: 5G Platforms are a useful tool to support the 5G European trials. These platforms can support the execution of 5G services and use cases, including for mass market and vertical sectors. Due to the high diversity of platforms, use cases, trials and maturity stages of technology, the 5G Platforms can be classified in three different levels, that is: (i) Research; (ii) End-to-End (E2E) Trials, *and*; (iii) pre-Commercial. A number of platforms have been designed in Europe (e.g. from EU-funded research projects) that can serve as a "basis" for 5G trials [13]. However, because the standardisation of 5G is an ongoing activity, 5G Platforms will have to evolve from existing and new platforms, requiring further investments. In such scenario, cooperation between platforms is a way to rapidly adapt to changes/improvements to standards, to reduce costs, permit large trials, and even to interconnect with sites in other regions. The 5G-PPP Trials WG is assessing the interest, feasibility conditions and possible solutions to create and maintain a pan-European platform, or a network of federated platforms, to be used for 5G pan-European trials.

5G Vertical Pilots Stream: 5G experimentation and trials will evidently address vertical applications and use cases. The vertical trials may be partly connected to the private trials and directly connected to the 5G available platforms (pre-Commercial and R&I). The selection of vertical pilots should take into account the sectors already mentioned in the 5GAP, including but not limited to, the media and entertainment, public safety, eHealth, automotive, transport and logistic sectors. It will also incorporate the progress already achieved by the 5G Infrastructure PPP on the 5G use by vertical sectors. The 5G-PPP Trials WG's aim is to support the selection of vertical and use cases for trials for a better understanding of the technical and technology requirements. In any case, the pre-definition of the vertical trials will address: (i) Description of vertical sectors; (ii) use cases addressed; (iii) technical requirements, *and*; (iv) technologies required for the provision of requirements. This step can enable a gap analysis to focus further R&I to overcome any remaining technology gaps.

5G International Trials Cooperation Stream: Multiple European 5G network trials and most of the 5G technologies under trials will be available for commercial deployment by 2020. In any case and beyond the 5G EU-focused developments, the 5G Pan-EU trials are implemented within a global context where several trials, pre-commercial and even commercial deployment initiatives are already taking place in other countries and regions outside the EU. Since 5G will be deployed worldwide, it is required to work not only towards accelerating global 5G standards, but also on trialing and interoperability with other main regions. EU-"X" joint trials, where "X" includes international counterpart countries like China, Japan, Korea, Brazil and US, are "key" to ensure a common understanding of 5G as well as global interoperability. On the private side, the 5G IA has already signed bilateral Memorandums of Understanding (MoUs) with the leading 5G visionary organisations in China (IMT-2020 5G promotion group), Korea (5G Forum), Japan (5G Mobile Communications Promotion Forum) and 5G Americas (North and South America). Specific joint experimentations and trials will be developed in the context of these MoUs.

5G/5GAP Regulation and Policy Stream: As the validation of 5G services and facilities is to take place via trials and experimentation, it is expected that this will also affect EU policies and relevant regulation. For certain domains like access to and use of selected frequency bands of spectrum, results are to be immediate, while for other cases results may affect further development of technical solutions as well as corresponding market policies.

The ongoing twenty-one (-21-) 5G-PPP *Phase 2* projects [7] (2017–2019) contribute to the prototyping, experimentation and trialing of 5G technologies and components for specific use-cases including vertical use-cases developed with vertical stakeholders. This infrastructure offers the suitable level of openness to allow vertical industries to test their innovative 5G business cases by using *ad-hoc* network resource control in an E2E interoperability framework. With the application-specific requirements and usage scenarios for 5G already identified, the experiments are investigating 5G functionalities spanning eMBB, uRLLC and mMTC. These requirements stem from an analysis of business aspects and applications driven by the verticals. In the automotive sector, *in particular*, industry stakeholders within the 5G-PPP are embracing connected and autonomous cars, vehicle-to-infrastructure, entertainment and corresponding media services. The anticipated impact is huge and extensive, as this promotes new ecosystems of commercial and public-sector product and service providers.

In the same scope, the 5G-PPP *Phase 3* of pan-EU 5G E2E facilities/platforms (ICT-17) projects [7] started in July 2018 and cover 20 platforms/nodes in EU (each one in a European city). Simultaneously, the three *Phase 3* corridors (under ICT-18) projects started in November 2018, address multiple EU "test corridors" [14]. The so called as the 5G corridors make Europe the biggest experiment area rolling out the 5G technology. This confirms Europe's leadership in large-scale testing and early deployment of 5G infrastructure also enabling connected and automated driving, *among others*. As of October 2018, 10 digital cross-border corridors have been identified for Connected and Automated Mobility (CAM).

As of October 2018, more than 140 trials and pilots have been reported as "being active" within the EU. In June 2019, 6–7 PPP *Phase 3* Vertical Pilots (ICT-19) projects will "target" large scale trials and pilots, including complete E2E 5G systems and leveraging the existing platforms projects. It is expected that additional 5G test corridors projects will be launched in the context of the PPP *Phase 3*. In addition to the 5G private trials and pilots reported in the EC EU 5G Observatory, the 5G Infrastructure PPP Verticals Cartography, launched in September 2018, tracks city-based 5G trials and pilots from 5G Infrastructure PPP *Phase 2* projects across eight vertical clusters: Automotive, Energy, Health, Industry, Media and Entertainment, Public Safety, Smart Cities, Transport and Logistics planned in 2018–2020 [15].

3   The Context of the 5G-DRIVE Project

The 5G-DRIVE project [16] aims to perform a "close" collaboration between EU and China to synchronise 5G technologies and spectrum issues before the final roll-out of 5G in order to "address" two most promising 5G deployment scenarios, namely enhanced Mobile Broadband (eMBB) and Vehicle-to-Everything (V2X) communications. The eMBB is one of three primary 5G New Radio (NR) use cases defined by the 3GPP [17] as part of its SMARTER (Study on New Services and Markets Technology Enablers) project [18]. This "addresses" the human-centric use cases for access to multi-media content, services and data. Actual technology trends purely "demonstrate" that the demand for mobile broadband will continue to increase, thus leading to eMBB. The related usage scenario covers a range of cases, including wide-area coverage and hotspot, which have different requirements. On the other hand, V2X communication is the transfer of information from a vehicle to any "entity" that may affect the vehicle, and *vice versa*. It is a vehicular communication system that integrates other more specific types of communication as V2I (Vehicle-to-Infrastructure), V2N (Vehicle-to-Network), V2V (Vehicle-to-Vehicle), V2P (Vehicle-to-Pedestrian), V2D (vehicle-to-Device) and V2G (Vehicle-to-Grid).

The 5G-DRIVE project falls within the context of the ICT-22-2018 Call ("EU China 5G Collaboration") [3]. The main scope is to conduct 5G trials addressing two specific scenarios: (i) Scenario no 1 - eMBB on the 3.5 GHz band, which is a priority band in the two regions for early introduction of very high rate services; and; (ii) Scenario no 2 - Internet of Vehicles (IoV) based on LTE-V2X using the 5.9 GHz band for V2V and the 3.5 GHz band for V2N. The overall goal is to evaluate in real setup innovative end-to-end 5G systems built on the outcomes of the previous phases of the 5G R&I. More specifically, the optimisation of the band usage in multiple scenarios with different coverage is a key target, so as the validation of the geographic interoperability of the 3.5 and 5.9 GHz bands for these use cases. Both scenarios shall be implemented in both regions (EU and China) through testbeds with interoperability forming the core of the R&I work.

The underlying trials' testing facilities shall implement the latest mature and broadly commonly agreed 5G systems, network architectures and technologies spanning from the core/transport networks, the radio access, up to the service, orchestration, management and security components. The trial facility shall not be restricted to innovative 5G radio access technology, but should include and enable the evolution of 5G networks innovations in network slicing, virtualisation, cross-domain orchestration, in view of supporting resource control from multiple tenants. In EU, trials are preferably implemented over the 5G end-to-end platforms developed under ICT-17-2018 [3]. The 5G trials' infrastructures shall facilitate the testing and validation of innovative applications for each of the defined scenarios, including efficiency solutions in the areas of spectrum usage, energy consumption and costs.

The main objective of the 5G-DRIVE context is to "bridge" current 5G developments in Europe and China through joint trials and research activities in order to facilitate technology convergence, spectrum harmonisation and business innovation before large scale commercial deployments of 5G networks take place. In order to achieve this goal, the 5G-DRIVE develops "key" 5G technologies and pre-commercial testbeds for eMBB and V2X services in collaboration with the "twinned" Chinese project led by *China Mobile*. Trials for testing and validating key 5G functionalities, services and network planning will be conducted in eight cities across the EU and China.

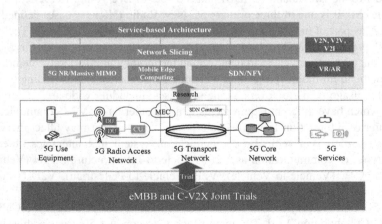

Fig. 3. Overall concept of the 5G-DRIVE project's approach.

5G-DRIVE's overall concept is illustrated in Fig. 3, which shows the three "core" streams and depicts the flow from research, to adaptation into existing testbeds and commercial testbed deployments, to the real-world trials of the 5G radio access network (RAN) and the wider 5G network. The project "brings together" solid research competence, commercial grade testbeds, and some of the stakeholders who will eventually become major customers of 5G systems.

In the 5G-DRIVE context there are partners with rather extensive 5G testbed installations - these are three facilities that have been defined, specified and deployed to "meet" the individual requirements of the involved three research organisations (UoS, VTT and JRC, as discussed in detail in the following sub-sections). In fact, three testbed sites have already been set up with commercial and experimental-grade equipment, supporting capacity provision in very dense deployments, network slicing and V2X, as well as testing of new technologies in any part of the network in a fully-controlled environment. While all three testbeds are set up with commercial grade equipment, each one has a special focus: the University of Surrey (UoS) testbed can support capacity provision in very dense deployments over a 4 km^2 area; the Espoo testbed (VTT) demonstrates the use of slicing and V2X; the JRC facility allows the testing of new technologies in any part of the network in a fully-controlled environment. All testbeds are defined in an evolutionary approach and allow the gradual introduction and testing of new equipment, as well as new mechanisms, algorithms and protocols.

These characteristics will be exploited in the entire 5G-DRIVE's context. In the research stream, the project will investigate network and RAN slicing, mobile edge computing (MEC), massive MIMO (Multiple Inputs, Multiple Outputs) for the 5G NR, as well as SDN and network function virtualisation (NFV) techniques applied to different traffic and load scenarios. Techniques and mechanisms in the research stream will be integrated into the most appropriate testbed. Wherever possible, 5G-DRIVE will endeavour to deploy such new mechanisms into all three testbeds.

The core objective of the project is to extensively trial eMBB and V2X service delivery under real world conditions. The stringent requirements for the delivery of such services will be defined jointly with the mobile operators in the consortium (Orange, OTE), as well as stakeholders from the automotive and intelligent transports markets (BMW, Vedia, Dynniq, ERT). These partners will be involved in the use case and trial requirements definition, as well as in its subsequent implementation and analysis. The inclusion of these stakeholders is imperative to ensure that the trials and solutions "do meet" the requirements from the vertical domains.

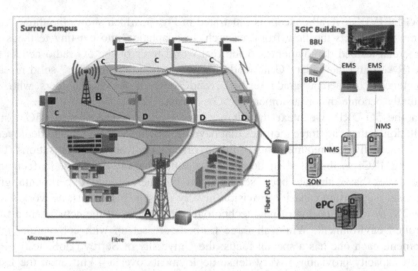

Fig. 4. High-level view of the University of Surrey's test network in the UK.

As shown in Fig. 4, the UoS trial site and the 5G Innovation Centre [19] includes a Cloud-RAN (C-RAN) test platform [20] which supports clusters of remote radio heads (RRH), supported by high performance core processing facilities for experimental research on advanced techniques such as joint transmission coordinated multi-point transmission and reception (CoMP) schemes [21]. In addition, the test network provides a unique environment to test operation of heterogeneous access networks in a real life environment. In the context of 5G-DRIVE, it will focus on the development and evaluation of the eMBB scenario. The testbed is connected to the Vodafone Core Network, Fujitsu Cloud Computing facilities and covers a 4 km^2 area for the testing of 5G technologies. The coverage area encompasses a stretch of motorway, rural, urban and dense urban radio environments. The outdoor deployment consists of 44 sites and 65 cells (of which 3 are macro cells, the remainder are small and ultra-dense cells). This end-to-end testbed incorporates a different range of frequency bands (3.5 GHz, 28 GHz and 60 GHz) and allows the testing and trialling of new air-interface solutions. Supported by a mix of wireless and fibre optic backhaul connectivity, trials can be matched to meet industry requirements. Finally, the platform can support interfacing to other testbeds, servers and databases for integration of different components provided by other consortium members and external experiments.

The Espoo trial site (see Fig. 5) provides 5G testing facilities built in several national projects under the 5GTNF (5G Test Network of Finland) framework. In the context of 5G-DRIVE, it will focus on the development and evaluation of both eMBB and V2X scenarios. The current network infrastructure is built on top of Nokia's NetLeap LTE test network [22]. It will be gradually upgraded to 5G networks when 5G NR and 5G core network components are available. The network contains both indoor and outdoor eNodeBs operating at 2.6 GHz, lamppost integrated small cell networks operating at 3.5 GHz and mm-wave bands at 26 GHz, as well as Wi-Fi networks operating at unlicensed 2.4 GHz and 5 GHz. This site enables creating a virtual mobile network with its own evolved packet core (EPC) and can utilize the edge computing platform for developing localized services.

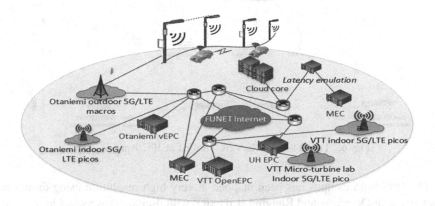

Fig. 5. Espoo trial site at Otaniemi Espoo in Finland.

The design of the test network is such that it is open for experimental EPCs. This enables multi-operator scenarios and testing of network slicing in the project. MEC platforms are currently being installed at the Otaniemi site. With the aid of an artificial delay element (network emulator), the performance of MEC for URLLC use cases can be tested in different latency scenarios. eNodeBs are connected to a 10 Gbps SDN-enabled backhaul and to an OpenStack cloud environment. The testbed in Espoo provides facilities and test environments for SDN/MEC, indoor positioning, latency reduction, reliability and other technology topics targeted by 5G-DRIVE.

The JRC Ispra site is a fully fenced research campus equipped with high-level safety and security features – a 167-hectare controlled environment for hands-on experimentation, testing and demonstration purposes. It features 36 km of roads under real-life driving conditions, as well as 9 Vehicle Emissions Laboratories (VELA 1–9) that can be used for calibration, electromagnetic compatibility/interference testing and other experimental activities. In the context of 5G-DRIVE, the JRC Ispra site will focus on the development and evaluation of V2X scenarios, with a particular focus on laboratory and field ITS-G5/LTE-V2X coexistence testing (see Fig. 6).

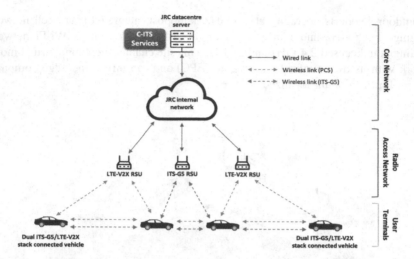

Fig. 6. The ITS-G5/LTE-V2X Testbed at JPC Ispra, in Italy.

The JRC Ispra campus has been mapped at very high resolution using drones and Laser Imaging Detection and Ranging (LiDAR), with digital maps available in various formats. This information will be used for network planning (i.e. predictions of radio propagation and network coverage), as well as vehicle localisation and intelligent routing. As far as network infrastructure is concerned, the JRC owns various LTE eNodeBs of both commercial and experimental grade, as well as a software-defined LTE core network to provide mobility, session management and user authentication services to internal test users. MEC infrastructure can be connected to the core network using either radio links or low latency fibre. These systems will take the form of small-form factor PCs featuring roadside sensing and fast computing capabilities. Finally, the JRC is also equipped with a production-level Public Key Infrastructure (PKI) which has already been used as the European Root Certification Authority for the EU Digital Tachograph project [23]. The JRC has been directly involved in drafting the Certificate Policy for the European V2X (referred to as the Cooperative Intelligent Transport Systems (C-ITS) Trust Model) [25].

4   Conclusion

The present paper has discussed the important role of trials and of dedicated platforms at the European level as fundamental "enablers" for the 5G deployment and validation within the EU. The work identified the important role that 5G is expected to perform, as essential part of the EU policy for evolution and growth, offering benefits to the European market and citizens. More specifically, within the context of the actual 5G-PPP initiative, we have assessed the specific measures proposed and the roadmap already applied -or scheduled- towards establishing the necessary framework for the realisation of pilot actions and/or related trials, to serve the expected transition to the 5G. The European Commission, in particular, emphasizes on the establishment of an adequate and well-defined framework, able to support 5G growth via suitable experimental efforts. The proper development of the 5G ecosystem in Europe is strongly dependent on a dedicated roadmap that is harmonised to the present EU research effort, being able to promote and enlarge all potential technological and business benefits. To this aim, we have discussed the distinct and separate streams affecting these actions, in parallel to corresponding standardisation efforts, promotion of research programs and events of global character.

The actual 5G pan-European trials roadmap [24] is covering a broader scope than the 5GAP and the 5G Infrastructure PPP *Phase 3* (2018–20+). Most of the roadmap implementation is -and will be- covered by the industry on private basis, with part of this implementation supported by EC through the 5GAP, EC 5G Infrastructure PPP *Phase 3*, EC 5G Investment Fund and by MSs through specific national programs. More specifically, the 5G Infrastructure PPP *Phase 3* platforms projects (2018–2021) provide a pan-European large-scale E2E 5G validation network infrastructure, covering about 20 European sites and nodes on a pan-European basis. This infrastructure will provide the adequate level of openness to make it possible for vertical industries to test their innovative 5G business cases using *ad-hoc* network resource control in an E2E interoperability framework. The future roadmap of actual 5G infrastructure deployment is highly dependent on the capability to up-date existing or deliver a new relevant and comprehensive set of platforms addressing the remaining gaps and challenges as well as to promote new architectures [26].

Part of the above PPP *Phase 3* context is also the case of the 5G-DRIVE project which intends to realise a collaborative framework between EU and China so that to achieve mutual synchronisation of 5G technologies and spectrum issues before the final roll-out of 5G, around two essential 5G deployment scenarios (namely enhanced Mobile Broadband (eMBB) and Vehicle-to-Everything (V2X) communications). In this scope, we have presented, in detail, the related 5G-DRIVE trial sites that have been proposed by this project, as a characteristic example of the actual EU initiatives for trials and as an indispensable part of the European strategic framework for the 5G validation in certain domains that can be of significant benefit for the European economy and society.

Acknowledgments. This work has been performed in the scope of the *5G-DRIVE* European Research Project and has been supported by the Commission of the European Communities/ *H2020, Grant Agreement No. 814956.*

References

1. European Commission: Communication of the Commission: A Digital Single Market Strategy for Europe. COM(2015) 192 final, 06.05.2015. European Commission (2015)
2. European Commission: Communication of the Commission: Connectivity for a Competitive Digital Single Market: Towards a European Gigabit Society, COM(2016) 587 final, 14.09.2016. European Commission (2016)
3. Horizon 2020 (H2020) Work Program. https://ec.europa.eu/programmes/horizon2020/en/news/horizon-2020-work-programme-2018-2020

4. Andrews, J.G., Buzzi, S., Choi, W., Hanly, S.V., et al.: What will 5G be? IEEE JSAC Spec. Issue 5G Wirel. Commun. Syst. **32**(6), 1065–1082 (2014)
5. European Commission: 5G: Challenges, Research Priorities, and Recommendations – Joint White Paper. European Commission, Strategic Research and Innovation Agenda (2014)
6. European Commission: Communication of the Commission: 5G for Europe: An Action Plan, COM(2016) 588 Final, 14 Sept 2016
7. The 5G Public Private Partnership (5G-PPP). https://5g-ppp.eu/
8. The European 5G Observatory. http://5gobservatory.eu/
9. 5G-PPP: Trials Roadmap. https://5g-ppp.eu/5g-trials-roadmap/
10. 5G Pan-European Trials Roadmap Strategy, Short Document, February 2017. https://5g-ppp. eu/wp-content/uploads/2018/05/5GInfraPPP_TrialsWG_Roadmap_Version3.0.pdf
11. The 3rd Generation Partnership Project (3GPP): 3GPP TR 21.915 v0.5.0, Release description; Release 15, December 2018
12. The 3rd Generation Partnership Project: 3GPP Release 16. http://www.3gpp.org/release-16
13. Verdone, R., Manzalini, A.: White Paper on 5G Experimental Facilities in EU. NetWorld 2020 ETP, March 2016
14. European Commission: Cross-Border corridors for Connected and Automated Mobility. https://ec.europa.eu/digital-single-market/en/cross-border-corridors-connected-and-automated-mobility-cam
15. Global 5G: Verticals Cartography. http://global5g.org/cartography
16. G-DRIVE: 5G harmoniseD Research and trIals for serVice Evolution between EU and China 5G-PPP Project, Grant Agreement No. 814956. https://5g-drive.eu/
17. The 3rd Generation Partnership Project (3GPP). http://www.3gpp.org/about-3gpp
18. The 3rd Generation Partnership Project (3GPP): 3GPP Specification 22.891: Study on New Services and Markets Technology Enablers – Technical Report (TR) - Release 14 (2015)
19. University of Surrey: 5G Innovation Centre (5G IC). https://www.surrey.ac.uk/5gic
20. Fujitsu Network Communications Inc.: The Benefits of Cloud-RAN Architecture in Mobile Network Expansion, Richardson, Texas, US (2014)
21. Singh, S., et al.: Coordinated multipoint (CoMP) reception and transmission for LTE-advanced/4G. Int. J. Comput. Sci. (IJCST) **3**(2), 212–217 (2012)
22. Aalto, Finland: Mobile test network for research (Netleap). https://www.aalto.fi/services/mobile-test-network-for-research-netleap
23. Joint Research Centre (JRC). https://dtc.jrc.ec.europa.eu/dtc_erca_st.php
24. 5G Infrastructure Association (5G IA): 5G pan-European Trials Roadmap v.4. https://5g-ppp.eu/wp-content/uploads/2018/11/5GInfraPPP_TrialsWG_Roadmap_Version4.0.pdf
25. European Commission: Intelligent Transport Systems: Cooperative, Connected and Automated Mobility (CCAM). https://ec.europa.eu/transport/themes/its/c-its_en
26. Redana, S., Kaloxylos, A., Galis, A. Rost, P., Marsch, P., Queseth, O., et al.: Views on 5G architecture, white paper of the 5G-PPP architecture WG, July 2016. 5G-PPP (2016)

A Techno-Economic Analysis of Employing a Central Coordinator Entity in 5G Networks

Christos Tsirakis[1], Mariana Goldhamer[2], Panagiotis Matzoros[3],
George Agapiou[3(✉)], Dimitris Varoutas[4], and Marinos Agapiou[4]

[1] OTE Academy S.A., Department of Informatics and Telecommunications,
National and Kapodistrian University of Athens, Athens, Greece
ctsirakis@oteacademy.gr, ctsirakis@di.uoa.gr
[2] 4GCelleX, Tel Aviv, Israel
marianna001@gmail.com
[3] OTE S.A., Athens, Greece
{pmatzoros, gagapiou}@oteresearch.gr
[4] Department of Informatics and Telecommunications,
National and Kapodistrian University of Athens, Athens, Greece
{D. Varoutas, sdi1400002}@di.uoa.gr

Abstract. This research work describes the role of the Central Controller and Coordinator (C3) entity and its potential techno-economic gain when implemented in the upcoming 5G networks. We investigate how viable could be for a C3 Producer and for a cellular network Operator to produce and implement respectively the C3 entity in its network. The performance of techno-economic analysis is estimated by considering various key parameters and some useful conclusions are drawn.

Keywords: 5G · C3 entity · Techno-economic analysis · Producer · Operator

1 Introduction

"Mobile data traffic will grow at a compound annual growth rate (CAGR) of 47% from 2016 to 2021", according to [1]. So mobile network operators are facing massive data growth, but their revenues are usually not following this trend directly. This means that the operators need to provide the required capacity in a more efficient way. Moreover, mobile operators need to re-evaluate their network architecture due to advanced requirements of various applications. So it is crucial to identify the most flexible and cost-effective infrastructure model for next-generation services. In particular, the new mobile network needs to provide capacity exactly when and where it is required. Another challenge is that despite the fact that LTE and next generations of mobile networks offer lower price per bit, operators cannot switch off their legacy 2G/3G networks. Thus operational costs need to be optimized by outsourcing or by shared operations.

There are also high expectations for new markets toward which the 5G technology is evolving [2, 3]. These markets are associated with Machine-to-Machine (M2M) type communication and Ultra-Reliable Communication (URLLC), but they are not yet well

© IFIP International Federation for Information Processing 2019
Published by Springer Nature Switzerland AG 2019
J. MacIntyre et al. (Eds.): AIAI 2019 Workshops, IFIP AICT 560, pp. 93–102, 2019.
https://doi.org/10.1007/978-3-030-19909-8_8

understood by operators. Therefore, flexibility of configuration and operation are probably the most profound features expected from future 5G networks in order to provide these new types of services. A new sharable architecture is needed which should be flexible and easily manageable to satisfy the needs of the end users. The network controller and its clients at the Radio Access Network (RAN) level have to be highly adjustable to accommodate changing traffic characteristics such as bandwidth and latency requirements.

The COHERENT project [4] focuses on developing a next generation unified programmable control and coordination framework for various heterogeneous radio access networks, with demonstrators based on LTE and Wi-Fi. It adopts the concept of resource and service virtualization across technology domains. The COHERENT architecture includes the C3 entity that exploits the software-defined networking (SDN) and virtualization concepts [5–7], and converts the existing wireless mobile networks to contemporary, flexible, scalable, efficient and interoperable 5G networks.

The main contribution of our research work is the techno-economic analysis of employing the C3 entity in the 5G networks that highlights the potential financial gain value from two different perspectives, namely of the C3 producer and of the cellular network Operator.

In this research work, we perform a techno-economic analysis of how employing the C3 entity in 5G networks could provide profit for producer and operator companies. In Sect. 2, the C3 entity and the architecture, where it is integrated, are indicated, whereas in Sect. 3, a detailed techno-economic analysis is performed from two different business perspectives. Finally, in Sect. 4, the results of this techno-economic analysis are presented, while interesting conclusions are drawn in Sect. 5.

2   COHERENT Architecture and C3 Entity

The COHERENT architecture [8] provides a programmable control and coordination that offers fine grain, real-time control. Scalability and timeliness for control and coordination are achieved by introducing two control mechanisms, namely Central Controller and Coordinator (C3) and Real-Time Controller (RTC), as shown in Fig. 1. By receiving status reports from low layer entities, C3 maintains a centralised network view of the governed entities, e.g., transport nodes (TNs) and Radio Transceivers (RTs) in the RAN. For example, an RT could be a legacy LTE eNodeB or a legacy WiFi Access Point (AP) or a New Radio Base Station (NR BS).

Based on the Centralised Network View (CNV), the SDN principles are applied in the design of the C3. For overcoming the delay limitation between the C3 and the individual access network elements, latency-sensitive control functionalities are off-loaded from the C3 to RTCs. The network entities connect to C3 and RTCs through the southbound interface (SBi).

As mentioned before, C3 is a logically centralised control entity because the C3 instances share the network graphs with each other. The communication between controllers (RTC-C3, C3-C3) for sharing network graphs and offloading control functions is through east-west interface (EWi).

The service plane is defined as a collection of specific network applications and Radio Access Technology (RAT) configurations. Different network slices contain different network applications and configuration settings as shown in Fig. 1. Through northbound interface (NBi), the C3 and/or RTCs provide the required network view, namely slice-specific network view (SNV), for the network service slices so that network service slices could express desired network behaviours (by programming) without being responsible themselves for implementing that behaviour (with hardware).

Some application modules in network slices may be latency-sensitive. For such a slice, these modules are located in the RTC. Additionally, monitoring modules which are latency-sensitive may need to operate close to the data source for reducing overhead and observe the network at high information granularity. The need for such monitoring modules may be service specific or operation specific. The examples of latency-sensitive network applications are flexible RAN function splitting in Cloud- RAN, MAC scheduling, handover decision, cell reconfiguration. In addition, most of the Mobile Edge Computing application areas [9] are also relevant to RTC, e.g., localisation, augmented reality, low latency IP service, etc. In general, we could have different views inside the same slice, according to what the application wants to do.

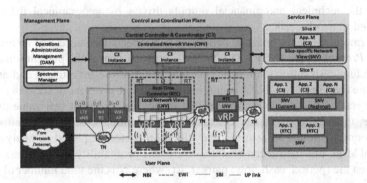

Fig. 1. COHERENT architecture [8].

While the COHERENT control and coordination plane makes control decisions for RAN functions and sends the decisions to the network entities for executing the decisions, the management plane usually focuses on monitoring, configuring and maintaining the long-term decisions for network entities in the infrastructure, e.g., queries the databases managed by the National Regulation Agency (NRA) for the spectrum usage rules in the spectrum manager [10]. The entities in management plane are connected to the C3 through NBi.

3 Techno-Economic Analysis

This section presents a detailed financial analysis of employing the C3 entity from two different business actors' point of view [11]:

 I. C3 Producer's point of view
 II. Operator's point of view

3.1 Financial Model

A key step in the process of planning a transition path towards COHERENT network deployment is the evaluation of the network economics. Specifically, C3 producers and network operators should consider choosing the evolution path that yields the most economic value, including revenues, capital expenditures (CapEx) and operating expenditures (OpEx) over the economic life of the system. Note that economic evaluation may have to be based on assumptions about the evolution of demand and service penetration.

To implement a financial model where all of the described aspects are properly taken into account, specially designed tools are normally used. This implies a sequence of steps to go through to associate values to the input parameters. Running the model generates the technical and financial outputs driven by geographical data, service demand and network costs.

Furthermore, the main financial parameter that reflects the success of an investment is the *Net Present Value (NPV)*. The NPV of an investment is the present (discounted) value of future cash inflows minus the present value of the investment and any associated future cash outflows. NPV is important because it gives more accurate solutions in the out years. This metric recognizes that money has different real value over time and makes the values of money constant by discounting costs and benefits over a specific period of time—an asset's life cycle or any selected period of analysis. On a less formal level, this metric can be indicative of the profitability of a business over the years. Given the (period, cash flow) pairs (t, Rt) where N is the total number of periods, the NPV is given by:

$$NPV(i,N) = \sum_{t=0}^{N} \frac{R_t}{(1+i)^t}$$

where, t – the time of the cash flow; cash flow equals to the revenues minus the costs.

i – the rate of return WACC; the opportunity cost of capital.
R_t – the cash flow at time t.

Finally, there is one more input parameter that is needed, namely the *Weighted Average Cost of Capital (WACC)* of the company for this investment. The WACC is the average rate of return that the company expects to compensate all its different investors. The weights are the fraction of each financing source in the company's target capital structure. The WACC can serve as a useful reality check for investors. In this analysis, the WACC for the C3 Producer and Operator Company is 10%.

3.2   C3 Producer

This subsection describes a techno-economic analysis of employing the COHERENT architecture and specifically the C3 entity from the C3 Producer's point of view.

The viability of the C3 Producer (i.e. Start-up Company) is going to be evaluated over a period of seven years. The C3 Producer is going to invest on this architecture (i.e. developing the product and selling its services to multiple operators) because it would like to gain some revenues. The results of this analysis will show the economic benefits of employing the COHERENT architecture from the C3 Producer's point of view. The costs and revenues of the C3 Producer are categorized into the following general groups, as shown in Fig. 2.

More specifically, each group is further explained below, after making the necessary realistic assumptions for business related works with similar cost-revenues methodology [12]:

I. *Cost of business*—includes the sum of the personnel-related cost, i.e. head count (15–25) and cost per employee (80 k€–84 k€), the fixed assets (10 k€–50 k€), the production cost (60 k€–150 k€) and the marketing cost (50 k€–100 k€), according to the COHERENT original approach. It is also taken into consideration a company overhead factor (e.g. accounting, depreciation, insurance, license fees, taxes, rent), which is usually 0,3–0,5.

The approach is that there is a basic functionality, such as mobility and load balancing, which can be enhanced by additional features. For each additional feature the producer revenue is defined as percentage of the infrastructure served by one C3 and a penetration factor. The producer will have revenues on both C3 and agents:

II. *Basic SW C3 + agent revenues*—the revenues from the C3 are assumed to be the total C3 server cost multiplied by the number of C3 servers. Additionally, the revenues from the SW agent are assumed to be 5% of the total infrastructure cost served by one C3 multiplied by the penetration percentage of SW agents. In this case, the penetration percentage is 100%, since the SW agents are installed at each micro/macro DU.

III. *Spectrum sharing revenues, infrastructure sharing revenues, RRM revenues, network slicing revenues*—include the added value multiplied by the basic SW C3 + agent revenues. Added value is the price that the product or service is sold at. The added value is assumed to increase from the initial 20% up to 50% for spectrum sharing, 30% for infrastructure sharing, 30% for RRM and network slicing. Also, the penetration percentage waves from 10% to 70% over the years for spectrum sharing and infrastructure sharing, from 20% to 40% for RRM, up to 50% for network slicing revenues. Note that, added value and penetration percentages follow the original COHERENT approach.

IV. *Maintenance revenues*—it is usual practice to assume that maintenance is the 10% over the sum of revenues (i.e. SW C3 + agent revenues plus infrastructure sharing revenues plus spectrum sharing revenues plus RRM revenues plus network slicing revenues).

3.3 Operator

This subsection describes a techno-economic analysis of employing the COHERENT architecture and specifically the C3 entity from the Operator's point of view.

The viability of the Operator is going to be evaluated through a 7-year analysis. The Operator is going to invest on this architecture (i.e. buying the product and services from the C3 Producer) because it would like to improve the performance of its network and at the same time gain some revenues. The results of this analysis will show the economic benefits of employing the COHERENT architecture from the Operator's point of view.

The costs and revenues of the Operator are categorized into the following general groups, as shown in Fig. 4.

More specifically, each group is further explained below, after making the necessary realistic assumptions for business related works with similar cost-revenues methodology [12]:

   I. *Infrastructure cost*—Infrastructure includes the micro DUs and macro DUs. Specifically, DU is a hardware box with MAC and PHY layers, radios and antennas. The micro DU and macro DU cost 600 € and 4.500 €, respectively, according to data provided by OTE S.A, Greece. The macro DU/micro DU ratio is considered to be 1/10.

   II. *Cost of business*—It is actually the price that the Operator will pay to the C3 Producer in order to employ the COHERENT architecture in his existing network. A C3 producer can sell to multiple Operators.

   III. *C3 + agent related ARPU*—First of all, it is assumed that the Operator deploys the new technology for providing coverage to customers; the increase in infrastructure coverage is reflected in the yearly increase of the customer number. Each year the customer base increases 10%. Also, the indicative average revenue per user (ARPU) is 25 €, which is reduced by 3% every year, according to data provided by OTE S.A, Greece. The income generated by ARPU is partially used (starting with 20% and increasing in time to 30%) for paying the infrastructure, C3 and agents costs. The SW cost is covered by the proportional part of the ARPU.

4 Results

This section demonstrates the results of the techno-economic analysis provided in Sect. 3. These results give the opportunity to a future C3 Producer or Operator to examine the case of investing on the C3 entity and COHERENT architecture in general.

At first, Fig. 2 presents the costs and revenues per year for the C3 Producer. It is observed that only after Year 3 the revenues-to-cost ratio is more than 1.5. The first two years, i.e. Year 1 and Year 2, the C3 Producer needs to cover this damage, i.e. difference between cost and revenue, with alternative ways, e.g. by taking a bank loan for the required capital. It is also shown that Year 4 and Year 5 have the highest performance, since these years the C3 production and relevant sales reach their peak. In fact, according to [11], in Year 4 and Year 5, the number of C3 servers has more than tenfold increase compared with the number of C3 servers in Year 1. Also, Fig. 3, which shows the net revenues per year for the C3 Producer, proves the peak performance of the Year 4 regarding the revenues. Therefore, from the C3 Producer's point of view, it seems that it is beneficial to employ the COHERENT architecture since the techno-economic analysis results reflect the success of this investment.

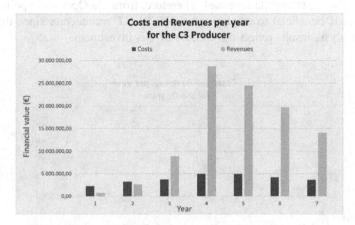

Fig. 2. Costs and revenues per year for the C3 Producer.

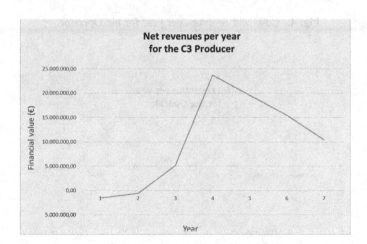

Fig. 3. Net revenues per year for the C3 Producer.

100   C. Tsirakis et al.

Then, Fig. 4 demonstrates the costs and revenues per year for the Operator. It is observed that the revenues exceed the costs from Year 3 onwards. Only the starting years, i.e. Year 1 and Year 2, both costs and revenues follow a similar trend, but then the revenues grow extremely during the whole next period analysis. The Operator starts with limited amount of money from the customer ARPU and invests strongly in the technology; in time the investments are reduced and the customer base increases significantly, such that the Operator gets significant earnings and has limited costs. Also, Fig. 5, that shows the net revenues per year for the Operator, proves again this almost exponential rise regarding the revenues. Therefore, from the Operator's point of view, it results that is beneficial to employ the COHERENT architecture since the techno-economic analysis results reflect the success of this investment.

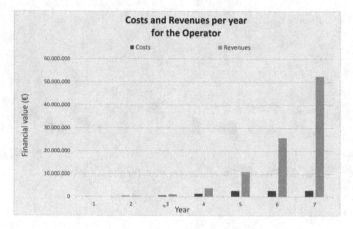

Fig. 4. Costs and revenues per year for the Operator.

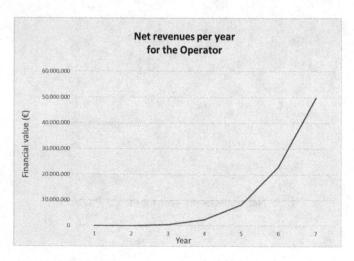

Fig. 5. Net revenues per year for the Operator.

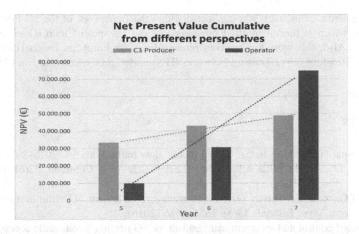

Fig. 6. Net present value cumulative for both C3 Producer and Operator.

Finally, in Fig. 6, it is observed that the gradient of the NPV cumulative is higher for the Operator than for the C3 Producer. Essentially, after Year 4 the revenues for the C3 Producer slows down since the market starts to reach a saturated level of this technology and the competition is stronger. On the contrary, the Operator can impressively increase its revenues and continuously acquire new customers by providing new attractive services on the top of the COHERENT architecture.

To summarize, through this 7-year detailed financial analysis, it was proved that the adoption of COHERENT architecture could be profitable in economic terms and a viable solution for the wireless ecosystem, for both C3 Producers and Operators but with different attributes. It is also important to note that the assumptions made were modest, neither pessimistic nor optimistic. Thus, the results of the techno-economic analysis reflect the success of the COHERENT investment from both C3 Producers' and Operators' point of view and can drive to great development for future wireless networks.

5 Conclusion

This research work described the role of C3 entity and its potential technical gain value if implemented in the existing wireless communications network. Additionally, the performed techno-economic analysis showed that it could be viable for both C3 producer and network operator to implement the C3 entity in their own network.

The C3 producer is expected to make a platform that provides a lot of opportunities in increasing the financial base. In the near future, when 5G will come into the arena of network operators, there will be the need for the operators to have a platform such as C3 that controls and orchestrates the infrastructure, slicing aspects and resources.

Regarding the Operator, the C3 solution will bring benefits to him in terms of providing less CapEx and OpEx since most of the EPC-based equipment will be replaced by C3. However, the high initial cost or the time period it will take to replace all the access infrastructures may be threats to the operator.

Acknowledgments. This work was conducted within the framework of the 5G-PPP COHERENT project, which is funded by the Commission of the European Union (Grant Agreement No. 671639). Also, this work has received funding from the European Union Horizon 2020-MCSA-ITN-2015 Innovative Training Networks (ITN) under grant agreement No. 675806 (5G-Aura).

References

1. Cisco Visual Networking Index: Global mobile data traffic Forecast, 2016–2021 (2017)
2. Andrews, J.G., et al.: What will 5G be? IEEE J. Sel. Areas Commun. **32**(6), 1065–1082 (2014)
3. Olwal, T.O., et al.: A survey of resource management toward 5G radio access networks. IEEE Comm. Surv. Tutorials **18**(3), 1656–1686 (2016)
4. Coordinated control and spectrum management for 5G heterogeneous radio access networks (COHERENT), EU H2020 5G-PPP project
5. Arslan, M., et al.: Software-defined networking in cellular radio access networks: potential and challenges. IEEE Commun. Mag. **53**(1), 150–156 (2015)
6. Granelli, F., et al.: Software defined and virtualized wireless access in future wireless networks: scenarios and standards. IEEE Commun. Mag. **53**(6), 26–34 (2015)
7. Trivisonno, R., et al.: SDN-based 5G mobile networks: architecture, functions, procedures and backward compatibility. Trans. Emerg. Telecommun. Technol. **26**(1), 82–92 (2015)
8. COHERENT, Deliverable 2.2: System Architecture and Abstractions for Mobile Networks (2016)
9. Patel, M., et al.: Mobile-Edge Computing – Introductory Technical White Paper ETSI (2014)
10. Lembo, S., et al.: Hierarchical network-level coordination for 5G radio access networks. In: IEEE International Symposium on Personal Indoor and Mobile Communications (PIMRC), Montreal, QC, Canada, October 2017
11. COHERENT, Deliverable 7.4: Exploitation and Techno-Economic Model (2018)
12. Kantor, M., et al.: General framework for techno-economic analysis of next generation access networks. In: International Conference on Transparent Optical Networks (2010)

Trustworthy AI for 5G: Telco Experience and Impact in the 5G ESSENCE

Maria Rita Spada[✉] and Alessandro Vincentini[✉]

Wind Tre S.p.A., Largo Metropolitana 5, 20017 Rho, MI, Italy
{mariarita.spada, alessandro.vincentini}@windtre.it
http://www.windtre.it/

Abstract. This paper discusses how it is possible to implement a general model to cope with the network and service management when the AI (Artificial Intelligence) capabilities are integrated in a trustworthy AI for 5G solutions framework. We discuss the general regulatory considerations related to the AI introduction in the 5G network management as this has been examined as part of the H2020 Project 5GESSENCE.

Keywords: 5G networks · AI · Agents · BSS · Neutral Host · OSS · Trust

1 Introduction

The telecommunications are one of the most interesting contexts involved in the process of the AI (Artificial Intelligence) development, because in real life situations it might happen that sensors, actuators and AI agents are away from each other and one - or more- telecommunications network(s) lay in between and connect them.

In general, the communications networks are clearly the infrastructure that transfers the information generated by the sensors to the remote AI agents. The new 5G and FTTH (Fibre-to-the-Home) networks are the main connective tissue of the artificial intelligence systems located throughout the territory.

When a Telco operator wants to use the new solution based on AI, it is important to take into account some "values" with which AI should comply to set out several concrete requirements (such as privacy, accountability and transparency) for AI systems integrated with other systems used to create value and to deal with the complexity of the information and communication aspects.

Given the complexity of the services offered, it is necessary to use policies on different levels so that to evaluate AI models and their integration in the normal context. When a Telco includes AI solutions it is necessary to develop governance frameworks in order to make sure that AI development does not infringe upon different aspects, like human rights, freedoms, dignity and privacy; there will be the possibility of programming, by using the AI solutions, co-robot ethics to legal and other questions, including liability and privacy concerns. In this framework, the Telecom Operator must have a reliable approach on trustworthy AI so that to offer solutions that "people can trust", according to transparency and responsibility requirements.

© IFIP International Federation for Information Processing 2019
Published by Springer Nature Switzerland AG 2019
J. MacIntyre et al. (Eds.): AIAI 2019 Workshops, IFIP AICT 560, pp. 103–110, 2019.
https://doi.org/10.1007/978-3-030-19909-8_9

The present paper is organized as follows: Sect. 2 describes the new approach for realizing trustworthy AI for 5G solutions; Sect. 3 describes some AI applications in the network, with a particular focus upon the 5G network; an overview of the general architecture and how this can be deployed is introduced in Sect. 4, taking into account as reference the 5G ESSENCE solution. Section 5 underlines the benefit of the new approach and the improvement of the realization and management of the network slicing concept -or of other aspects- correlated when using the AI solution.

2   Approaches for Realizing Trustworthy AI for 5G Solutions

It is important to take into account the concept of the model for network management that can be implemented by using the 5G capabilities, when it is also possible to integrate the AI capabilities.

In fact, when we design the network slicing model for a Telco, or more generally for a Neutral Host, an intermediate provider between manufacturer or RF equipment provider and Mobile Operators/Service Providers, we have to deal with the possible conflict in the network between special services and equally worthy of protection, such as that which is given to an electro-medical device or to a machine that can manage the braking system of a vehicle. Which of the two applications is more appropriate to give priority in case of problems? How is this decision made? To date, there is no clear answer; perhaps the only principle that can be considered is that it should be established *a priori* in order to define some rules that will be applied, when we have millions of people using such services. The first aspect to be defined is that of the relationship(s) between the network operators, the software and hardware developers, the deployers and the customer(s). Everyone among these has a central but different role, and everyone has different responsibilities.

The network indeed can experience congestion or outages and, when this occurs, the transferred information can be delayed or even discarded. Networks, in fact, are dimensioned when using the criteria adopted to define the slices.

From a Telco's point of view, two important safety properties must be guaranteed and these have already been explored by the researchers, that is: the *"safe interruptibility"* and the *"distributional shift"*, where:

1. Safe interruptibility is the ability to interrupt an intelligent agent and override its actions at any time.
2. Distributional shift is the ability of the AI system to behave robustly when the environment where it operates differs from the training environment.

According to this vision, a Telco is not responsible for any failure not being able to achieve the two properties, as mentioned above. The reason why networks cannot be considered as responsible of the possible fallacies of the ensemble "sensors-actuators-AI agent" is that zeroing the probability of congestion would require infinite network resources, which is clearly impossible. A fall-back strategy for the AI agent in this scenario is in charge to developers, expected "by design": it is important to create a strong ecosystem to share this approach. The AI equipment should sense the "hiccup information" of the surrounding congested networks and swiftly stop what it is doing, thus applying the principle of safe interruptibility.

This applies even more when the consequences of wrong decisions made by an AI used are well diverse, depending on the field these are made. Wrong decisions in a medical context are clearly much worse than a wrong suggestion provided to a consumer by a recommender system. It is important to share common guidelines to cope with these aspects; besides it should be requested to have clear and unequivocal criteria to support an electronic communications network operator so that to make choices when network resources are insufficient to manage one or more mission critical services that transit networks simultaneously.

In the event an inconvenience is unavoidable anyway, e.g. when humans are damaged, injured or killed due to a decision taken by AI systems, AI system must decide with fairness.

Another issue, important from a Telco's point of view, is the correct assessment of the security measures to be provided for AI systems when we include this in the operational context integrating the new features in the different systems. In particular, it might be useful to define a classification of AI systems according to their intended use in order to define the security measures adequate to the context of applications, as discussed in "Ethics guidelines for the development and use of artificial intelligence" [1].

It is also important to define security measures to ensure the availability and integrity of data throughout the life cycle of the entire AI system. Among the measures that help to ensure the robustness of the AI system is necessary to foresee the segregation of all environments, including those provided for the AI training.

According to Telco's experience, the human supervision is only one of the possible instances of governance of all these elements; with more experience, it could be possible to evaluate the hypothesis of the aid of other AI systems to support human supervision, which carry out extemporaneous (therefore unpredictable) redundancy checks in environments separated by AI system to be governed in a sort of "logic" of "assisted governance". The autonomy of the AI system also depends on its ability to interact: that is, some context in the network management could be used as first field for the application of this approach.

This concept of governance then extends to the autonomous interaction of the AI system with other systems networks and devices; in this way it could be possible in the near future that network systems could be equipped with the capacity to autonomously expand their interactions within a predefined "evolutionary perimeter" during the design phase.

The AI, equipped with its own start-up of a minimum set of connections to protect potential vulnerabilities, could independently activate further systemic interactions to increase its evolutionary degree. The improvement in efficiency would correspond to a reduction in risks related to vulnerability. This will improve the capacity to include the AI in the Telco's context to manage better the network and the final services to the end-users.

In particular, we believe that an assessment lists should be enriched by items to detect the correct application of "*safe interruptibility*" and "*distributional shift*", or other applicable procedures to avoid danger in case of outage of communication networks.

Further fine tuning should be applied on supervised machine learning algorithms and AI's essentially learn what they are taught. Therefore, for them to be fair and non-discriminatory, a proper choice of the training set is crucial to avoid imbalances and inequalities when classifying (i.e. with the term "imbalance" we mean that the classification results are not distributed evenly across all the classes forming the domain of the classification problem).

Since miss-classification might lead to uneven decisions and bias reinforcement, an approach to mitigate the risk of miss-classification could consist in the assessment of the training sets in search of imbalances not necessarily intended.

Moreover, we generally agree on the principle that it is needed to guarantee not only the concept of "privacy by design" but also the concept of "ethics by design"; in this way, we require ethical principles (and privacy) to be embedded in AI products and/or services, right at the beginning of the design process.

In fact, ethics must be embedded into the design and development process from the very beginning of the AI creation and those ethics must be aligned with the values and ethical principles of a society or of the community it affects. For this reason, it could be necessary to use the same approach in Europe to guarantee the process. Each company has to share a common vision and follow an internal procedure to guarantee principles for trust and transparency. By adopting and practicing this approach, it could be more clear and transparent about how to use the AI solutions in different contexts.

3   AI Packed Approach to 5G Business Case

Artificial Intelligence requires an ongoing and interdisciplinary effort to cover all the effects in the different ecosystems where the new approach will be introduced. Guidelines should give clear and unequivocal criteria to support a communications network operator so that to make choices when network resources are insufficient in order to manage one or more mission critical services that transit networks, simultaneously: the consequences of wrong decisions made by an AI are well diverse depending on the field they are made. Wrong decisions, in a medical and/or transport contexts, are clearly much worse than others. Therefore, we think that the regulation of the safety topic should be domain specific.

In the same way, it is important to realise "Trustworthy AI" according to a shared framework compatible with the general architecture described in [2]. We look at the opportunities of enhancing our tools for the management of the network and to improve our OSS (Operations Support Systems) services -or in other sectors- so that AI can be "trained" to help improve diagnoses -or other outcomes- to improve the quality of the final services in different contexts (such as smart mobility, smart cities or industry 4.0).

The OSS/BSS (Operational and Business Support Systems) service provides Operating and Business supports functions in order to manage the network infrastructure (OSS) as well products, customers and customer life cycle (i.e.: Orders, Upgrades, Complains, Usage & Invoicing, Leave) of the services provided by the operators (BSS).

The need for highly automated processes is particularly stressed from a telco's point of view, due to frequency/network/IT (Information Technology) resource sharing in deployment and provisioning processes, having in mind the maximisation of the customer experience, services and network resources.

As the network infrastructure moves towards virtualized infrastructures, OSS and BSS systems evolve the virtualization path based on IaaS (Infrastructure-as-a-Service), PaaS (Platform-as-a-Service) or SaaS (Software-as-a-Service), by using a common commercial hardware and storage and by providing separate virtualized infrastructure, virtualized platform and virtualized software to a set of tenants using the shared physical infrastructure. Specific application environments can be then made available for vertical implementations, including Artificial Intelligence and Machine Learning functionalities in order to provide enhanced analytics needed for a quick service time to market. In the following we discuss a few examples of telco's contexts in which we think that the introduction of AI will be an important challenge to improve the Telco's role:

1. Network Management: More and more data are generated by devices across the network and used to manage itself; other network sources can provide insight into how networks are performing. The way how that data is collected and analyzed to provide meaningful and actionable information is the "key" to make a difference in network operations. The AI tools can help Telcos to monitor and evaluate network performance and these tools are comprehensive enough to deliver a complete and holistic picture of the entire network (from the user terminal to the cloud through the edge).

2. Product Management: A Telco organization is typically responsible for managing the Product/Service Catalogue through the assembly and update of products utilizing available components. The definition of a "product" is an item that satisfies a market's want or need. The introduction of the AI approach will improve the Telco's ability to create and maintain products that can be sold to customers in the target market. It could be possible via using the AI approach to model the structure of a product, creating and managing this in a "catalog" of products or a number of components associated together to create new opportunities to reduce the time to market. According to this, some of the components within a product will be enabled by shared/common/reusable resources (e.g., network exchange) that may be managed by different parts of the organization, improving the global efficiency of a Telco organization.

3. Customer Contact Management: Another context in which the introduction of an AI approach is important, is the "customer contact management" dealing with the retention and loyalty aspects; the Customer Relationship Management (CRM) suite allows a telco operator to create, update and view the customer's information (i.e.: names, addresses, phone numbers, organizational hierarchy), as well as to record and view all customer interactions across different communication channels and department. The AI solution will offer better capabilities to highlight customers as risk of switching to an alternative carrier and provide comparisons with other operator's service packages, allowing customer care agents to provide advantages for the business intelligence platforms.

4. Customer Order Management: Starting from the telecoms experience, the introduction of AI solutions will help in the design, price and the lifecycle of the proposed services. Besides, the AI will offer support to negotiation and closure of a formal contract with the customers to deal with the creation of the customer's contract and of any associated service level agreements, including approval of custom language, customer contract sign-off, appropriate counter signature and contract expiration taking into account all the "smart" elements coming from an analysis based upon AI tools. In particular, Customer Order Management application handles order requests to suspend, resume, change ownership, amend, add, change and discontinue existing ordered products. By using AI it will be easier to deal with repackaging of the purchased offers into alternate product offering (may require sales/contract negotiation).

In the telco contexts in which we think that the introduction of AI will be an important challenge to improve the Telco's role, as discussed, the AI is going to be part of any application and network controller. In 5G scenarios we can assume that AI solutions can be part of business proposition of specific use case. In particular, proposition depends upon specific use case; when assuming a Network Slice for a Smart City scenario the proposition could include specific AI services for sensor to be deployed on edge or in the scenario of broadband network slice AI-based monitoring within vEPC (virtualised Evolved Packet Core) solution.

4   The 5G ESSENCE Solution

The 5G ESSENCE project [3] addresses the paradigms of Edge Cloud computing and Small Cell as-a-Service (SCaaS) by fueling the drivers and removing the barriers in the Small Cell (SC) market, forecasted to grow at an impressive pace up to 2020 and beyond and to play a "key role" in the 5G ecosystem. The project defines the baseline system architecture and interfaces for the provisioning of a cloud-integrated multi-tenant Small Cell network and a programmable radio resources management (RRM) controller.

The introduction of AI solutions will improve the capability of the system to development of the centralized software-defined radio access network (SD-RAN) controller to program the radio resources usage in a unified way for all CESCs (Cloud-Enabled Small Cells) and to distribute service management in a multi-tier architecture.

As already introduced, the 5G ESSENCE offers an innovative architecture, capable of providing Small Cell coverage to multiple operators "As-a-Service", enriched with a two-tier architecture: a first distributed tier for providing low latency services and a second centralized tier for providing high processing power for compute-intensive network applications. To that end, 5G ESSENCE envisages to virtualize and to partition Small Cell capacity while, *at the same time*, it aims to support enhanced edge cloud services by enriching the network infrastructure with an edge cloud.

The introduction of the approach based on AI techniques in a project like the 5G ESSENCE will improve the capabilities of the solution not only to cope with the complex network based on the combination of MEC (Mobile Edge Computing) and

NFV (Network Function Virtualisation) concepts with Small Cell virtualization in 5G networks, but also to cope better with the complex ecosystem required for supporting multi-tenancy and for increasing the network capacity and the available computational resources at the edge.

The proposed solution allows multiple network operators (tenants) to provide services to their users through a set of Cloud Enabled Small Cells deployed, owned and managed by a third party (i.e., the CESC provider). Figure 1 shows a high level view of the envisaged architecture.

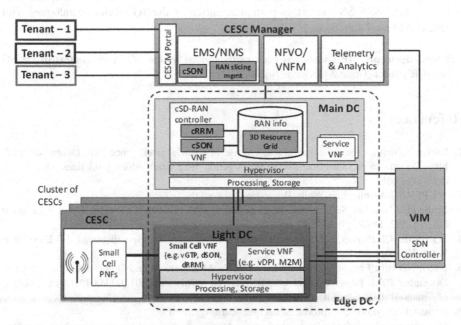

Fig. 1. 5G ESSENCE architecture

In the 5G ESSENCE architecture [4] The NFVI (Network Function Virtualization Infrastructure) spans across the Main Data Centre-DC (i.e., the core cloud) and Light DCs (i.e., edge clouds), and this requires dealing with wide distribution and heterogeneity. The high dynamicity characterizing the system calls for an efficient, distributed and adaptable monitoring system. The monitoring data is provided to an analytics engine to extract insights for the support of orchestration decisions and to enable efficient resource allocation across the overall infrastructure. An end-to-end orchestration of infrastructure and services is crucial for reliable deployment and execution of services. The 5G ESSENCE orchestration platform also manages the lifecycle of services and it fully supports an ETSI-based view of the MANO (MANagement and Orchestration) [5]. For all these reasons this context could be a good reference point to start in the evaluation of the AI introduction, to improve the global systems using an approach like the Machine Learning as a Service (MLaaS) or the ML Market Places; it could be possible to install specific algorithm at edge level or in the distributed sensors or to use specific APIs, as suggested by some already available solutions described in [6] or in [7].

5   Conclusion

The integration of such AI capabilities demonstrates how the new integrated approach contributes to 5G architectural concepts such as, for example, the improvement of the realization and management of the network slicing concept or the other aspects correlated to the BSS/OSS context, in particular enriching the 5G services catalogues with different AI-based functions.

Acknowledgements. This work has been partly funded by the EC in the context of the 5G ESSENCE project (Grant Agreement No. 761592).

References

1. Ethics Guidelines for the development and use of artificial intelligence (AI), December 2018. https://ec.europa.eu/futurium/en/system/files/ged/ai_hleg_draft_ethics_guidelines_18_december.pdf
2. 5G-PPP-5G-Architecture-White-Paper-Jan-2018-v2.0
3. Embedded Network Services for 5G Experiences (5G ESSENCE) Project, Grant Agreement No. 761592, DoW
4. 5G ESSENCE Project, D2.2: Overall System Architecture and Specifications, 5G ESSENCE WP2, February 2018
5. ETSI, Network Functions Virtualisation (NFV); Management and Orchestration 001 V1.1.1, December 2014. https://www.etsi.org/deliver/etsi_gs/nfv-man/001_099/001/01.01.01_60/gs_nfv-man001v010101p.pdf
6. https://cloud.google.com/products/machine-learning/?hl=it
7. https://azure.microsoft.com/en-us/resources/videos/an-overview-of-the-azure-machine-learning-marketplace/

Regulatory Considerations in the 5G Era: The 5GCity Neutral Host Case

Ioannis Neokosmidis[1(✉)], Theodoros Rokkas[1], Dimitrios Xydias[1], and Maria Rita Spada[2]

[1] inCITES Consulting, 130 Route d'Arlon, 8008 Strassen, Luxembourg
i.neokosmidis@incites.eu
[2] Wind Tre S.p.A., Largo Metropolitana 5, Rho, Milan, Italy

Abstract. The need for densification in 5G networks will necessitate the installation of large amounts of small cells in dense urban environments in order to meet future demands for capacity. The Neutral Host model has been proposed as a potential solution to this problem. This paper discusses the general regulatory considerations of 5G networks and specific considerations that relate to the Neutral Host model as this has been examined as part of the H2020 Project 5GCity.

Keywords: 5G networks · Network densification · Neutral Host · Regulation · Spectrum sharing

1 5G and the Need for Densification

5G is the latest generation of mobile networks which will enable faster and more reliable mobile networks as compared to the existing ones. Initial deployments of 5G networks will depend on existing infrastructure and will be based on Non-Standalone (NSA) 5G new radio standards. NSA new radio refers to a 5G network which uses a 4G core and radio anchor with a 5G small cell mobile broadband (MBB) capacity boost, while Standalone (SA) new radio refers to a 5G network which only depends on 5G technology both for its core and radio anchor. NSA standards will enable the enhanced mobile broadband (eMBB) use case family. This type of network is expected to be very popular in the early years of 5G as mobile network operators demand backward network compatibility. Subsequently, the industry will start launching SA 5G networks to support the strictest criteria regarding the technical specifications, such as latency, data rate, capacity, spectrum efficiency and mobility, to support massive machine-type communications (mMTC) and ultra-reliable low-latency communication (URLLC) [1].

5G will not be a revolutionary technology, but rather a fine orchestration of existing technologies, such as Software Defined Networking (SDN) [2], Network Functions Virtualisation (NFV) [3], Mobile Edge Computing (MEC) and Cloud Computing [4]. 5G is also going to use two new frequency bands, namely, 3.6 GHz and 26 GHz [5], which will be essential to achieve the advanced specifications it promises. Achieving the specifications in these bands will only be possible with network densification by deploying a large number of small cells. This is due to the shorter transmission range

© IFIP International Federation for Information Processing 2019
Published by Springer Nature Switzerland AG 2019
J. MacIntyre et al. (Eds.): AIAI 2019 Workshops, IFIP AICT 560, pp. 111–120, 2019.
https://doi.org/10.1007/978-3-030-19909-8_10

that higher frequencies can achieve. Network densification will be particularly necessary in dense urban environments where the demand for capacity will be higher. Demand for more small cell antennas, however, outpaces the supply of available sites in many cities. This creates an imbalance in the market, which could potentially drive up rental fees for those sites to the benefit of their owners. In such cases, the development of parallel small cells networks by operators will be prohibitively expensive and potentially not feasible.

An alternative to building parallel networks will be the Neutral Host (NH) model [6], whereby a single entity, the NH, deploys and operates the network (through self-operation or outsourcing) and then provides wholesale access to those interested in providing their services. The hosting aspect refers to an entity that provides a certain set of resources that are made available to clients, such as Mobile Network Operators (MNO)s, allowing them to provide uninterrupted services to their clients at the expense of reduced flexibility and complex billing relationships. The "neutrality" aspect refers to the host acting as a shared platform to multiple hosted clients. Neutrality in this context does not imply strict equality between hosted clients, as the resources offered to each client are subject to the commercial agreement between the NH and the client, and policy-based management may be applied. From a hosted client's point of view, the system behaviour and services using the resources of a NH should be available without user intervention and, ideally, they should be seamless and identical to those provided by their hosted clients' dedicated resources.

Towards this direction, 5GCity [7] architecture employs distributed cloud technologies to build its combined edge and network infrastructure, providing a multi-tenant, cost-effective platform for deploying virtualized, heterogeneous services. The 5GCity architecture allows the exploitation of the NH model, employing features of the different layers:

- Application Layer: offers the tools and functions available for the infrastructure operators, customers, subcontractors, and third-party actors
- Orchestration and Control Layer: allows management of a non-homogeneous set of physical resources, abstraction of physical resources, operation of horizontal slicing to provide coherence cast end-to end services tailored to a multi-tenant framework
- Access Layer: the Neutral Host model requires network information on how to deal with the access layer (end-user devices - physical resources providing connectivity); in the Service Level Agreement (SLA) between the NH and the operator it is necessary to define how the network deals with the end-to-end chain from Radio elements and Fronthaul network to the end user devices in order to control for the availability and quality of the service.

5GCity will offer an infrastructure dashboard providing operators and verticals the ability to create slices according to their needs. 5GCity goes one step further by providing a Software Development Kit (SDK) that allows developers to create network functions and services, and service providers to combine pre-existing functions in order to develop new services.

Moreover, both infrastructure and services dashboards will also provide advanced functionalities, such as billing, offering increased flexibility to mobile operators and other interested parties and motivating them to adopt the NH model.

2 Regulatory Considerations in the 5G Era

Past regulatory practice was generally based on the requirements of physically larger high-power macrocells. This approach will likely not be appropriate in the case of networks with smaller cells, such as the NH model. Enabling the deployment of small cell networks requires streamlined federal, state and local permitting, rights-of-way, application submission timelines, application fees, application review timelines and appeals processes to make it economically feasible for operators to deploy 5G across communities. Some of the issues that need to be addressed by regulatory authorities to facilitate the smooth transition to 5G networks are as follow.

2.1 Network Equipment Certification and Permits

To enable the deployment of a large number of new antennas, a simplified and easily-replicable certification process could be considered. For instance, the height of the installed antenna and the Effective Isotropic Radiation Power (EIRP) metric are already being used in many countries as criteria for certification exemption or process simplification. The enforcement of the simplification should be done at a national level, though specific local considerations should be taken into account. This would allow for a flexible regulatory agenda which also respects local laws, given that the latter do not impede the development of new networks.

Indicative examples of metrics used as thresholds for the need for declaration or installation permission are:

- Antenna height: Canada (15 m), Germany (10 m), the Netherlands (5 m), France (12 m), United Kingdom (4 m/15 m)
- Power level: Chile (low power), France (up to 5 W simple declaration is needed), Japan (low power type approved, 20mW), Malaysia (EIRP of 2 W), Germany (10 W)
- A combination of height and power: United States
- Regional-based simplified procedures: Spain

Before overhauling the certification and permitting procedures, considerations such as street furniture aesthetics should also be taken into account. In particular it could be examined if the installation of multiple small cells can be facilitated at once, taking into account their relatively small size and visual impact.

Some additional recommendations made by the Small Cells Forum [8] and GSMA [9] in order to accelerate the deployment of small cell networks are as follow:

1. Use of generic permits or exemptions based on internationally standardized equipment classes (e.g. IEC 62232 Ed.2.0 installation classes).
2. Harmonization of the rules and administrative processes for planning permissions across different authority domains in accordance with the Digital Single Market (DSM) strategy [10] for Europe.
3. Simplified administrative processes for small cell deployments through use 'one stop shop' application procedures, reducing the decision-making time and paperwork.

4. Proving tacit approval if local authorities do not oppose an authorization request within a certain number of days or weeks.
5. Maintaining a database of qualified candidate site locations to speed-up site identification and further simplify processing of applications.
6. Incentivizing small cell deployments through revision or full exemptions of base station taxes and recurring fees originally devised for macro base stations.

In the United States (US), according to Federal Communications Commission (FCC) rules, small cells can be exempt from environmental assessment in case they meet certain size and visibility criteria. In addition, the FCC has set time limits for the authorities to decide on permit applications in case of collocation (90 days) and new installations (150 days). The United Kingdom (UK), in a radical move for European standards, has removed all restrictions for placing small cell antennas on commercial buildings/structures to support mobile network rollout. This has simplified network investment considerations for the MNOs which now can expand their 4G mobile networks and better prepare for 5G.

During the site identification phase, a site owner might be reluctant to provide access to all interested parties that want to install equipment and instead sign an exclusive agreement with only one of the operators. Such anticompetitive practices should also be taken care of by regulatory authorities to ensure a level playing field for all players.

The relevant public authorities should, therefore, work closely together with a view to simplify administrative procedures, reduce delays and lower the cost for operators, while protecting public interests.

2.2 Site Availability

Regulating access to existing sites raises significant challenges for National Regulatory Authorities (NRAs), both in dense urban areas where the site availability is limited and some site owners might have significant negotiating power over the contract terms, as well as in rural areas where it is uneconomic to develop parallel networks. An alternative solution to alleviate some of the regulatory challenges is to increase the number of available sites for network installation. To achieve that, the NRA must collaborate with local municipalities or the relevant state authority to reconsider planning rules which should accommodate the small size and radiation impact of small cell antennas in both indoor and outdoor environments. What is more, the public authorities should enable the cost-effective access to street furniture elements, such as lamp posts and masts, to ensure that the supply of sites suitable for antenna installations is enough to counter any market cornering or market power concentration incidents.

2.3 Electrical Power

One of the biggest challenges that the industry is likely to face with 5G installations is the need for electrical power on each cell site. To tackle this problem, the authorities could facilitate the deployment of small cells near sites with electrical power like bus stops, street-lamps or ducts. To address this potential problem, operators are investigating off-grid network deployments including power over Ethernet, the construction of power generators or the use of renewable sources, suitable for installations in remote areas. In some countries, such as Luxembourg, on top of the above-mentioned problems, 5G stakeholders have highlighted that the necessity to deploy an electricity meter for each small cell antenna would increase both the complexity and deployment costs considering the number of small cells needed to be installed.

2.4   Access to Public Furniture and Fiber Networks

Depending on the use case that 5G networks need to support, this might include installing a large number of macrocells, small cells or line-of-sight connections. The need to deploy more antennas and new network equipment will be accompanied by issues associated with gaining access to sites, public and private infrastructure as well as with backhauling. These issues should be addressed from an early stage, during the network planning phase, to avoid impeding 5G network deployments.

Very high on the 5G ecosystem stakeholders' agenda are issues related to locating new available installation sites and agreeing on the contract terms with landlords, which apparently is a very lengthy and cumbersome process. Thus, easy access to public buildings, street furniture and street-lamps can significantly accelerate the deployment of 5G networks and especially small cells networks. Access to passive infrastructure, however, such as ducts and masts will also be required.

Addressing the need for backhauling will also be important. Although an alternative solution with microwaves has been suggested, this technology depends on weather conditions, as it can be impacted by heavy rainfall. Thus, access to fibre, depending on availability, will be necessary to address the need for backhauling. Hence, fibre sharing will need to be facilitated and regulated in order to accelerate 5G deployment.

2.5   Spectrum

Timely availability and price of spectrum will be critical factors for the deployment of 5G. Hence, it is essential to set up a roadmap for the grant of spectrum as early as possible and to investigate solutions beneficial for both the regulator and interested spectrum buyers. A 'spectrum fee holiday', that is to provide free access to spectrum for a predefined period provided that spectrum owners allocates pre-defined capital resources in 5G, could be among the potential regulatory considerations to lower the cost burden for operators. For instance, Italy auctioned 5G spectrum frequencies in October 2018, raising an astounding 6.5 billion euro, over a 14-days long bidding process, raising concerns regarding the operators' capacity to further invest in infrastructure over the coming years. Taking Italy as counter-example, the French regulator, ARCEP (Autorité de régulation des communications électroniques et des Postes), committed to working out a way to keep spectrum prices low, to encourage healthy competition and the much-needed investments in next generation infrastructure.

Another consideration related to spectrum, has to do with the active sharing of a future small cells network, whereby regulation permitting, or even obliging, spectrum sharing between the network operators and small cell operators, should be in place. This would allow the more efficient usage of spectrum, one of the main regulatory concerns as we move to 5G. Here, the use of a Licensed Shared Access (LSA) agreement could be in place, whereby the spectrum owner (mobile network operator) allows the small cell operator to use their spectrum in areas where it is unused by the MNO. Another alternative is for the small cell networks to use unlicensed spectrum though this solution runs the risk of causing interference with other equipment which could impair the small cell network's ability to deliver the specifications of a 5G network, such as low latency and high reliability.

Spectrum licensing for private indoor 5G networks that will be deployed in the future should also be considered. Regulators need to ensure that the spectrum bands used for private 5G networks should ideally be compatible across all European Union (EU) member states. Apart from the spectrum bands used, the way of licensing spectrum for private networks should also be considered. Spectrum sharing on an unprotected basis, raises concerns regarding the reliability of using such spectrum given the potential interference from existing users of unlicensed spectrum. Hence, there appears to be a need for private 5G networks to use spectrum bands that are distinct from existing uses of shared spectrum. However, given the potential limited interference that indoor private networks could have to outdoor spectrum users, there could be considerations to licence private networks as secondary spectrum users. This would ensure that the spectrum is shared on a non-interfering basis with network operators being the primary spectrum users. More specifically, the propagation characteristics of millimeter Wave (mmWave) bands limit any potential for interference while beamforming and massive MIMO techniques could also assist in reducing interference with other users.

2.6 Radiation

Organisations like the World Health Organisation (WHO) have issued recommendations and suggested limits for the allowed radio frequency exposure [11] that are also endorsed by the EU and other national governments. To meet the advanced specifications that 5G networks promise, a large number of small cell antennas and the use of intelligent beaming techniques, such as beamforming and massive Multiple Input Multiple Output (MIMO), might result in higher power levels when and where needed and lower levels once the needs are reduced. Hence, the 5G ecosystem stakeholders have raised concerns whether the existing radiation limit will still be relevant when 5G networks are introduced. Therefore, the new technology could trigger an adaptation of the existing regulatory framework, while respecting health-related laws and mandates.

3 Spectrum Auction in Italy and the NH Model

5G development can benefit from synergies among pioneer bands in frequencies:

1. Coverage-oriented band: 2×30 MHz Frequency Division Duplex (FDD) and up to 20 MHz SDL in the 694–790 MHz band
2. Intermediate band: 400 MHz Time Division Duplex (TDD) in the 3.6–3.8 GHz band
3. Capacity-oriented band: 1 GHz TDD in the 26.5–27.5 GHz band

Italy was the first country in Europe to auction spectrum in all three frequency bands concurrently, a process which took place in September 2018. All mobile operators participated in the 5G spectrum auction where a simultaneous multi-band award procedure was running. All spectrum assignments for all the bands were part of a single award procedure, which was divided in two phases. Firstly, the 700 MHz band was awarded and subsequently the remaining lots on the other bands were auctioned. The licence duration was set in a way that it offers enough time for the operators to recoup their investments in 5G networks within a reasonable timeframe. The expiry date of the allocated licenses is 31st December 2037 for all the assigned lots.

The financial exposure taken on in the Italian auction was huge, and all telcos will be impacted in the medium term as it happened in other countries after the 3G bands were auctioned in the early 2000s. This could affect the creation of a 5G ecosystem for the different actors because of the high price the operators had to pay, which squeezed their cash reserves. Operators have to explore new opportunities based on different use cases and business models in mission critical services, in massive IoT or in other verticals like Media and Energy. Possible synergies must be explored to cooperate with regulators and policymakers to deploy 5G in a more economically-efficient way.

A reliable 5G infrastructure is fundamental to offer the benefits enabled by the new technologies for different contexts.

Telcos have to follow not only the auction obligations but also to implement a new strategy for smart deployments, such as the one described in 5GCity by:

- sharing small cells networks
- prioritizing site construction according to the business models
- using more information coming from the business analysis of the customers
- creating smart partnerships to capture the economic benefits of the 5G technology.

4 Neutral Host-Specific Regulatory Considerations

Regulating the NH model is a complex task given the various facets that need to be considered. Few considerations that NRAs should take into account are as follow:

4.1 Ensure Neutrality

The NH should be obliged to provide wholesale access to all interested parties, e.g. network operators or other service providers, on a non-discriminatory basis. In other words, no operator or other party should be refused access to the NH's infrastructure, subject to regulatory approval. Neutrality doesn't necessarily mean providing the same level of service to everyone, since different bundles of services could be available to the hosted clients, but rather to provide the same level of service to those who have subscribed to the same service bundle.

4.2   No Retail Services

The NH should be prohibited from offering retail services that would put them in direct competition with existing MNOs, as this would defeat the purpose of the NH's very existence. Allowing a NH to exist in dense urban areas or rural areas where it is uneconomic to build individual networks ensures that MNOs have access to the NH's resources which complement their network to ensure improved coverage and service delivery. Direct competition between the two would turn operators away from trying to do business with the NH, making its existence not viable.

4.3   Price Regulation

The wholesale access prices offered by the NH should be regulated to ensure transparency, reasonableness and equal treatment of all parties. The NH's significant market power in its niche market could give it the ability to charge extraordinary prices to provide wholesale access to other interested parties, squeezing their profit margins and creating distortions in the market. Hence, a transparent rate card with 'reasonable' prices for the different levels of service should be in place. Several pricing schemes could also be investigating, such as the 'pay as you grow', 'pay as you use' or one with a flat annual fee.

4.4   Spectrum Ownership

Spectrum used by the NH should also be carefully regulated. Here, what needs to be clarified is who is going to be the spectrum owner in the case a NH exists. We have identified four alternative scenarios that vary in the form of the relationship between the operator and NH.

The Operator Owns the Spectrum. The operator acquires a spectrum license from the NRA, while the NH has zero spectrum holdings. Should the operator decide to use the NH's network, the latter uses the frequency bands acquired by the former. In this scenario, the NH minimizes its expenses and avoids participating in the complex task of spectrum management.

The NH Owns the Spectrum. The NH acquires a local spectrum license on its own. This scenario gives the NH significant market power which needs to be regulated so that it offers competitive prices.

Both the Operators and the NH Own Spectrum. In this case the operator will use its spectrum and NH's infrastructure. On the other hand, the NH can provide spectrum to verticals and other interesting parties that do not have their own license or complement operators' spectrum if needed.

A Third Entity Owns the Spectrum. In this case, the NH plays the role of the plays the role of the intermediary which increases the complexity since the NH undertakes the spectrum management task. A similar approach can be followed for the infrastructure.

4.5   Stakeholders Opinion About NH Regulatory Considerations

In order to investigate stakeholders' opinion and confirm the initial NH regulatory considerations, 5GCity project conducted a survey through questionnaires during MWC19. Regarding the need for proper regulation of the Neutral Host, 73% of respondents believe that the NH services/products should be regulated. This likely relates to the potential exhaustive pricing and potential preferential treatment of the wholesale customers that the NH would have in case its products/services were not regulated. Should the NH products/services be regulated, this would enabled fair and equal treatment of all actors requesting access, stimulating healthy competition in the market. Concerning billing, the majority of respondents believe that the billing relationship between the NH and operators should be based on the resources used from the latter. Only 13% of respondents believe in a fixed fee relationship. This is likely due to the fact that operators/verticals prefer dynamic billing systems, which are tailored to their changing needs for access. Surprisingly, more respondents believe that the NH should be the spectrum owner, in contrast to the current model in which operators are the sole owners and are subject to strict regulation for its use. This is likely due to expectations that there would be less complexity in the process, should the NH own spectrum.

5   Conclusions

Although Europe, USA and Asia are competing about the leadership in the 5G era, there are still several challenges that should be addressed before the deployment and the commercialization of 5G networks. In this paper, the need for the NH model in this new environment was briefly discusses. The NH model supported by the H2020 5GCity project was then described. Regulatory considerations were investigated and several guidelines that will be useful for network operators to accelerate the deployment of 5G networks and adopt the NH model were provided.

Acknowledgement. We like to acknowledge the efforts of all the partners of the 5GCity project consortium. This project has received funding from the European Union's Horizon 2020 research and innovation programme under grant agreement No 761508.

References

1. Elayoubi, S.E., et al.: 5G service requirements and operational use cases: analysis and METIS II vision. In: 2016 European Conference on Networks and Communications (EuCNC), Athens, pp. 158–162 (2016)
2. Mosharaf, N.M., Chowdhury, K., Boutaba, R.: A survey of network virtualization. Comput. Netw. **54**(5), 862–876 (2010)
3. Nunes, B.A.A., Mendonça, M., Ngyen, X.-N., Obraczka, K., Turletti, T.: A survey of software-defined networking: past, present, and future of programmable networks. IEEE Commun. Surv. Tutor. **16**(3), 1–18 (2014)

4. Frascolla, V., et al.: Millimeter-waves, MEC, and network softwarization as enablers of new 5G business opportunities. In: 2018 IEEE Wireless Communications and Networking Conference (WCNC), Barcelona, pp. 1–5 (2018)
5. https://ec.europa.eu/digital-single-market/en/news/commission-decides-harmonise-radio-spectrum-future-5g
6. Neokosmidis, I., et al.: Are 5G networks and the neutral host model the solution to the shrinking telecom market. In: Iliadis, L., Maglogiannis, I., Plagianakos, V. (eds.) AIAI 2018. IAICT, vol. 520, pp. 70–77. Springer, Cham (2018). https://doi.org/10.1007/978-3-319-92016-0_7
7. www.5gcity.eu
8. https://scf.io/en/documents/195_-_Small_cell_siting_challenges_and_recommendations.php
9. https://www.gsma.com/publicpolicy/resources/policy-recommendations-enable-small-cell-deployments-2
10. https://ec.europa.eu/digital-single-market/en/news/digital-single-market-strategy-europe-com-2015-192-final
11. http://www.who.int/emf/

8th Mining Humanistic Data Workshop (MHDW 2019)

Preface

8th Mining Humanistic Data Workshop (MHDW 2019)

The abundance of available data that is retrieved from or is related to the areas of humanities and the human condition challenges the research community in processing and analyzing it. The aim is two fold: on the one hand, to extract knowledge that will help us understand human behavior, creativity, ways of thinking, reasoning, learning, decision-making, socializing and even biological processes; on the other hand, to exploit the extracted knowledge by incorporating it into intelligent systems that will support humans in their everyday activities.

The nature of humanistic data can be multimodal, semantically heterogeneous, dynamic, time- and space-dependent, and highly complicated. Translating humanistic information, e.g., behavior, state of mind, artistic creation, linguistic utterance, learning and genomic information into numerical or categorical low-level data is a significant challenge on its own. New techniques, appropriate for dealing with this type of data, need to be proposed and existing ones adapted to its special characteristics.

The workshop aims to bring together interdisciplinary approaches that focus on the application of innovative as well as existing data matching, fusion and mining as well as knowledge discovery and management techniques (like decision rules, decision trees, association rules, ontologies and alignments, clustering, filtering, learning, classifier systems, neural networks, support vector machines, preprocessing, post-processing, feature selection, visualization techniques) to data derived from all areas of humanistic sciences, e.g., linguistic, historical, behavioral, psychological, artistic, musical, educational, social etc., and ubiquitous computing and bioinformatics.

Ubiquitous computing applications (aka pervasive computing, mobile computing, ambient intelligence, etc.) collect large volumes of usually heterogeneous data to effect adaptation, learning, and in general context awareness. Data matching, fusion, and mining techniques are necessary to ensure the functionality of human-centered applications.

An important aspect of humanistics centers around managing, processing, and computationally analyzing biological and biomedical data. Hence, one of the aims of this workshop is to also attract researchers that are interested in designing, developing, and applying efficient data and text mining techniques for discovering the underlying knowledge existing in biomedical data, such as sequences, gene expressions, and pathways. The topics of interest are listed here https://conferences.cwa.gr/mhdw2019/workshop-aim/.

We would like to thank the Steering Committee of the 8th Mining Humanistic Data workshop, Professors Spyros Sioutas, Katia Lida Kermanidis, and Dr. Ioannis Karydis, for their important contribution to the organization of this high-quality and mature event. Also, we would like to thank Professors Christos Makris, Phivos Mylonas, and Dr. Andreas Kanavos for doing an excellent job as senior members of the Program Committee. The MHDW attracts more and more high-quality research papers every year under the framework of the EANN and AIAI conferences.

Organization

8th Mining Humanistic Data Workshop (MHDW 2019)

Steering Committee

Ioannis Karydis	Ionian University, Greece & Creative Web Applications P.C., Greece
Katia Lida Kermanidis	Ionian University, Greece
Spyros Sioutas	University of Patras, Greece

Program Chairs

Luis Miguel Campos	PDMFC, Portugal
Andreas Kanavos	University of Patras, Greece
Christos Makris	University of Patras, Greece
Phivos Mylonas	Ionian University, Greece

Program Committee

Ioannis Anagnostopoulos	University of Thessaly, Greece
Mohamed Bader-El-Den	University of Portsmouth, UK
Georgios Drakopoulos	Ionian University, Greece
Ioannis Hatzilygeroudis	University of Patras, Greece
Ioannis Livieris	Technological Educational Institute of Western Greece, Greece
Manolis Maragoudakis	University of the Aegean, Greece
Alaa Mohasseb	University of Portsmouth, UK
Iosif Mporas	University of Hertfordshire, UK
Panayotis Pintelas	University of Patras, Greece
Evaggelos Spyrou	National Technical University of Athens, Greece
Giannis Tzimas	Technological Educational Institute of Western Greece, Greece

An Approach for Domain-Specific Design Pattern Identification Based on Domain Ontology

Vassiliki Gkantouna[1]([✉]) [iD], Vaios Papaioannou[1] [iD],
Giannis Tzimas[2] [iD], and Zlatan Sabic[3]

[1] Department of Computer Engineering and Informatics,
University of Patras, 26504 Patras, Greece
gkantoun@ceid.upatras.gr
[2] Department of Computer and Informatics Engineering,
Technological Educational Institute of Western Greece, 26334 Patras, Greece
[3] World Bank Group, Washington, D.C., USA

Abstract. In this work, we present an approach for supporting the identification of domain-specific design patterns based on domain's ontology, since the latter encapsulates the knowledge about the problem domain. More specifically, the proposed approach automatically analyzes the designs of a collection of domain-specific websites in terms of all the recurrent patterns occurring among them, both in the organization of their content and the front-end interface of their pages, resulting in a set of reusable design solutions which are commonly used in them by designers as building blocks for addressing typical domain problems. Then, evaluation is performed according to a number of inspection steps. At a first level, the recurrent patterns occurring at content organization, i.e., the common configurations of domain concepts occurring among website pages are evaluated by matching them against the domain's ontology and selecting the ones which are in alignment with the domain's context. At a second level, the recurrent patterns occurring at front-end organization (i.e., the common configurations of front-end design elements) are evaluated towards their consistent and effective use in designs of the collected websites. Finally, the approach categorizes the various reusable design solutions and recommends the ones with the best evaluation results as candidate domain-specific design patterns.

Keywords: Domain ontologies · Domain-specific design patterns ·
Content Management Systems

1 Introduction

Domain-specific design patterns (Pree 1997) are a powerful conceptual tool for designing web applications of high quality in a certain application domain. By using them, developers can gain a number of important advantages, such as increased design quality, reduced development and maintenance costs, and better communication since they provide a common vocabulary to discuss the various design alternatives. However, despite their numerous advantages, there is still an absence of techniques to

© IFIP International Federation for Information Processing 2019
Published by Springer Nature Switzerland AG 2019
J. MacIntyre et al. (Eds.): AIAI 2019 Workshops, IFIP AICT 560, pp. 125–137, 2019.
https://doi.org/10.1007/978-3-030-19909-8_11

systematically assist domain designers with their identification. To this end, we here propose an approach which automatically supports the identification of domain-specific design patterns, by providing designers with recommendations about candidate patterns. More specifically, we propose an approach that automatically analyzes the designs of domain-specific websites in terms of the various reusable design solutions which are used in them by designers as building blocks for addressing common domain problems. Then, in order to verify and validate that the identified design solutions truly lie and are applicable in the target domain, we evaluate them against the domain ontology and also apply a number of evaluation metrics on them. Finally, the approach categorizes the various reusable design solutions and recommends the ones with the best evaluation results as candidate domain-specific design patterns.

In order to automate the process of capturing the designs of domain-specific websites, we have narrowed down the scope of the approach to the area of Content Management Systems (CMSs) and illustrate its potential on websites built on top of Joomla! CMS. To explain the concepts of the proposed methodology, we focus on the domain of academic websites and refer to various instances of real Greek academic websites. The remaining of this paper is organized as follows: Sect. 2 provides an overview of the related work and discusses the contribution of this work. Section 3 presents in detail the approach, while Sect. 4 discusses conclusions and future work.

2 Related Work and Contribution

The main objective of this work is to assist domain designers with the identification of domain-specific web design patterns. Therefore, we have developed an approach to provide them with automatically identified recommendations about candidate patterns based on the domain's ontology. By reviewing the literature for studies concerning the identification of domain-specific design patterns, one can find out that the research in the field is still not mature enough. To begin with, despite the fact that there are many catalogues of web design patterns (Tidwell 2010; Van Welie 2019; Toxboe 2019), we noticed that only a small percentage of the patterns included in them are domain-specific and the domains explored are very few. Another issue is that the identification of domain-specific design patterns relies on a completely manual process (Van Welie and Klaasse 2004; Pontico et al. 2008; Cremonesi et al. 2017) and the whole burden of the process is carried by designers, requiring a great amount of time and effort. Here lies the main contribution of the proposed approach, since it aims to assist domain designers by attempting to support the pattern identification process in an automated way. More specifically, the proposed approach supports the automated design analysis of various websites in a particular application domain, as well as, the automated identification of the reusable design solutions which are commonly used in them for addressing typical domain problems. As a result, by simply providing a list of URLs that belong to domain-specific websites, domain designers can have access to a set of reusable micro-architectures which are used in the website designs as building blocks for addressing recurring domain problems.

3   The Approach

The approach can be divided in three main steps as depicted in Fig. 1. First, we identify all the recurrent patterns occurring in the organization of content and front-end interfaces of a collection of domain-specific websites, resulting in a set of reusable design solutions revealing potential design practices which are commonly used by designers in the domain for supporting the realization of domain functionalities (common domain-specific tasks). Then, in order to verify which of them are effectively used, denoting the existence of domain-specific design patterns, we validate and match them against domain's ontology, apply a number of evaluation criteria on them, and finally, recommend the ones with best evaluation results as candidate patterns.

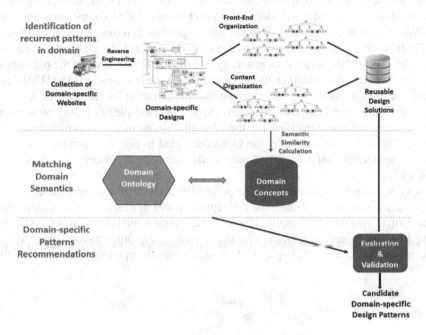

Fig. 1. The approach overview.

3.1   Identification of Recurrent Patterns in Domain-Specific Designs

The identification of recurrent patterns in the designs of the collected domain-specific websites is carried out in the following four phases:

Phase 1: Domain-Specific Websites Collection & Extraction of Domain Concepts
In the first phase, we create the collection of websites in the target application domain by employing a web crawler which, given a list containing the URLs of domain-specific websites, traverses all of their pages and makes a local copy of them on the user's computer. Subsequently, based on the semantics that is encapsulated on the pages of the collected domain-specific websites, we automatically capture domain

concepts by applying a semantic similarity measurement technique on their contents. To support this task, we have developed a tool which first collects the content of every page in the website collection, and then applies a WordNet-based semantic similarity measurement technique (Simpson and Dao 2005) on them in order to extract the common semantic concepts to which they refer. We consider all the computed common semantic concepts as domain concepts and store them in a database table, called domain dictionary. This way, a domain concept is assigned to every page of the collected websites.

Phase 2: Capturing the Designs of Domain-Specific Websites
In the second phase, we capture the designs of the collected domain-specific websites by automatically extracting their conceptual model at hypertext level, which specifies the organization of their front-end interfaces in terms of pages, made of a number of predefined structural and navigational design elements, called components and modules. When used in a page, all these types of components and modules, can be found in its HTML code as <div> elements, having characteristic HTML class attribute values (i.e., <div class = "value">). As a result, by parsing the HTML code of the pages of the collected websites and locating the occurrences of these characteristic HTML class attribute values in them, we can retrieve the organization of the various front-end design elements that compose their hypertext. For example, Fig. 3(a) presents the hypertext organization identified for the "Faculty" page of an academic department website. This task is supported by the toolset depicted in Fig. 2, which retrieves in the reverse engineering way described above the conceptual model of the collected websites.

Next, in order to facilitate the subsequent identification of recurrent patterns in the designs of the collected websites, the conceptual model of every website is represented in the form of two directed graphs. The first graph representation captures their designs at the level of content organization in them, that is, the organization of the various domain concepts among their pages. The second graph representation captures their

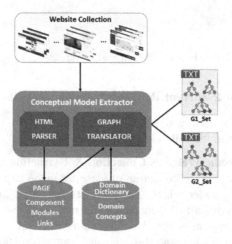

Fig. 2. The conceptual model extraction process.

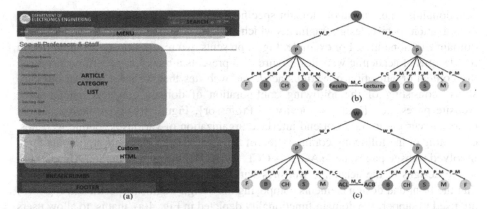

Fig. 3. (a) The organization of a page in terms of Joomla! component and modules. (b) The first graph representation of the page at the level of content organization. (c) The second graph representation of the page at the level of front-end interface organization.

designs at the level of hypertext organization, that is, the organization of the various design elements in the front-end interfaces of their pages. This task is supported by the "Graph Translator" unit depicted in Fig. 2. An example can be found in Fig. 3(b) and (c) which present an instance of the two graph representations produced for the conceptual model of an academic department website. Finally, the tool produces as output two TXT files containing the two graph representations produced for the conceptual model of every website in the collection. These two graph datasets are provided as input to the graph mining algorithm utilized in the next phase, in order to perform their pattern-based analysis and obtain the identification of the recurrent patterns in the organization of their content and hypertext interfaces.

Phase 3: Identification of Recurrent Patterns In Content and Hypertext Organization
In the third phase, we analyze the designs of the collected websites in terms of the recurrent patterns occurring in them, both at the level of content and hypertext organization. To achieve this, we reduce the problem of pattern identification in the two graph datasets produced in the previous phase to the subgraph isomorphism problem, synopsized in its general form into finding whether the isomorphic image of a subgraph exists in a larger graph. Intuitively, the isomorphic subgraphs occurring within a graph dataset is an alternative way to obtain the identification of the recurrent patterns among its graphs. Quite a few heuristics have been proposed to solve it, among which we have selected the most prominent one, that is, the gSpan algorithm (Yan and Han 2002). Thus, by applying gSpan (Philippsen 2011) on the two graph datasets, we identify all the recurrent patterns occurring in the content and hypertext organization of the collected domain-specific websites. We must note that the recurrent patterns in the content organization of the websites specify information flows which determine domain

functionalities, i.e., common domain-specific tasks, whereas the patterns in hypertext organization specify design fragments which are used to support the realization of these domain functionalities. For example, Fig. 4 presents two recurrent patterns identified in the designs of academic websites. Figure 4(a) presents a recurrent pattern occurring in the content organization of various academic websites that we have used in our case study, consisting of the following configuration of domain concepts among three website pages, i.e., {Staff → Faculty → Professor}. Figure 4(b) presents a recurrent pattern occurring in the front-end interface organization of various academic websites, consisting of the following configuration of front-end design elements among the three involved website pages, i.e., {ACL → CCL → SC}. If the pattern in Fig. 4(b) coexists in the designs of the academic websites with the pattern of Fig. 4(a), we can assume that the front-end design elements composing the design fragment specified in Fig. 4(b) are used to support the domain functionality depicted in Fig. 4(a), that is, to allow users to find the contact details of the various professors included in the faculty staff category of an academic department. As a result, in order to identify the commonly used design practices in the collection of domain-specific websites, we examine the occurrences of the identified recurrent patterns in the two graph datasets and identify those patterns that coexist, i.e., they occur simultaneously both at content and hypertext organization level.

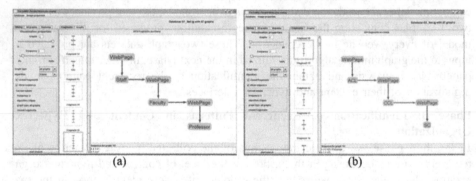

(a)   (b)

Fig. 4. Recurrent patterns in the designs of academic websites. (a) A pattern occurring in the content organization of academic websites. (b) A pattern occurring in the front-end interface organization of academic websites.

At the at the end of this phase, for every domain functionality (recurrent configuration of domain concepts), we identify a list of all the various recurrent design fragments which are commonly used in the designs of the collected websites in order to support its realization. Every possible combination of a design fragment in this list at the hypertext organization of the websites with the particular information flow of this domain functionality at their content organization can possibly result in a reusable design solution that is commonly used in the domain for addressing a certain domain problem. Have in mind that behind such a reusable design solution, there may be hidden a good design practice used by designers in the domain under study for addressing typical domain problems, signifying the existence of a possible domain-specific design pattern. To verify this, in the next phase, we proceed with the evaluation of the identified reusable design solutions.

Phase 4: Evaluation

In this step, we apply a number of evaluation criteria on the previously identified recurrent patterns in order to determine which of them can be considered as effective design solutions for the target application domain. Evaluation is performed in two steps. First, we evaluate the various configurations of domain concepts, captured as recurrent patterns in the content organization of the websites, by matching them against the domain's ontology. Then, we evaluate the various recurrent design fragments, captured as recurrent patterns in hypertext organization, towards (i) their consistent use in the designs of the website and (ii) the degree of their design similarity, since the underlying design reuse among them possibly reveals designers attempt to apply a certain design practice, indicating a possible domain-specific design pattern.

3.1.1 Evaluation Based on Domain Ontology

Domain ontology encapsulates the knowledge about the problem domain. It is an intentional semantic structure that encodes the set of objects and terms that are presumed to exist in the semantic domain, the relationships that hold among them, and the implicit rules constraining the structure of this (piece of) reality (Giaretta and Guarino 1995). Therefore, in order to validate that the identified recurrent configurations of domain concepts are actually within the context of the target domain, we cross-check the semantic concepts composing them against the concepts of domain ontology.

To define the domain ontology, we either use an already developed domain ontology as basis for domain reference or we define the domain ontology in OWL using Protégé (Noy et al. 2001). Then, based on the domain ontology definition, we either programmatically query the ontology repository for matched terms between the ontology's concepts and the identified configurations of domain concepts with SPARQL queries (Fig. 5), or, given the output of the previous phase in OWL format, we perform an ontology matching algorithm (Fig. 6) to check the validity of the terms composing the identified configurations of domain concepts. Figures 5 and 6 provide some relevant examples. In Fig. 5, the user validates an identified configuration of domain concepts by programmatically querying this configuration against the domain ontology of the academic domain. We can validate all terms included in an identified configuration of domain concepts one by one, such as in Fig. 5. Assuming that the concept "Professor" is one of these concepts, the toolkit validates this concept via a SPARQL query. It also suggests the concept "Lecturer", since this is also a subclass of the class Academic staff.

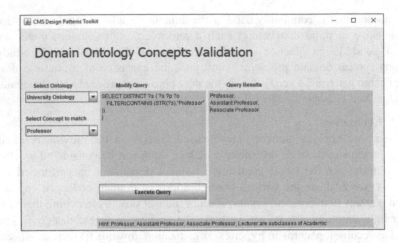

Fig. 5. Querying the domain ontology.

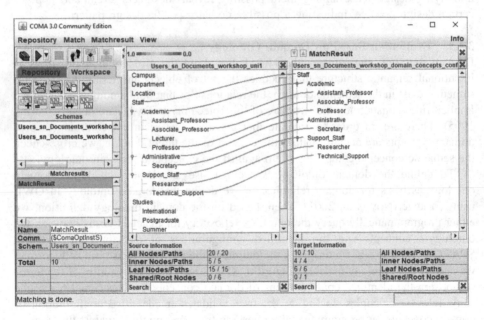

Fig. 6. An example of ontology mapping. (Color figure online)

Figure 6 presents an example of ontology matching approach based on the open-source API implementation of COMA (Massmann et al. 2011). In Fig. 6, the entire configuration of domain concepts belongs to the University ontology with estimated matching value of 1.0 (ranging from 0.0 to 1.0, green color). Thus, the configuration of domain concepts is totally matched against the domain ontology. The matching results shows that this configuration lies in the semantic context of the domain and it can also be optionally enhanced. For example, the concept of "Lecturer" is missing from the original discovered domain concept configuration (no connection line) and now can be utilized.

In both cases (either in programmatically querying ontology or in ontology mapping), the matching results can fall into three cases:

1. The identified domain concepts composing a recurrent pattern are a subset of the domain ontology's concepts, verifying that the websites composing the collection truly fall under the umbrella of the target application domain under consideration. Web designers can either use this configuration as it has been identified or even extend it with additional concepts specified in the domain ontology. For example, if the following configurations of domain concepts have been identified in a collection of academic websites, {Professor → Associate} and {Professor → Assistant}, then by matching them against the University Ontology, a further examination of the Academic class hierarchy can reveal the concept of "Lecturer" which can be used to extend the identified configuration of domain concepts.
2. The identified domain concepts in a configuration do not belong in the set of domain ontology's concepts, denoting either that the website collection is invalid for this domain or that the semantic analysis of the contents of website pages has produced invalid results.
3. The identified domain concepts composing the recovered patterns partially belong to the set of domain ontology's concepts. In this case, web designers can decide on how to make use of the identified domain concepts and even enhance them with concepts of the domain ontology. For example, the semantic analysis of domain concepts concluded to the term Professor among other academic terms, but no other types of Academic staff were discovered. In this case, web designers might examine the academic staff class hierarchy, and finally include Associate Professor and Assistant professor in their domain concepts configuration.

This way, we validate and verify which of the identified configuration of domain concepts truly lie in the specific context of the target application domain, and select those which are in alignment with its semantics.

3.1.2 Evaluation Based on Consistent Use and Effectiveness

After selecting the design fragments which are used to deliver to end-users the configurations of domain concepts which are valid according to the domain ontology evaluation of the previous step, the next step is to evaluate them towards their consistent use in the designs of the collected website, as well as, towards the degree of their design similarity.

3.1.2.1 Consistent Use of Recurrent Design Fragments

To determine which of the design fragments are effectively used for the realization of the identified domain functionalities (i.e., configurations of domain concepts), we evaluate them towards their consistent use in the website designs with respect to their starting and ending variants. More specifically, in phase 3 of Sect. 3.1, when obtaining the identification of the recurrent patterns in the graph datasets, except from the pattern's core specification (i.e., invariant composition of design elements), we also identify its starting and ending variants, extending the core specification of the pattern with all the valid modalities in which it can start or terminate. Intuitively, these variants correspond to the various design structures with which it is connected (on its left or right side) in the collected websites in order to execute a domain functionality. Thus, to verify the consistent use of a recurrent design fragment in the various website designs, we need to consider it with respect to its starting and ending variants.

To this end, we have defined two metrics called Start-Point Metric (SPM) and End-Point Metric (EPM), respectively. Assuming that a recurrent design fragment can have N starting and M ending variants, these metrics compute the statistical variance of the occurrences of these variants in the website designs, normalized with respect to the best-case variance. They are calculated according to the following formulas:

$$SPM = \sigma_S^2/\sigma_{S,BC}^2 \qquad EPM = \sigma_E^2/\sigma_{E,BC}^2 \qquad (1)$$

σ_S^2 and σ_E^2 is the statistical variance of the N starting variants occurrences and the M ending variants occurrences respectively, calculated according to the formula (2):

$$\sigma_S^2 = \frac{1}{N}\sum_{i=1}^{N}\left(p_i - \frac{1}{N}\right)^2 \qquad \sigma_E^2 = \frac{1}{M}\sum_{i=1}^{M}\left(p_i - \frac{1}{M}\right)^2 \qquad (2)$$

where p_i is the percentage of occurrences for the i-th pattern variant. $\sigma_{S,BC}^2$ and $\sigma_{E,BC}^2$ are instead the best-case variances for the starting and ending variants, calculated by the formula (2) assuming that only one variant has been coherently used throughout the website. We have also defined a measurement scale specifying a mapping between the numerical results obtained through the calculus method and a set of (predefined) meaningful and discrete values, as defined in Table 1.

Table 1. The measurement scale for the SPM and EPM metrics.

SPM/EPM range	Measurement scale value
$0 \leq$ SPM/EPM < 0.2	Optimum
$0.2 \leq$ SPM/EPM < 0.4	Good
$0.4 \leq$ SPM/EPM < 0.6	Discrete
$0.6 \leq$ SPM/EPM < 0.8	Weak
$0.8 \leq$ SPM/EPM ≤ 1	Insufficient

We compute the SPM and EPM metrics for all the starting and ending variants of the recurrent design fragments supporting the various domain functionalities and select only the ones having SPM and EPM values less than 0.6, and store the results in the "Results Repository". This way, we obtain a first level categorization of them based on the consistent use of their variants.

3.1.2.2 Design Similarity of Recurrent Design Fragments

Another important factor that must be taken into account in order to determine whether the identified recurrent patterns can be considered as candidate domain-specific patterns is their design similarity. This is due to the fact that high design similarity among them implies underlying design reuse which possibly occurs due to developers attempts to maintain a common design practice in the domain for the realization of a domain functionality, thus, signifying the existence of domain-specific design patterns. To this end, we perform a second level categorization of the previously selected recurrent design fragments based on the degree of their design similarity. To compute the degree of design similarity among a list of recurrent design fragments (i.e., configurations of design elements) that support a domain functionality, we adopt the vector space model. More specifically, every design fragment is represented as a vector $d_i = (x_{1,i}, x_{2,i}, \ldots, x_{n,i})$, where the compounds comprise all the distinct Joomla! design elements occurring among the various design fragments included in the list. These compounds are considered as unigrams and are weighted by the frequency of each respective unigram, that is, the number of times in which the design element (to which they correspond) occurs in the recurrent design fragment under consideration. Then, we compute the degree of design similarity between every possible pair of recurrent design fragments in the list, by calculating the cosine of the angle between their corresponding vector representations d_i and d_j. The latter is calculated according to the following formula:

$$Similarity(d_i, d_j) = \cos(d_i, d_j) = \frac{d_i \cdot d_j}{|d_i| \cdot |d_j|} = \frac{\sum_{t=1}^{n} w_{t,i} \cdot w_{t,j}}{\sqrt{\sum_{t=1}^{n} w_{t,i}^2} \cdot \sqrt{\sum_{t=1}^{n} w_{t,j}^2}}, \in [0, 1]$$

where $|d_i|$ and $|d_j|$ are the norms of the two vectors. To quantify the degree of this similarity, we have defined five similarity levels, presented in Table 2. The higher the level of design similarity among the design fragments, the more possible the design reuse occurring in them to capture a common design practice in the domain for the realization of the domain functionality.

Table 2. Design fragments categorization based on design similarity.

Design similarity level	Design fragments composed by:
1	■ totally different configurations of design elements
2	■ configurations of design elements identical up to 25%
3	■ configurations of design elements identical up to 50%
4	■ configurations of design elements identical up to 75%
5	■ identical configurations of design elements

At the end of this step, for every identified list of recurrent design fragments that supports a domain functionality, we locate all the sets of similar design fragments in the list, and identify the various design reuse schemes occurring in them. Then, we categorize them according to their design similarity level, and present the results in descending order. This way, we manage to capture the various common design practices which are used in the domain for addressing the domain functionalities. In order to reduce the large number of the identified design fragments, we select only the ones that occur in design fragments having a design similarity above the third level. By inspecting the identified design reuse schemes, domain designers can have a global picture of the various design practices that are commonly used in the domain for realizing the various domain functionalities. By combining these results with the results concerning their consistent use in the designs of the collected websites, it becomes easier for designers to determine which of the identified reusable design solutions can be considered as good design practices for the target domain, signifying the existence of candidate domain-specific design patterns.

4   Conclusions and Future Work

In this work, we have presented an approach that recommends automatically identified candidate reusable design solutions to domain designers in order to assist them with the identification process of domain-specific design patterns. To obtain these recommendations, it automatically analyzes the designs of a collection of websites in a target application domain, identifies and evaluates all the reusable design solutions occurring among them for addressing typical domain problems. For the evaluation of the recovered design solutions, we have relied on the domain ontology in order to capture those which are in alignment with the domain's semantics, on their consistent use and on their design similarity. Finally, the approach categorizes the various reusable design solutions and recommends the ones with the best evaluation results as candidate domain-specific design patterns. By having access to the results, domain designers can have an overview of the common design practices used in the domain for addressing typical domain problems, among which they can possibly recognize best practices and capture domain-specific design patterns. In future, we plan to apply the methodology in various application and extend it, so that it can be applied in websites built on top of other popular CMS platforms, such as Drupal and WordPress.

References

Cremonesi, P., Elahi, M., Garzotto, F.: User interface patterns in recommendation-empowered content intensive multimedia applications. Springer Multimedia Tools Appl. **76**(4), 5275–5309 (2017)

Giaretta, P., Guarino, N.: Ontologies and knowledge bases towards a terminological clarification. In: Towards Very Large Knowledge Bases: Knowledge Building & Knowledge Sharing, vol. 25, no. 32, pp. 307–317 (1995)

Massmann, S., Raunich, S., Aumüller, D., Arnold, P., Rahm, E.: Evolution of the COMA match system. In: Proceedings of the 6th International Conference on Ontology Matching, vol. 814, pp. 49–60, October 2011. CEUR-WS. org

Noy, N.F., Sintek, M., Decker, S., Crubézy, M., Fergerson, R.W., Musen, M.A.: Creating semantic web contents with protege-2000. IEEE Intell. Syst. **16**(2), 60–71 (2001)

Philippsen, M.: ParSeMiS - the Parallel and Sequential Mining Suite (2011). https://www2.cs.fau.de/EN/research/zold/ParSeMiS/index.html. Accessed 16 Mar 2019

Pontico, F., Winckler, M., Limbourg, Q.: Organizing user interface patterns for e-Government applications. In: Gulliksen, J., Harning, M.B., Palanque, P., van der Veer, Gerrit C., Wesson, J. (eds.) DSV-IS/EHCI/HCSE -2007. LNCS, vol. 4940, pp. 601–619. Springer, Heidelberg (2008). https://doi.org/10.1007/978-3-540-92698-6_36

Pree, W.: Essential framework design patterns. Object Mag. **7**, 34–37 (1997)

Simpson, T., Dao, T.: WordNet-based semantic similarity measurement (2005). http://www.codeproject.com/Articles/11835/WordNet-based-semantic-similarity-measurement. Accessed 16 Mar 2019

Tidwell, J.: Designing Interfaces. O'Reilly Media, Inc., Sebastopol (2010)

Toxboe, A.: User interface design pattern library. http://ui-patterns.com/patterns. Accessed 16 Mar 2019

Van Welie, M.: Web Design Patterns. http://www.welie.com/patterns/. Accessed 16 Mar 2019

Van Welie, M., Klaasse, B.: Evaluating museum websites using design patterns. Technical report, Internal Report IR-IMSE-001 (2004)

Yan, X., Han, J.: gSpan: graph-based substructure pattern mining. In: Proceedings of ICDM 2002, pp. 721–724 (2002)

Pre-processing Framework for Twitter Sentiment Classification

Elias Dritsas[1], Gerasimos Vonitsanos[1], Ioannis E. Livieris[2(✉)],
Andreas Kanavos[1,2], Aristidis Ilias[1], Christos Makris[1],
and Athanasios Tsakalidis[1]

[1] Computer Engineering and Informatics Department,
University of Patras, Patras, Greece
eldritsas@gmail.com,
{mvonitsanos,kanavos,aristeid,makri,tsak}@ceid.upatras.gr
[2] Computer and Informatics Engineering Department,
Technological Educational Institute of Western Greece, Antirrion, Greece
livieris@teiwest.gr

Abstract. Twitter Sentiment Classification is undergoing great appeal from the research community; also, user posts and opinions are producing very interesting conclusions and information. In the context of this paper, a pre-processing tool was developed in Python language. This tool processes text and natural language data intending to remove wrong values and noise. The main reason for developing such a tool is to achieve sentiment analysis in an optimum and efficient way. The most remarkable characteristic is considered the use of emojis and emoticons in the sentiment analysis field. Moreover, supervised machine learning techniques were utilized for the analysis of users' posts. Through our experiments, the performance of the involved classifiers, namely Naive Bayes and SVM, under specific parameters such as the size of the training data, the employed methods for feature selection (unigrams, bigrams and trigrams) are evaluated. Finally, the performance was assessed based on independent datasets through the application of k-fold cross validation.

Keywords: Classification · Microblogging · Pre-processing ·
Sentiment analysis · Supervised machine learning · Twitter

1 Introduction

The rapid development of modern computing systems along with Internet access and high communication capabilities, has turned these schemes into an integral part of human everyday life. Nowadays, users can express their personal opinion on any matter whenever they wish as well as share their thoughts and feelings. It is no coincidence that most websites encourage their users to review their services or products while social media accounts have significantly increased.

© IFIP International Federation for Information Processing 2019
Published by Springer Nature Switzerland AG 2019
J. MacIntyre et al. (Eds.): AIAI 2019 Workshops, IFIP AICT 560, pp. 138–149, 2019.
https://doi.org/10.1007/978-3-030-19909-8_12

In particular, a user through websites can be informed, express their personal views on a variety of topics and simultaneously interact with other users. Hence, this kind of interaction produces a large amount of data that is of particular interest for further process and analysis. Companies have started to poll these microblogs to get a sense and understand the general sentiment towards their product. Often, these companies study user replies and in following reply on the corresponding microblogs. The challenge is to build tools that can detect and summarize an overall sentiment, so that valuable conclusions and information on various kinds of issues can be drawn. For example, one can consider demographic and social conclusions, information of economic nature such as the prevailing view of a product or service, or even results of political content.

Sentiment analysis constitutes a subtle field in information mining. It is considered a computational analysis and categorization of opinions, feelings and attitudes that are drawn up in text format. The use of Natural Language Processing techniques is sought through polarity performance, while polarity can be characterized by many different classes. Specifically, the positive and negative terms, which correspond to the positive or negative view that a user has, are utilized in terms of a specific event or topic.

It is widely noted that the emotional analysis has many applications, as an individual may have a view on a huge range of issues of a different nature, such as economic, political, religious, and so on. For this reason, the positive and negative classes are not the only ones used, as aforementioned. It constitutes a basic way of studying and analyzing such data. Indeed, in recent years, the great volume of raw information generated by Internet users has increased the interest in processing such data. In other words, it is the process of mining and categorizing subjective data so as to extract information about the polarity and overall emotion expressed in natural language in text form [14].

Data mining is considered an important part of the data analysis [24]. It largely consists of collection, processing and modeling of data and is aimed at the objectives shown in Fig. 1. Its characteristics are the export of information from a dataset, its following transformation in a comprehensible structure with

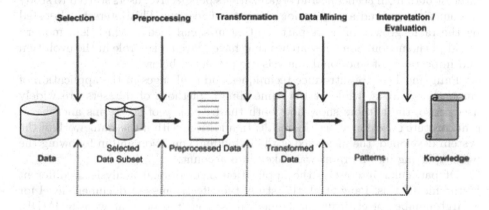

Fig. 1. KDD process for knowledge mining from data [12]

the use of various techniques (machine learning, statistics, etc.) which facilitate analysis, and finally the conclusions export as well as the decision-making.

In this present work, the main contributions concern the following aspects. Concerning data pre-processing techniques, tweets face several new challenges due to the typical short length and irregular structure of such content. Hence, data pre-processing constitutes a crucial step in the corresponding field of sentiment analysis, since selecting the appropriate pre-processing methods, the correctly classified instances can be increased [6]. To properly implement the data analysis process, it is necessary to process the raw data collected in a variety of ways. Initially, it should be decided what data will be used depending on the purpose of the analysis. In following, it is necessary to eliminate the abnormalities and deal with incorrect values and/or incomplete inputs. Subsequently, the processed data are modified in a form suitable for mining them. Therefore, we focus on designing an efficient pre-processing tool which facilitates the sentiment analysis conducted based on supervised machine learning algorithms. Another contribution is the application of Latent Dirichlet Allocation (LDA) based probabilistic system to discover latent topics from the conversations in connection to the event we take into account.

The proposed research is organized as follows: Sect. 2 describes the background topics and the challenges faced, while Sect. 3 explains the process of information retrieval from Twitter platform. The same section analyzes the tool for data pre-processing, which is the main contribution of this work. Furthermore, Sect. 4 presents the experimental results and main conclusions extracted from the study and the analysis. Finally, Sect. 5 portrays conclusions and draws directions for future work.

2   Related Work

Sentiment Analysis can be considered as a field of data mining, which intends to determine the polarity of a subjective text, through the use of various algorithms. In the recent years, this particular branch of science has started to gain increasing interest both from academic and organizations perspective; users started to study the emotions around a subject for a variety of reasons. This interest is boosted by the rapid growth of users participating in social media, which is a modern world phenomenon. Some researches that have played a key role in the evolution and importance of emotional analysis are presented below.

Pang and Lee [16] introduce techniques and challenges in the application of emotional analysis, while at the same time a plethora of datasets are widely used. Also, the authors show how both the frequency of the terms and the n-gram feature selection affect the result. In addition, within the framework of the system developed, the incidence of the individual condition and in following the posts splitting into n-grams was taken into account.

Of particular interest is the application of emotional analysis to different hierarchical levels. Pang et al. [17] study the effectiveness of document-level for a large number of critically acclaimed films from the popular website IMDB.

Turney et al. [19] examine the polarity of a file through its proposals. Phrases that include adjectives and/or adverbs, or other features and parts of speech that are highly likely to express the author's emotion, are selected. Concretely, user reviews on a variety of topics such as movies, travel destinations, banks and cars, were utilized. Wilson et al. [21] analyzed the views of the MPQA corpus along with a set of data containing journal articles from different sources that have been rated in terms of their emotion. An important part of their work was the separation of neutral phrases in polar and objective and then, the polarity analysis of subjective phrases to extract the overall feeling of the text.

Furthermore, the emotional analysis can also be applied in the field of economic interest, in sets of journalistic content and critical films [7,22,23], as well as for political aspects [18,20]. Initially, authors in [23] studied reviews for mobile applications and in following exported important features for their nature. Then, in [7], product reviews to identify consumer's sentiment in terms of certain characteristics and the products themselves were analyzed. Authors in [22] constructed a model for emotional analysis based on travelers reviews about the destinations they visited. In a similar way, a system that analyzes the sentiment of publications of real-time Twitter users to predict the results of the 2012 presidential election in the United States of America was created [20]. Finally, in [18], researchers used messages (not real-time data) that included reference to German political parties in 2009.

Previous works regarding emotional content are the ones presented in [8–10], in which the authors presented various approaches for the automatic analysis of tweets and the recognition of the emotional content of each tweet based on Ekman emotion model; based on Ekman emotion model, the existence of one or more out of the six basic human emotions (Anger, Disgust, Fear, Joy, Sadness and Surprise) is specified. Finally, a novel distributed framework implemented in Hadoop as well as in Spark for exploiting the hashtags and emoticons inside a tweet is introduced in [11]. Moreover, Bloom filters are also utilized to increase the performance of the proposed algorithm.

3 Tools and Environment

The pre-processing methods evaluated by the current research are three different data representations, namely unigrams, bigrams and trigrams. Two well-known machine learning algorithms were selected for classification, namely Naive Bayes and Support Vector Machine (SVM) as shown in the following section.

3.1 Twitter

The platform that is being studied in this work is Twitter. This is a platform for posting posts, exchanging messages between users, and modifying their private profiles according to their needs. There is the possibility of communicating links, images and audiovisual material to the posts. Twitter has gained considerable interest on a global scale, due to the services it provides its users with.

A special feature that makes emotional analysis quite difficult in its context is the small length of suspension that it allows its users. It is therefore perceived that studying the polarity of users' publications, beyond the general challenges and difficulties faced, is even more difficult due to their limited length.

3.2 Publications Mining Tools

The mining of posts was done using the Tweepy library which through the Twitter interface allows managing a user's profile, collecting data by optionally using certain search keywords, and finally creating and studying a stream of posts over a specific time interval.

In this work, posts were stored in a CSV file, where rows contain the posts that were extracted, while the columns contain the values of the different attributes of each post (e.g., date, text, username, etc.).

Useful tools in the context of this work were the following:

1. The Natural Language Tool Kit is a natural language processing library, which offers classification, parsing, tagging, and clipping stemming possibilities.
2. Scikit-Learn is a library that addresses the implementation and development of machine learning techniques and text editing tools. This library interacts with the Python, NumPy and SciPy computational and scientific libraries enhancing its efficiency and speed significantly.
3. Pickle is a library that converts objects in a form understandable only by the Python language, in order to limit the space they occupy in memory; this is due to certain features (e.g. JSON format) to be stored and reused whenever necessary. In this work, this library was used to allow the usage of objects returned after the classifier training, without retraining, whenever necessary.

3.3 Pre-processing Scheme

In order to facilitate the mining process of the collected data, it is necessary to apply several pre-processing steps [3]. The main parts of this process are the following.

Pandas Library: It was utilized to facilitate the management of input files having the components of the publications. Then, a dataframe was created only with the most important components for our analysis, i.e. records were removed, either with incorrect values or the ones not rated.

Regular Expressions: They were utilized to remove the urls and references to other users' username. Also, it was possible to find and replace/remove alphanumeric characters that match a predefined search pattern and remove unnecessary spaces. The repetition of suffix characters that were used for emphasis reason and numeric characters, which do not facilitate Sentiment Analysis, were removed as well.

Emoticons: Emoticons are characters, such as punctuation and parentheses, which in turn form representations of expressions of the human face, e.g. cheerful person {:-)}, but also different representations that play an important role in analyzing the feelings of each publication. Emoticons are widely used in social media, especially on the Twitter, to express feelings and impressions in a short way. Therefore, a set of regular expressions containing a large part of these representations was created. Additionally, a set of widely used unofficial abbreviations was generated in order to replace words that users make up. For example, the lol expression, which was replaced by its equivalent full form, namely, laugh out loud.

Autocorrect Library: This library uses a list of words found in recognized dictionaries, and given an input word, compares its similarity to the words on that list. If the input word is correctly spelled, it is returned as a whole. If it is not correctly spelled, then its similarity is checked with the words in the list; if its similarity is greater than a certain threshold, then it is replaced by the word in the list. Otherwise, it is returned as a whole, without any changes.

Pycontractions Library: It detects a set of successive characters in which the apostrophe is contained and replaces it with the full form of expression. Expressions with the {'s} special character complicate emotional analysis since they express two or more words, which makes tokenization, as well as, normalization, particularly difficult. For effective mining, contractions are written in their original form no matter how complicated it is. In case the set has a single possible replacement, then the expression is transformed into its original full form. Using a grammatical controller and Word Mover's Distance [13], a method of calculating the distance between the original text and the texts produced, called "compatibility" metric, is derived. The substitution applied is the one with the highest value.

Emoji Library: They are Unicode characters in the form of an icon representing face expressions, and many kinds of objects. This part differentiates our work from others, as in most other studies, emoticons and emojis are not taken into account. However, they are used in most publications in opinion mining. This library uses a mapping list, as created by the Unicode Consortium. Unicode characters included in a text are reviewed, and if they are in this list, they are replaced with the text form of their representation.

Part-of-Speech Tagging: Each word of the text is tagged according to the part of the speech that it constitutes (adverb, verb, object). This process uses the context of the text to be analyzed as well as a set of aggregated elements (corpus), to evaluate and attribute the part of speech to the particular term being studied.

Lemmatization: It is the process in which lexical and morphological analyses of words are taken into account in order to remove complex suffixes and to retrieve the lexical form of the term. It is applied after POS tagging and facilitates the emotional analysis through the application of machine learning algorithms. In the context of this work, POS tagging labels are Penn Treebank format.

Tokenization: It is the separation of sentences into a list of symbol terms that can be used to reform the original sentence. Both emoticons and emojis that have now been converted to text characters are taken as tokens, without being divided into individual characters or punctuation marks. The tokenization process is applied to all sentences, and their terms are stored in the same token list. Essentially, the tokens list is created for each post. Once the publication's details are now in a list in the order they appear in it, some more conversions are made to optimize and improve the viewing process.

Punctuation: These are also tokens of the list. Generally, punctuation marks do not attach any emotional significance to the publication and thus, they are removed.

Stopwords: These are words appearing very often, without expressing some form of feeling. The reason why such words are removed is because the whole attempt is to examine meaningful words in order to determine the overall emotion expressed in publication.

3.4   Features

N-grams are one of the most common structures used in text mining and natural language processing fields. They constitute a set of co-occuring words within a given window. In addition, as already known, a Markov assumption is the assumption that the probability of a word depends only on the previous word. So, Markov models are these probabilistic models that with their use, the probability of a future aspect without looking too far into the past can be predicted. The most popular ones are the bigrams, which search for one word from the past, the trigrams, which search for two words from the past, and the n-grams, which search for $n1$ words from the past.

The "bag-of-words" approach is considered a very simple and flexible representation of text that describes the occurrence of words within a document. It involves a vocabulary of known words as well as a metric of the presence of these known words. The model considers only the existence of the known words in the document, and not the exact place where to be found in the document. The intuition is that documents are similar if they have similar content.

The Summed Term Frequency constitutes the sum of all the term frequencies in the documents. In the proposed paper, it is utilized as

$$SummedTermFrequency = \sum_{d \in D} TF_{n-gram} \tag{1}$$

In addition, the "Apply Features" method has been taken into consideration in order to obtain a feature-value representation of the documents. Concretely, this method is used in order to apply a "positive" or a "negative" label to each feature of the training data.

3.5   Topic Modeling

One other aspect we want to take into consideration in our proposed work is the verification of whether all the posts discuss the specific topic. Topic modeling considers a document as a "bag-of-topics" representation, and its purpose is to cluster each term in each post into a relevant topic. Variations of different probabilistic topic models [1,15] have been proposed and LDA [2] is considered to be a well known method.

Concretely, the LDA model extracts the most common topics discussed that are represented by the words most frequently used, by simply taking as input a group of documents. The input is a term document matrix, and the output is composed of two distributions, namely document-topic distribution θ and topic-word distribution ϕ. EM [5] and Gibbs Sampling [4] algorithms were proposed to derive the distributions of θ and ϕ. In this paper, we use the Gibbs Sampling based LDA. In this approach, one of the most significant steps is updating each topic assignments individually for each term in every documents according to the probabilities calculated using Eq. 2.

$$\mathbb{P}(z_i = k | z_{-i}, w, \alpha, \beta) \propto \frac{(n_{(k,m,\cdot)}^{-i} + \alpha)(n_{(k,\cdot,w_i)}^{-i} + \beta)}{n_{(k,\cdot,\cdot)}^{-i} + V\beta} \quad (2)$$

where $z_i = k$ shows that the i_{th} term in a document is assigned to topic k, z_i signifies all the assignments of topic except the i_{th} term, $n_{(k,m,\cdot)}^{-i}$ is the number of times that the document d contains the topic k, $n_{(k,\cdot,w_i)}^{-i}$ is the number of times that term v is assigned to topic k, V represents the size of the vocabulary as well as α and β are hyper-parameters for the document-topic distribution and topic-word distribution respectively.

The number of the Gibbs sampling iterations performed for every terms in the corpus is N; after this component, the document-topic θ and topic-word ϕ distributions are estimated using Eqs. 3 and 4 respectively.

$$\hat{\theta}_{m,k} = \frac{n_{(k,m,\cdot)} + \alpha}{K\alpha + \sum_{k=1}^{K} n_{(k,m,\cdot)}} \quad (3)$$

$$\hat{\phi}_{k,v} = \frac{n_{(k,\cdot,v)} + \beta}{V\beta + \sum_{v=1}^{V} n_{(k,\cdot,v)}} \quad (4)$$

4   Evaluation

In Table 1, the two datasets studied as well as their characteristics are presented. There are 5 different categories whereas the first dataset contains tweets for all of them and the second dataset contains tweets for the 3 of them. The total number of tweets studied per each dataset is also considered.

The first dataset consists of tweets about self-driving cars[1]. The sentiment is categorized into 5 categories, ranging from very positive to very negative.

---

[1] https://www.kaggle.com/c/twitter-sentiment-analysis-self-driving-cars.

The second dataset consists of the feelings that travelers have in February 2015 towards the problems of each major U.S. airline[2]. The sentiment in the tweets of this dataset is categorized as positive, neutral or negative for six US airlines.

Table 1. Datasets details

Sentiment	Selfdriving cars dataset	Airlines dataset
Positive	1262	2363
Slightly positive	1452	
Neutral	4245	3099
Slightly negative	1498	
Negative	1076	9178
Total number of tweets	9533	14640

The results of our work are presented in the following Tables 2, 3 and 4. The Accuracy, in terms of percentage, is used as the evaluation metric of the two different algorithms (Naive Bayes and SVM) for the different setup (Unigrams, Bigrams and Trigrams). Also, the percentage of training and test set is taken into account when considering the two datasets.

In Table 2, the results of the RapidMiner platform[3] are presented. We have used RapidMiner as a baseline to emphasize the improvement of our proposed methodology. Furthermore, in RapidMiner we cannot include features that are utilised in our paper, such as emojis and emoticons, etc. We observe that SVM performs better than Naive Bayes for the three different setups and for both datasets. Secondly, in both datasets, Unigrams and Bigrams achieve better accuracy than Trigrams; this is expected as tweets usually have small length due to the number restriction that characters have and thus, Trigrams cannot be considered as a qualitative metric.

Table 2. RapidMiner results - accuracy

Setup	Selfdriving cars dataset	Airlines dataset
Naive Bayes (Unigrams)	62.13	64.95
Naive Bayes (Bigrams)	64.37	62.40
Naive Bayes (Trigrams)	58.89	50.66
SVM (Unigrams)	69.56	75.50
SVM (Bigrams)	71.78	73.20
SVM (Trigrams)	71.49	70.95

---

[2] https://www.kaggle.com/crowdflower/twitter-airline-sentiment.
[3] https://rapidminer.com/.

Table 3. Accuracy for different training - test set ratios

Setup	Selfdriving cars dataset			Airlines dataset		
	70–30	75–25	80–20	70–30	75–25	80–20
Naive Bayes (Unigrams)	71.99	72.73	74.04	82.60	83.72	85.18
Naive Bayes (Bigrams)	77.83	79.49	80.76	77.78	78.55	80.94
Naive Bayes (Trigrams)	76.57	77.93	79.44	59.45	59.70	60.72
SVM (Unigrams)	73.50	74.45	74.15	77.45	77.57	78.44
SVM (Bigrams)	76.43	77.77	78.76	68.90	69.43	69.56
SVM (Trigrams)	75.70	77.27	78.67	64.94	65.28	65.82

In following, Table 3 presents the results for different ratio of training versus test set. We have utilised three different cases, with training set having values equal to 70, 75 and 80 whereas test set has values equal to 30, 25 and 20 respectively. Worth noting is the fact that our proposed methodology outperforms the results from RapidMiner as regarding Selfdriving Cars Dataset, for both classifiers and the three different setups, the accuracy has lower value equal to 72% and higher equal to 80%. On the other hand, for the Airlines dataset, we observe high rate fluctuations as the higher and the lower percentages are depicted. Concretely, Naive Bayes (Trigrams) achieves the lowest accuracy with almost 60% and Naive Bayes (Unigrams) achieves the highest accuracy with 85% (for training-test ratio equal to 80–20). Furthermore, we notice that for all cases, as the percentage of training set increases, so does the accuracy. This is something that we expect as higher values of training set increase the classifier's results.

Finally, Table 4 presents the Accuracy results when splitting with 10-Fold Cross-Validation. The concept of using this technique is that important information can be removed from the training set. In addition, this method is simple to understand and generally results in a less biased or less optimistic estimate of the model skill than other methods, such as a simple train/test split. As in Table 3, Naive Bayes outperforms SVM, while it achieves the higher percentage with value equal to 85%. What is more, for both datasets, Naive Bayes has values close to 79% whereas SVM has different values for the three setups.

Table 4. 10-fold cross-validation

Setup	Selfdriving cars dataset	Airlines dataset
Naive Bayes (Unigrams)	78.66	85.38
Naive Bayes (Bigrams)	79.92	79.99
Naive Bayes (Trigrams)	79.29	74.26
SVM (Unigrams)	73.04	77.26
SVM (Bigrams)	76.59	69.32
SVM (Trigrams)	75.93	65.25

5   Conclusions and Future Work

In this paper, we proposed a pre-processing framework for Twitter sentiment classification. We chose Twitter because of tweets' short length and content's diversity. We used supervised machine learning techniques for the analysis of the raw data in the user posts and incorporated emojis and emoticons if order to enrich our features. Furthermore, we applied the Latent Dirichlet Allocation (LDA) based probabilistic system to discover latent topics from the conversations. Two popular classifiers (Naive Bayes and SVM) were used for three different data representations (unigrams, bigrams and trigrams) in order to perform our experiments in two datasets.

In the near future, we plan to extend and improve our framework by exploring more traits that may be added in the feature vector and will increase the classification performance. Moreover, we plan to compare the classification performance of our solution with other classification methods. Another future consideration is the adoption of other heuristics for handling complex semantic issues, such as irony that is typical of messages on Twitter.

Acknowledgement. Elias Dritsas was funded by General Secretariat for Research and Technology (GSRT) and Hellenic Foundation for Research and Innovation (HFRI) and supported by University of Patras. Andreas Kanavos, Aristidis Ilias and Christos Makris are co-financed by the European Union (European Social Fund) and Greek national funds through the Operational Program Research and Innovation Strategies for Smart Specialisation - RIS3 of "Partnership Agreement (PA) 2014-2020".

References

1. Blei, D.M.: Probabilistic topic models. Commun. ACM **55**(4), 77–84 (2012)
2. Blei, D.M., Ng, A.Y., Jordan, M.I.: Latent Dirichlet allocation. J. Mach. Learn. Res. **3**, 993–1022 (2003)
3. García, S., Luengo, J., Herrera, F.: Data Preprocessing in Data Mining. Intelligent Systems Reference Library, vol. 72. Springer, Heidelberg (2015). https://doi.org/10.1007/978-3-319-10247-4
4. Griffiths, T.L.: Gibbs sampling in the generative model of latent Dirichlet allocation (2002)
5. Griffiths, T.L., Steyvers, M.: Finding scientific topics. Proc. Natl. Acad. Sci. **101**(Suppl. 1), 5228–5235 (2004)
6. Haddi, E., Liu, X., Shi, Y.: The role of text pre-processing in sentiment analysis. In: 1st International Conference on Information Technology and Quantitative Management (ITQM), pp. 26–32 (2013)
7. Hu, M., Liu, B.: Mining opinion features in customer reviews. In: Proceedings of the Nineteenth National Conference on Artificial Intelligence (AAAI), pp. 755–760 (2004)
8. Kanavos, A., Perikos, I., Hatzilygeroudis, I., Tsakalidis, A.: Integrating user's emotional behavior for community detection in social networks. In: International Conference on Web Information Systems and Technologies (WEBIST), pp. 355–362 (2016)

9. Kanavos, A., Perikos, I., Hatzilygeroudis, I., Tsakalidis, A.: Emotional community detection in social networks. Comput. Electr. Eng. **65**, 449–460 (2018)

10. Kanavos, A., Perikos, I., Vikatos, P., Hatzilygeroudis, I., Makris, C., Tsakalidis, A.: Conversation emotional modeling in social networks. In: IEEE International Conference on Tools with Artificial Intelligence (ICTAI), pp. 478–484 (2014)

11. Kanavos, A., Nodarakis, N., Sioutas, S., Tsakalidis, A., Tsolis, D., Tzimas, G.: Large scale implementations for twitter sentiment classification. Algorithms **10**(1), 33 (2017)

12. Kavakiotis, I., Tsave, O., Salifoglou, A., Maglaveras, N., Vlahavas, I., Chouvarda, I.: Machine learning and data mining methods in diabetes research. Comput. Struct. Biotechnol. J. **15**, 104–116 (2017)

13. Kusner, M.J., Sun, Y., Kolkin, N.I., Weinberger, K.Q.: From word embeddings to document distances. In: Proceedings of the 32nd International Conference on Machine Learning (ICML), pp. 957–966 (2015)

14. Liu, B., Zhang, L.: A survey of opinion mining and sentiment analysis. In: Aggarwal, C., Zhai, C. (eds.) Mining Text Data, pp. 415–463. Springer, Boston (2012). https://doi.org/10.1007/978-1-4614-3223-4_13

15. Murphy, K.P.: Machine Learning: A Probabilistic Perspective. Adaptive Computation and Machine Learning. MIT Press, Cambridge (2012)

16. Pang, B., Lee, L.: Opinion mining and sentiment analysis. Found. Trends Inf. Retrieval **2**(1–2), 1–135 (2008)

17. Pang, B., Lee, L., Vaithyanathan, S.: Thumbs up? Sentiment classification using machine learning techniques. In: ACL Conference on Empirical methods in Natural Language Processing (EMNLP), pp. 79–86 (2002)

18. Tumasjan, A., Sprenger, T.O., Sandner, P.G., Welpe, I.M.: Predicting elections with twitter: what 140 characters reveal about political sentiment. In: Proceedings of the Fourth International Conference on Weblogs and Social Media (ICWSM) (2010)

19. Turney, P.D.: Thumbs up or thumbs down? Semantic orientation applied to unsupervised classification of reviews. In: Proceedings of the 40th Annual Meeting of the Association for Computational Linguistics (ACL), pp. 417–424 (2002)

20. Wang, H., Can, D., Kazemzadeh, A., Bar, F., Narayanan, S.: A system for real-time twitter sentiment analysis of 2012 U.S. presidential election cycle. In: Annual Meeting of the Association for Computational Linguistics, pp. 115–120 (2012)

21. Wilson, T., Wiebe, J., Hoffmann, P.: Recognizing contextual polarity in phrase-level sentiment analysis. In: Conference on Human Language Technology and Empirical Methods in Natural Language Processing (HLT/EMNLP), pp. 347–354 (2005)

22. Ye, Q., Zhang, Z., Law, R.: Sentiment classification of online reviews to travel destinations by supervised machine learning approaches. Expert Syst. Appl. **36**(3), 6527–6535 (2009)

23. Zhang, L., Hua, K., Wang, H., Qian, G., Zhang, L.: Sentiment analysis on reviews of mobile users. In: 9th International Conference on Future Networks and Communications (FNC)/11th International Conference on Mobile Systems and Pervasive Computing (MobiSPC), pp. 458–465 (2014)

24. Zhao, J., Wang, W., Sheng, C.: Data-Driven Prediction for Industrial Processes and Their Applications. Springer, Heidelberg (2018). https://doi.org/10.1007/978-3-319-94051-9

Computing Long Sequences of Consecutive Fibonacci Integers with TensorFlow

Georgios Drakopoulos[1(✉)], Xenophon Liapakis[2], Evaggelos Spyrou[3], Giannis Tzimas[4], Phivos Mylonas[1], and Spyros Sioutas[5]

[1] Department of Informatics, Ionian University, Corfu, Hellas
{c16drak,fmylonas}@ionio.gr
[2] Interamerican SA, Marousi, Hellas
liapakisx@interamerican.com
[3] NCSR "Demokritos", Athens, Hellas
espyrou@iit.demikritos.gr
[4] Technological Educational Institute of Western Greece, Patras, Hellas
tzimas@teimes.gr
[5] Computer Engingeering and Informatics Department, University of Patras, Patras, Hellas
sioutas@ceid.upatras.gr

Abstract. Fibonacci numbers appear in numerous engineering and computing applications including population growth models, software engineering, task management, and data structure analysis. This mandates a computationally efficient way for generating a long sequence of successive Fibonacci integers. With the advent of GPU computing and the associated specialized tools, this task is greatly facilitated by harnessing the potential of parallel computing. This work presents two alternative parallel Fibonacci generators implemented in TensorFlow, one based on the well-known recurrence equation generating the Fibonacci sequence and one expressed on inherent linear algebraic properties of Fibonacci numbers. Additionally, the question of using lookup tables in conjunction with spline interpolation or direct computation within a parallel context for the computation of the powers of known quantities is explored. Although both parallel generators outperform the baseline serial implementation in terms of wallclock time and FLOPS, there is no clear winner between them as the results rely on the number of integers generated. Additionally, replacing computations with a lookup table degrades performance, which can be attributed to the frequent access to the shared memory.

Keywords: Fibonacci sequence · Linear recurrence equations · Finite differences · Google TensorFlow · GPU computing · Parallel computing

© IFIP International Federation for Information Processing 2019
Published by Springer Nature Switzerland AG 2019
J. MacIntyre et al. (Eds.): AIAI 2019 Workshops, IFIP AICT 560, pp. 150–160, 2019.
https://doi.org/10.1007/978-3-030-19909-8_13

1   Introduction

The sequence of Fibonacci integers $\langle f_k \rangle$ appears often in a broad spectrum of engineering applications including coding theory, cryptography, simulation, and software management. Additionally, Fibonacci numbers are very closely tied to the golden ratio φ which is frequently encountered in nature, such as in population growth models and in botanics. Moreover, in architecture φ is almost considered synonymous to harmony. Thus, Fibonacci integers are arguably among the most significant sequences. Although their defining linear recurrence equation is simple, serially generating a long sequence of consecutive Fibonacci integers is by no means a trivial task.

However, with the advent of GPU computing, the efficient parallel generation of $\langle f_k \rangle$ has been rendered feasible. Indeed, by exploiting known properties of the Fibonacci integers it is possible to build parallel generators which exploit the underlying hardware potential to a great extent, achieving low response times. This requires specialized scientific software such as TensorFlow which not only contains very efficient libraries, but also facilitates the development of high quality custom source code.

The primary research contribution of this work is twofold. First, it lays the groundwork for two parallel Fibonacci integer generators, one based on a closed form for each number in the sequence and one based on certain linear algebraic properties of Fibonacci integer pairs. The performance of the two proposed generators developed in TensorFlow for Python is evaluated in terms of both total turnaround time and FLOPS against a serial implementation with the same software tools. Second, it explores the question whether it is worth substituing the computation of known quantities with a lookup table.

This conference paper is structured as follows. Section 2 reviews current scientific literature regarding the computational aspects of Fibonacci numbers. Their fundamental properties are described in Sect. 3. The TensorFlow implementation is presented in Sect. 4, whereas future research directions are outlined in Sect. 5. Table 1 summarizes the notation of this work. Concerning notation, matrices and vectors are depicted with boldface uppercase and boldface lowercase respectively, whereas roman lowercase is reserved for scalars.

Table 1. Notation of this conference paper.

Symbol	Meaning
$\triangleq$	Definition or equality by definition
$\|\mathbf{x}\|$	Norm of vector $\mathbf{x}$
$\det(\mathbf{A})$	Determinant of matrix $\mathbf{A}$
$\mathrm{tr}(\mathbf{A})$	Trace of matrix $\mathbf{A}$
φ	Golden ratio
$\langle s_n \rangle$	Sequence of integers s_n

2   Previous Work

The Fibonacci sequence of integers, examined among others in [6] and [30], has perhaps the most applications not only in computer science and in engineering but in science as a whole. Closed forms for the spectral norms of circulant matrics whose entries are either Fibonacci or Lucas integers are derived in [21]. In data structure analysis the Fibonacci heap [19] and the associated pairing heap [18] have efficient search and insertion operations with numerous applications such as network optimization. A pair of successive Fibonacci numbers are known to be the worst case in Euclidean integer division algorithm as shown in [9] as well as in [29]. Fibonacci numbers play a central role in estimating task duration and, consequently, task difficulty in scrum based software engineering methodologies [27,28], including inaccurate estimation discovery [25] and using agile methodologies to predict student progress [26]. Moreover, Fibonacci numbers are very closely linked to the golden ratio φ^1 as well as to symmetry of many geometric shapes, the latter having important implications in group theory [16]. Many identities in combinatorics regarding Fibonacci numbers can be found in [31] as well as in the most recent works [5] and [23]. Finally, the Lucas sequence $\langle \ell_k \rangle$ is closely associated with the Fibonacci sequence $\langle f_k \rangle$ since the two integer sequences constitute a Lucas complementary pair and share similar properties such as growth rate and generation mechanism [3,4].

TensorFlow, originally developed by Google for massive brain circuit simulation, is an open source computational framework whose algorithmic cornerstone is the dataflow paradigm as described in [1,2], or [20]. A library for generating Gaussian processes in TensorFlow is presented in [24]. For a genetic algorithm implementation in TensorFlow for heuristically discovering community structure, a problem examined in [10], in large multilayer graphs, such as those presented in [12] and in [11], see [15]. In [14] the ways insurance and digital health markets can benefit from blockchain and GPU computing are explored. For a path and triangle based graph resilience metric in TensorFlow see [13]. A very popular front end for the low level TensorFlow is keras, which allows the easy manipulation of neural network layers, including connecticity patterns and activation functions [8]. Model training and prediction generation is done also easily in keras in four stages [22]. Convolutional kernels whose lengths depend on their relative location inside the neural network architecture for computational vision purposes implemented in keras are introduced [7].

3   Fibonacci Numbers

The n-th integer in the Fibonacci sequence $\langle f_n \rangle$ is defined as:

$$f_n = f_{n-1} + f_{n-2}, \quad f_0 = 0, f_1 = 1 \tag{1}$$

---

[1] OEIS sequence A001622.

Theorem 1. *The n-th Fibonacci number f_n has the closed form:*

$$f_n = \frac{1}{\sqrt{5}}\left(\frac{1+\sqrt{5}}{2}\right)^n - \frac{1}{\sqrt{5}}\left(\frac{1-\sqrt{5}}{2}\right)^n = \frac{\varphi^n + (1-\varphi)^n}{\sqrt{5}} \tag{2}$$

Proof. The characteristic polynomial of (1) is:

$$z^2 = z+1 \Leftrightarrow z^2 - z - 1 = 0 \tag{3}$$

And its two real and distinct roots are:

$$r_{0,1} = \frac{1 \pm \sqrt{5}}{2} \tag{4}$$

Therefore, it follows that:

$$f_n = \alpha_0 r_0 + \alpha_1 r_1 = \frac{1}{\sqrt{5}}\left(\frac{1+\sqrt{5}}{2}\right)^n - \frac{1}{\sqrt{5}}\left(\frac{1-\sqrt{5}}{2}\right)^n \tag{5}$$

The constants α_0 and α_1 are computed using the initial conditions derived by the first two Fibonacci numbers as follows:

$$\alpha_0 + \alpha_1 = f_0 = 0$$
$$\alpha_0 r_0 + \alpha_1 r_1 = f_1 = 1 \tag{6}$$

The above conditions yield:

$$\alpha_0 = \frac{1}{r_0 - r_1} = \frac{1}{\sqrt{5}}$$
$$\alpha_1 = -\alpha_0 = \frac{1}{r_1 - r_0} = -\frac{1}{\sqrt{5}} \tag{7}$$

$\square$

Another way to prove Theorem 1 is the following:

Proof. Another way to directly compute the n-th Fibonacci number f_n is to rewrite the Fibonacci definition of Eq. (1) and the identity $f_n = f_n$ combined in matrix-vector format as follows:

$$\begin{bmatrix} f_n \\ f_{n-1} \end{bmatrix} = \begin{bmatrix} 1 & 1 \\ 1 & 0 \end{bmatrix}\begin{bmatrix} f_{n-1} \\ f_{n-2} \end{bmatrix} = \mathbf{A}\begin{bmatrix} f_{n-1} \\ f_{n-2} \end{bmatrix} = \mathbf{A}f_{n-2} \tag{8}$$

The eigenvalues λ_1 and λ_2 (recall that $\det(\mathbf{A}) = \lambda_1\lambda_2$ and that $\operatorname{tr}(\mathbf{A}) = \lambda_1+\lambda_2$) and the corresponding eigenvectors $\mathbf{e}_1$ and $\mathbf{e}_2$ are:

$$\lambda_1 = \frac{1+\sqrt{5}}{2} \overset{\triangle}{=} \varphi \qquad \lambda_2 = \frac{1-\sqrt{5}}{2} = 1 - \varphi \tag{9}$$

$$\mathbf{e}_1 = \frac{1}{\sqrt{1+\lambda_1^2}}\begin{bmatrix}\lambda_1\\1\end{bmatrix} \qquad \mathbf{e}_2 = \frac{1}{\sqrt{1+\lambda_2^2}}\begin{bmatrix}\lambda_2\\1\end{bmatrix} \tag{10}$$

Notice that $\|\mathbf{e}_1\|_2 = 1$ and $\|\mathbf{e}_2\|_2 = 1$ and, additionally, $\mathbf{e}_1^T\mathbf{e}_2 = 0$. From the spectral decomposition of $\mathbf{A}$ it follows that:

$$\mathbf{A} = \lambda_1\mathbf{e}_1\mathbf{e}_1^T + \lambda_2\mathbf{e}_2\mathbf{e}_2^T$$
$$\mathbf{A}^n = \lambda_1^n\mathbf{e}_1\mathbf{e}_1^T + \lambda_2^n\mathbf{e}_2\mathbf{e}_2^T$$
$$\mathbf{A}^n\mathbf{f}_0 = \mathbf{f}_{n-1} = \lambda_1^n(\mathbf{e}_1^T\mathbf{f}_0)\mathbf{e}_1 + \lambda_2^n(\mathbf{e}_2^T\mathbf{f}_0)\mathbf{e}_2 \tag{11}$$

Observe that the first element of vector $\mathbf{f}_{n-1}$ is f_n and it is equal to:

$$f_n = \lambda_1^{n+1}\frac{1+\lambda_1}{1+\lambda_1^2} + \lambda_2^{n+1}\frac{1+\lambda_2}{1+\lambda_2^2} \tag{12}$$

Finally, the structure of $\mathbf{A}^n$ can be shown by induction to be:

$$\mathbf{A}^n = \begin{bmatrix} f_n & f_{n-1}\\ f_{n-1} & f_{n-2}\end{bmatrix} \tag{13}$$

□

Despite form (5), Fibonacci numbers as evident by the initial conditions and their generation mechanism. Another way to see this is the following theorem:

Theorem 2. *Fibonacci numbers are integers.*

Proof. Applying the Newton binomial theorem to (5) yields:

$$f_n = \frac{1}{\sqrt{5}}\sum_{k=0}^n \binom{n}{k}2^{-n}\underbrace{\left(\sqrt{5}^k - \left(-\sqrt{5}\right)^k\right)}_{\gamma_k} \tag{14}$$

When $k \equiv 0 \pmod 2$ then γ_k is zero, whereas if $k \equiv 1 \pmod 2$ then γ_k equals $2\cdot 5^{\frac{k+1}{2}}$. Therefore:

$$f_n = \sum_k \binom{n}{k}2^{1-n}5^{\frac{k}{2}}, \qquad k \equiv 1 \pmod 2 \tag{15}$$

□

4 TensorFlow Implementation

As stated earlier, TensorFlow relies on the dataflow algorithmic paradigm, which essentially utilizes a potentially large operations graph in order to break down the desired computational task to smaller manageable components. Dataflow graphs have the following properties:

- Vertices represent a wide array of mathematical operations including advanced ones such as eingenvector computation, singular value decomposition, and least squares fitting.
- Edges describe the directed data flow between operation results.
- The operands between the various graph operations are tensors of aritrary dimensions as long as they are compatible.

TensorFlow r1.12 was installed to Ubuntu 18.04 LTS for Python 3.6 using the pip package installer. An NVIDIA Titan Xp GPU based on Pascal architecture was available in the system and was successfully discovered by TensorFlow as gpu0.

Three Fibonacci generators were implemented in total. Each such generator yields a batch consisting of the first n consecutive Fibonacci integers. In the experiments, n ranged from 2 to 1024 with an exponentially increasing distance between two successive batch sizes. Since the particular GPU has 3840 CUDA cores, the parallelism potential is high. The generators are:

- A serial implementation which consists of a single loop which adds one new Fibonacci number with each pass.
- A parallel implementation which directly computes the k-th element of the sequence $\langle f_k \rangle$ based on Eq. (11).
- A second implementation which relies on the slightly simpler closed expression of Eq. (2).

Figure 1 shows the total number of floating point operations which were required for each batch size. The values are the arithmetic mean of ten executions for each batch size. Preceding each such execution there was a trial run not taken into consideration in the final results which served the single purpose of loading the data into system cache. Since the serial implementation is a loop, the number of additions is linear in terms of n. On the contrary, the parallel implementations require a number of auxiliary floating point operations, most notably the exponentiation of certai parameters. Thus, they require more operations whose number is a polynomical function, approximately quadratic, of batch size, with the second generator clearly always being more expensive in terms of operations.

However, the fact that a generator requires more floating point operations does not necessarily makes it slower in terms of total execution time. Instead, the results shown in Fig. 2 indicate that both parallel generators achieve considerably lower wallclock execution time in milliseconds. Since the computation of $\langle f_k \rangle$ is GPU-bound process and the design of both parallel generators entail very low communication across the memory hierarchy, ordinary wallclock time in this case consists almost entirely ot time spent to actual computations.

Notice that, unlike the previous figure, no parallel implementation appears to be ideal for every batch size. Specifically, the second implementation is better for lower sized batches, whereas the first one becomes more preferable as batch size grows despite its more complex formula. This can be attributed to the fact that

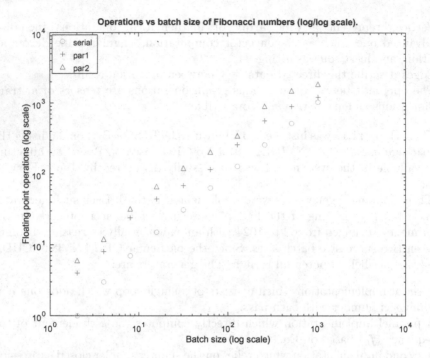

Fig. 1. Number of operations vs batch size of Fibonacci numbers.

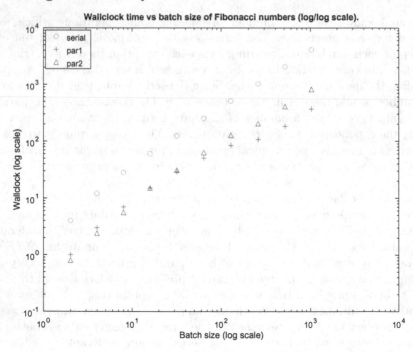

Fig. 2. Wall clock time (msec) vs batch size of Fibonacci numbers.

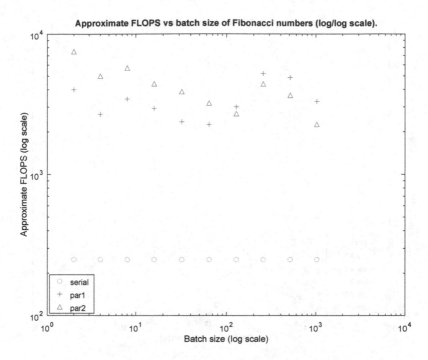

Fig. 3. Approximate FLOPS vs batch size of Fibonacci numbers.

the second generator achieves more locality as certain parameters are common across each batch size.

This difference in performance can be also seen by dividing the number of floating point operations to the wallclock time, yielding an approximation of the FLOPS for each generator as seen in Fig. 3. Although by no means a single absolute benchmark, especially within a parallel computation context, FLOPS are in this case indicative since the algorithmic core is purely computational. The difference from the serial implementation is now obvious, as is also the fact that the second generatorfor large batches performs better.

Notice that in both parallel implementations appear many consecutive powers of known quantities. In order to save floating point operations, a lookup table could have been used according the design principles found for instance in [17]. In order to evaluate the impact of relying on a lookup table to the total FLOPS for the two parallel generators, two variants of each were also implemented. The first version used locally half the known quantities required, whereas the second only one quarter of them. In both cases, and in order to achieve comparable result accuracy for fairness reasons, spline interpolation was used. As it can be seen from Fig. 4, the introduction of a lookup table for both generators downgraded their FLOPS counter. This can be explained from the facts that TensorFlow has an efficient multipication algorithm especially for large numbers and that frequently accessesing the shared GPU memory eventually slowed computations down.

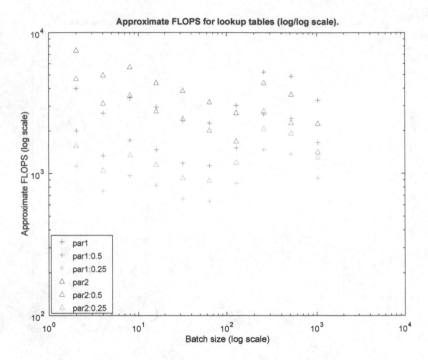

Fig. 4. Approximate FLOPS for two lookup table options.

5   Conclusions and Future Work

This conference paper presented two parallel Fibonacci integer generators for TensorFlow running over Python 3.6 and an NVIDIA Titan Xp GPU and discussed certain implementation aspects. Both generators yield batches of n integers, with n ranging from 2 to 1024. The maximum batch size is smaller than the number of cores in the GPU, increasing thus parallel potential. The baseline was a serial implementation for TensorFlow consisting of a single loop generating one new Fibonacci integer in each pass.

The primary finding of the experiments is the superior performance of parallel generators. Although requiring more floating point operations in total, both parallel implementations outperform the baseline in terms of wallclock time and of FLOPS. This is attributed to the efficient use of parallelism. A secondary finding was that replacing actual computations with frequent accesses to a shared lookup table led to lower FLOPS values. This can be explained by the latency caused by a large number of threads asking for the same information.

Concerning future research directions, there is a number of options which can be followed. Experiments with larger batch sizes should be conducted, especially with sizes which exceed the number of GPU cores. Additionally, more algorithmic schemes should be tested, such as those constructing Fibonacci integers bitwise, as they may led in generators with higher parallelism. Finally, the performance of the proposed algorithms to other parallel architectures can be evaluated, in order to understand whether a given hardware architecture is more appropriate for particular algorithmic principles.

Acknowledgements. This research was conducted within the project "Development of technologies and methods for cultural inventory data (ANTIKLIA)" under the EPAnEK 2014–2020 Operational Programme Competitiveness, Entrepreneurship, Innovation.

Additionally, this conference paper is part of Project 451, a long term research initiative whose primary objective is the development of novel, scalable, numerically stable, and interpretable tensor analytics.

Moreover, the authors gratefully acknowledge the support of NVIDIA Corporation with the donation of the Titan Xp GPU used for this research.

References

1. Abadi, M.: TensorFlow: learning functions at scale. ACM SIGPLAN Not. **51**(9) (2016)
2. Abadi, M., et al.: TensorFlow: a system for large-scale machine learning. In: OSDI, vol. 16, pp. 265–283 (2016)
3. Akbary, A., Wang, Q.: A generalized Lucas sequence and permutation binomials. Proc. Am. Math. Soc. **134**(1), 15–22 (2006)
4. Bilgici, G.: Two generalizations of Lucas sequence. Appl. Math. Comput. **245**, 526–538 (2014)
5. Bolat, C., Köse, H.: On the properties of k-Fibonacci numbers. Int. J. Contemp. Math. Sci. **5**(22), 1097–1105 (2010)
6. Capocelli, R.M., Cerbone, G., Cull, P., Holloway, J.L.: Fibonacci facts and formulas. In: Capocelli, R.M. (ed.) Sequences, pp. 123–137. Springer, New York (1990). https://doi.org/10.1007/978-1-4612-3352-7_9
7. Chollet, F.: Xception: deep learning with depthwise separable convolutions. In: CVPR, pp. 1251–1258 (2017)
8. Chollet, F., et al.: Keras: deep learning library for theano and TensorFlow (2015)
9. Dixon, J.D.: The number of steps in the Euclidean algorithm. J. Number Theory **2**(4), 414–422 (1970)
10. Drakopoulos, G., Gourgaris, P., Kanavos, A.: Graph communities in Neo4j: four algorithms at work. Evolving Syst. (2018). https://doi.org/10.1007/s12530-018-9244-x
11. Drakopoulos, G., Kanavos, A., Karydis, I., Sioutas, S., Vrahatis, A.G.: Tensor-based semantically-aware topic clustering of biomedical documents. Computation **5**(3) (2017)
12. Drakopoulos, G., Kanavos, A., Tsolis, D., Mylonas, P., Sioutas, S.: Towards a framework for tensor ontologies over Neo4j: representations and operations. In: IISA, August 2017
13. Drakopoulos, G., Liapakis, X., Tzimas, G., Mylonas, P.: A graph resilience metric based on paths: higher order analytics with GPU. In: ICTAI. IEEE, November 2018
14. Drakopoulos, G., Marountas, M., Liapakis, X., Tzimas, G., Mylonas, P., Sioutas, S.: Blockchain for mobile health applications: acceleration with GPU computing. In: Vlamos, P. (ed.) GeNeDis 2018. Springer, Heidelberg (2018)

15. Drakopoulos, G., et al.: A genetic algorithm for spatiosocial tensor clustering: exploiting TensorFlow potential. Evolving Syst. (2019). https://doi.org/10.1007/s12530-019-09274-9
16. Dunlap, R.A.: The Golden Ratio and Fibonacci Numbers. World Scientific (1997)
17. Fateman, R.J.: Lookup tables, recurrences and complexity. In: International Symposium on Symbolic and Algebraic Computation, pp. 68–73. ACM (1989)
18. Fredman, M.L., Sedgewick, R., Sleator, D.D., Tarjan, R.E.: The pairing heap: a new form of self-adjusting heap. Algorithmica 1(1–4), 111–129 (1986)
19. Fredman, M.L., Tarjan, R.E.: Fibonacci heaps and their uses in improved network optimization algorithms. J. ACM 34(3), 596–615 (1987)
20. Goldsborough, P.: A tour of TensorFlow. arXiv preprint arXiv:1610.01178 (2016)
21. İpek, A.: On the spectral norms of circulant matrices with classical Fibonacci and Lucas numbers entries. Appl. Math. Comput. 217(12), 6011–6012 (2011)
22. Ketkar, N.: Introduction to keras. In: Ketkar, N. (ed.) Deep Learning with Python, pp. 97–111. Springer, Heidelberg (2017)
23. Koshy, T.: Fibonacci and Lucas Numbers with Applications. Wiley, Hoboken (2019)
24. Matthews, D.G., et al.: GPflow: a Gaussian process library using TensorFlow. J. Mach. Learn. Res. 18(1), 1299–1304 (2017)
25. Raith, F., Richter, I., Lindermeier, R., Klinker, G.: Identification of inaccurate effort estimates in agile software development. In: APSEC, vol. 2, pp. 67–72. IEEE (2013)
26. Rodríguez, G., Soria, Á., Campo, M.: Measuring the impact of agile coaching on students' performance. Trans. Educ. 59(3), 202–209 (2016)
27. Rubin, K.S.: Essential Scrum: A Practical Guide to the Most Popular Agile Process. Addison-Wesley, Boston (2012)
28. Schwaber, K., Sutherland, J.: The scrum guide. Scrum Alliance 21 (2011)
29. Sorenson, J.: An analysis of Lehmer's Euclidean GCD algorithm. In: International Symposium on Symbolic and Algebraic Computation, pp. 254–258. ACM (1995)
30. Takahashi, D.: A fast algorithm for computing large Fibonacci numbers. Inf. Process. Lett. 75(6), 243–246 (2000)
31. Zhang, W.: Some identities involving the Fibonacci numbers. Fibonacci Q. 35, 225–228 (1997)

Employing Constrained Neural Networks for Forecasting New Product's Sales Increase

Ioannis E. Livieris[1]([✉]), Niki Kiriakidou[2], Andreas Kanavos[1,3], Gerasimos Vonitsanos[3], and Vassilis Tampakas[1]

[1] Computer and Informatics Engineering Department,
Technological Educational Institute of Western Greece, Antirrion, Greece
livieris@teiwest.gr, vtampakas@teimes.gr
[2] Department of Statistics and Insurance Science, University of Piraeus,
Piraeus, Greece
niki.c.kiriakidou@gmail.com
[3] Computer Engineering and Informatics Department, University of Patras,
Patras, Greece
{kanavos,mvonitsanos}@ceid.upatras.gr

Abstract. An intelligent sales forecasting system is considered a rather significant objective in the food industry, since a reasonably accurate prediction has the possibility of gaining significant profits and better stock management. Many food companies and restaurants strongly rely on their previous data history for predicting future trends in their business operations and strategies. Undoubtedly, the area of retail food analysis has been dramatically changed from a rather qualitative science based on subjective or judgemental assessments to a more quantitative science which is also based on knowledge extraction from databases. In this work, we evaluate the performance of weight-constrained neural networks for forecasting new product's sales increase. These new prediction models are characterized by the application of conditions on the weights of the network in the form of box-constraints, during the training process. The preliminary numerical experiments demonstrate the classification efficiency of weight-constrained neural networks in terms of accuracy, compared to state-of-the-art machine learning prediction models.

Keywords: Artificial neural networks · Machine learning ·
Sales forecasting · Food retail industry · Constrained optimization ·
Limited memory BFGS

1 Introduction

From the beginning of the 21st century, there has been an increasing interest on the application of modern information technology and artificial intelligence to food retail analysis. Food retail market has grown continuously rapidly and

J. MacIntyre et al. (Eds.): AIAI 2019 Workshops, IFIP AICT 560, pp. 161–172, 2019.
https://doi.org/10.1007/978-3-030-19909-8_14

steadily during the last decades. Nevertheless, the number of retail outlets forced out of business has also increased. In this competitive environment, it is necessary and vital for marketing managers in the food retail industry to utilize intelligent and efficient tools for better decision-making. Sales forecasting and product promotion activity constitute two of the most interesting and challenging problems in the field which significantly continue to grow in scale. As a result, a variety of promotional techniques are being used by companies in their marketing communication campaigns. A conventional measure of sales promotion effectiveness is to analyze sales patterns before and after promotion [14].

Nowadays, many food companies and restaurants try to build their business strategy by exploiting huge information stored in a data warehouse. For example, the largest retailer in the United States, Walmart, has a customer database which contains more than 460 terabytes of transactional data stored on Teradata mainframes, made by NCR [13]. The vigorous development of the Internet as well as the significant storage capabilities of electronic media, enabled the accumulation and storage of large repositories of data. On the one hand, many businesses and organizations realized that the knowledge in these data constitutes the key to various strategic decisions; but much of this knowledge is hidden and untapped. On the other hand, significant pressure on marketing decision-makers has been created by the intense competition. Therefore, there has emerged an attractive need to encourage customers to engage in a long-term relationship. This new trend has lead to the realization that food businesses must tailor their services and products according to customers' preferences by leveraging a large volume of transactional data.

During the last decades, several methodologies have been applied in the field of food retail marketing for extracting useful knowledge from transactional data, while most sophisticated analysis employs machine learning algorithms in order to provide a more meticulous view. Artificial Neural Networks (ANNs) constitute one of the most dominant machine learning algorithms for extracting useful knowledge; thus they have been extensively applied and evaluated across an impressive spectrum of applications (see [8–10,19] and the references therein). Due to their excellent capability of self-learning and self-adapting, they are very appealing to address challenging real-world problems with poorly defined system models, noisy data and strong presence of non-linear effects.

In this work, we examine and evaluate the performance of weight-constrained neural networks for forecasting new product's sales increase. To this end, we conducted a series of experiments and compared the performance of these newly proposed prediction models against state-of-the-art machine learning prediction models. The reported numerical experiments demonstrate the classification accuracy of these models, providing evidence that the application of the bounds on the weights of the network, provides more stable and reliable learning.

The remainder of this paper is organized as follows: Sect. 2 presents a survey of recent studies concerning the application of machine learning in food retail analysis. Section 3 analyzes the weight-constrained neural networks, while Sect. 4 presents the dataset utilized in our study. Section 5 presents the numerical experiments. Finally, Sect. 6 presents the conclusions and our proposals for future research.

2   Related Work

During the last decades, a number of decision-making models have been proposed in the literature to assist marketing managers in order to decide a business strategy based on the model's outcome. Several rewarding studies have been carried out in recent years and some useful outcomes are briefly presented below.

Hasin et al. [5] presented a fuzzy ANN approach to predict the sales of a number of selected products (including perishable foods) in a retail chain, in Bangladesh. Based on their numerical experiments, the authors concluded that the prediction performance of fuzzy ANN is better than Holt-Winter's model. Additionally, they claimed that as the forecasting period becomes smaller, the proposed model provides more accurate predictions.

Žliobaitė et al. [25] introduced an intelligent two-level sales prediction approach which utilizes a mechanism for model switching, depending on the sales behavior of a product. For recognizing the behavior, they formulated three types of categorical features: behavioral, shape-related, and relational, which allow the categorization of the products sufficiently and accurately to beat the baseline in the final prediction. In their study, they utilized real data from the food wholesales company Sligro Food Group N.V. and illustrated the superiority of their approach compared to the baseline predictor as well as an ensemble of predictors. Additionally, they presented in detail the trade-offs between the risk and benefit to the final accuracy, while moving the categorization threshold.

Lee et al. [6] evaluated the performance of three prediction models, namely Logistic Regression, Moving Average and ANNs, for forecasting fresh food sales in a point of sales database for convenience stores. The data utilized in their study were collected from 35 days of fresh food sales from the database of the Hi-Life convenience stores, including the number of sales and the amount of fresh food discarded. Their extensive experimental analysis revealed that Logistic Regression presented the highest overall classification performance.

Shukla and Jharkharia [20] investigated the applicability of ARIMA models in wholesale market models to forecast the demand for vegetables on a daily basis. In their study, they utilized sales data over a period of twenty five months from Ahmedabad wholesales market in India. Their numerical experiments showed that the proposed models are highly efficient in forecasting the demand for vegetables on a day-to-day basis. Therefore, the authors claimed that this model may be used to facilitate farmers and wholesalers in effective decision making.

In more recent works, Tsoumakas [21] provided an excellent survey presenting the most elaborate machine learning algorithms, which have been applied for food sales prediction and the appropriate measures for evaluating their accuracy. Additionally, the significant design decisions of a data analyst working on forecasting food sales were discussed in detail, such as the temporal granularity of sales data, the input variables for predicting sales and the representation of the sales output variable. Finally, the main challenges and opportunities in the domain of food sales prediction were also presented.

3   Weight-Constrained Neural Networks

Recently, Livieris [7] proposed a new approach for improving the generalization of ability of ANNs by applying conditions on the weights of the network in the form of box-constraints, during the training process. The motivation behind this approach focuses on defining the weights of the trained network more consistently, in order to explore and exploit all inputs and neurons of the network. More specifically, by placing constraints on the values of weights, the likelihood that some weights will "*blow up*" to unrealistic values is considerably reduced, improving, the generalization ability of the network.

Therefore, the mathematical problem of training an ANNs is re-formulated as the following constrained optimization problem:

$$\min\{E(w) \, : \, w \in \mathcal{B}\}, \tag{1}$$

with

$$\mathcal{B} = \{w \in \mathbb{R}^n \, : \, l \leq w \leq u\}, \tag{2}$$

where $E(w)$ is the error function which depends on the connection weights w of the network, $l \in \mathbb{R}^n$ is the vector of the lower bounds on the weights and $u \in \mathbb{R}^n$ is the vector of the upper bounds on the weights.

Furthermore, in order to evaluate the efficacy and the efficiency of this approach, Livieris proposed the Weight-Constrained Neural Network (WCNN) training algorithm which is based on the L-BFGS-B method [11].

At each iteration, WCNN algorithm approximates the error function $E(w)$ by a quadratic model $m_k(w)$ at a point w_k, namely

$$m_k(w) = E_k + g_k^T(w - w_k) + \frac{1}{2}(w - w_k)^T B_k(w - w_k), \tag{3}$$

where $E_k = E(w_k)$, g_k is the gradient of the error function at w_k and B_k is a positive-definite L-BFGS Hessian approximation [11].

Next, the algorithm performs a minimization procedure of the approximation model $m_k(w)$ to compute the new vector of weights, which consists of three distinct stages. In Stage I, the model (3) is approximately minimized subject to the feasible domain $\mathcal{B}$ utilizing the gradient projection method in order to compute the generalized Cauchy point w^C. Eventually, the active set $\mathcal{A}(w^C)$ is calculated which consists of the indices of weights whose values at w^C are at lower or upper bound. In Stage II, the quadratic model $m_k(w)$ is minimized with respect to the non-active variables utilizing a direct primal method [11]. It is worth noticing that the minimization is performed at a subspace of the feasibility domain $\mathcal{B}$ by considering as free variables, the variables which are not fixed on limits while the rest variables are fixed on their boundary value obtained during the previous stage. Finally, in Stage III, the algorithm calculates the new vector of weights w_{k+1} by performing a line search procedure.

Algorithm 1. WCNN

1. Initiate w_0, c_1, c_2 and vectors l and u.
2. Set $k = 0$.
3. **repeat**
4.   Calculate the error function value E_k and its gradient ∇E_k at w_k.
5.   Set the quadratic model (3) at w_k.
      /* STAGE I: CAUCHY POINT COMPUTATION */
6.   Calculate the generalized Cauchy point w^C.
7.   Define the active set $\mathcal{A}(w^C)$.
      /* STAGE II: SUBSPACE MINIMIZATION */
8.   Minimize the quadratic model $m_k(w)$

$$\overline{w}_{k+1} = \arg \min_{w \in D_S} m_k(w)$$

    where $D_S = \{w \in \mathbb{R} \,|\, l_i \leq w_i \leq u_i, \,\forall i \notin \mathcal{A}(w^C)\}$.
    /* STAGE III: LINE SEARCH */
9.   Set $d_k = \overline{w}_{k+1} - w_k$.
10.   Compute the learning rate η_k satisfying the strong Wolfe line search conditions

$$E_{k+1} \leq E_k + c_1 \eta_k \nabla E_k^T d_k,$$
$$|\nabla E_{k+1}^T d_k| \leq c_2 |\nabla E_k^T d_k|.$$

    with $0 \leq c_1 \leq c_2 < 1$.
11.   Update the weights $w_{k+1} = w_k + \eta_k d_k$.
12.   Set $k = k + 1$.
13. **until** (stopping criterion).

---

4 Dataset

The data collected from the IBM Watson Analytics[1] concerning a self-service fast food restaurant, located in the Connaught Place area of New Delhi with several branches all over Delhi. The chain plans to add a new product to its menu, therefore it decided three possible marketing campaigns for promoting the new product. In order to determine which promotion has the greatest effect on sales, the new item is introduced at locations in several randomly selected markets. A different promotion is used at each location and the weekly sales of the new item are recorded for the first four weeks.

---

[1] https://www.ibm.com/communities/analytics/watson-analytics-blog/marketing-campaign-eff-usec_-fastf//.

Table 1 presents a set of the six (6) specific attributes utilized in our study. The first two attributes concern a unique identifier for each market and the size of market area based on sales. The following two attributes concern a unique identifier for store location and the age of store in years. The last attribute concerns one of three tested promotions. Finally, the sales for each promotion and each store were classified utilizing a three-level classification scheme:

- "*Low*": the total amount of sales is less than 170 thousands (30 instances).
- "*Average*": the total amount of sales is between 170 and 200 thousands (44 instances).
- "*High*": the total amount of sales is more than 200 thousands (63 instances).

Table 1. List of attributes

Attribute	Type	Values
Market ID	Integer	1–10
Market size	Nominal	{Small, Medium, Large}
Location ID	Integer	1–10
Age of store	Integer	1–28
Promotion	Nominal	1, 2, 3
Sales (in thousand)	Nominal	{Low, Average, High}

Additionally, the class distribution is presented in Fig. 1.

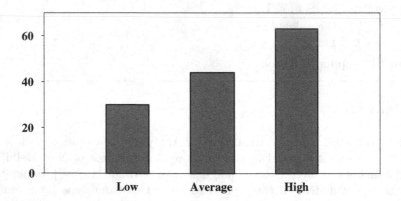

Fig. 1. Class distribution

5   Experimental Results

In this section, we present an experimental analysis in order to evaluate the performance of weight-constrained neural networks for forecasting new product's sales increase against the most popular and efficient prediction models.

The classification accuracy was evaluated using the standard procedure called *stratified 10-fold cross-validation* [18] i.e., this approach involves randomly dividing the set of instances into ten groups (folds), of approximately equal size, so that each fold has the same distribution of classes as the entire data set. Each fold is treated as a testing set, and the classification algorithm is fit on the remaining nine folds. The results of the cross-validation process are summarized with the mean of the prediction model skill scores.

The performance of all classification models was evaluated utilizing the following two performance metrics: F_1-*score* and *accuracy*. It is worth noticing that F_1-score consists of a harmonic mean of precision and recall while accuracy is the ratio of correct predictions of a classification model [7].

Our experimental results were obtained by conducting a two-phase procedure: In the first phase, the classification performance of the WCNN algorithm was evaluated against the most popular state-of-the-art neural network training algorithms; while in the second phase, we compare the performance of the weight-constrained neural networks trained with WCNN algorithm against the most popular and frequently utilized machine learning classification algorithms.

5.1   Performance Evaluation of Weight-Constrained Neural Networks Against Classical Neural Networks

In the sequel, we compare the classification accuracy of WCNN algorithm against state-of-the-art ANN training algorithms, i.e. Resilient backpropagation [17] and Levenberg-Marquardt training algorithm [4]. In other words, we evaluate the performance of weight-constrained neural networks against classical neural networks.

The implementation code was written in Matlab 7.6 and the simulations have been carried out on a PC (2.66GHz Quad-Core processor, 4Gbyte RAM) running Linux operating system, while the results have been averaged over 100 simulations. All networks had logistic activation functions and received the same sequence of input patterns and the weights were initiated using the Nguyen-Widrow method [12]. It is worth noticing that all training algorithms were utilized with their default parameter settings.

Furthermore, since a small number of simulations tend to dominate these results, the cumulative total for a performance metric over all simulations does not seem to be too informative. For this reason, we utilize the performance profiles of Dolan and Morè [2] to present perhaps the most complete information in terms of robustness, efficiency and solution quality. The use of performance profiles eliminates the influence of a small number of simulations on the benchmarking process and the sensitivity of results associated with the ranking of solvers [2]. The performance profile plots the fraction P of simulations for which any given method is within a factor τ of the best training method.

More analytically, let us assume that there exist n_s solvers and n_p problems for each solver s and problem p, requiring a baseline for comparisons, Dolan and Morè compared the performance $a_{p,s}$ (based on a metric) by solver s on problem p with the best performance by any solver on this problem; namely, using the performance ratio

$$r_{p,s} = \frac{a_{p,s}}{\min\{a_{p,s} \, : \, s \in S\}}.$$

The performance of solver s on any given problem might be of interest, but we would like to obtain an overall assessment of the performance of the solver. Next, the function ρ_s was the (cumulative) distribution function for the performance ratio is defined by

$$\rho_s(\alpha) = \frac{1}{n_p}\text{size}\,\{p \in \mathcal{P} \, : \, r_{p,s} \leq a\}.$$

where $\mathcal{P}$ is the set of all problems. Notice that the performance profile $\rho_s : \mathbb{R} \to [0,1]$ for a solver was a non-decreasing, piecewise constant function, continuous from the right at each breakpoint [2].

In other words, the performance profile plots the fraction P of problems for which any given algorithm is within a factor α of the training algorithm. The horizontal axis of each figure gives the percentage of the simulations for which a training algorithm achieved the best performance (efficiency). Regarding the above rules and discussion, we can conclude that one solver whose performance profile plot lies on top right, outperforms the rest of the solvers.

- "RPROP" stands for Resilient back propagation.
- "LM" stands for Levenberg-Marquardt training algorithm.
- "WCNN$_1$" stands for Algorithm 1 and bounds on the weights $-1 \leq w_i \leq 1$.
- "WCNN$_2$" stands for Algorithm 1 and bounds on the weights $-2 \leq w_i \leq 2$.
- "WCNN$_3$" stands for Algorithm 1 and bounds on the weights $-5 \leq w_i \leq 5$.

Figures 2 and 3 present the performance profiles based on F_1-score and accuracy, respectively, investigating the efficiency and robustness of each training method. Firstly, it is worth noticing that all versions of the WCNN outperformed the classical training algorithms, presenting the highest probabilities of being the optimal solvers, relative to both performance metrics. More specifically, WCNN$_1$, WCNN$_2$ and WCNN$_3$ report 28%, 52% and 42% of simulations with the best F_1-score, respectively; while RPROP and LM report 26% and 15%, respectively. As regards the classification accuracy, WCNN$_1$, WCNN$_2$ and WCNN$_3$ exhibit 55%, 63% and 59% of simulations with the highest accuracy, respectively; while RPROP and LM report 35% and 20%, respectively. Thus, we conclude that the application of the bounds on the weights of the neural network, increased the overall classification accuracy.

Furthermore, regarding the performance of the proposed algorithm, WCNN$_2$ illustrates the best performance, followed by WCNN$_1$ and WCNN$_3$. Therefore,

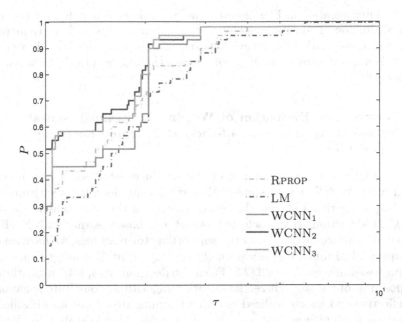

Fig. 2. Log_{10} scaled performance profiles for RPROP, LM, WCNN$_1$, WCNN$_2$ and WCNN$_3$ based on F_1-score

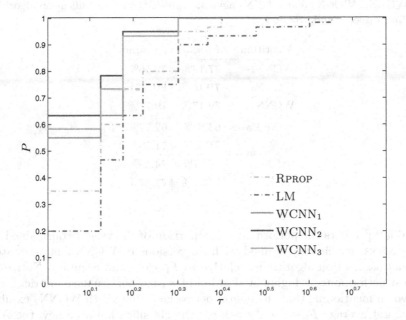

Fig. 3. Log_{10} scaled performance profiles for RPROP, LM, WCNN$_1$, WCNN$_2$ and WCNN$_3$ based on accuracy

from the interpretation of Figs. 2 and 3, we are able to conclude that the application of the bounds on the weights of a neural network significantly increased the overall classification accuracy. Nevertheless, in case the bounds were too tight, this did not substantially benefit much the classification performance of the networks.

5.2 Performance Evaluation of Weight-Constrained Neural Networks Against State-of-the-Art Machine Learning Algorithms

Next, we evaluate the performance of the weight-constrained neural networks trained with WCNN against state-of-the-art machine learning algorithms. The Naive Bayes algorithm [3] was the representative of the probabilistic classifiers while kNN algorithm [1] was selected as instance-based learner with Euclidean distance as distance metric. From the support vector machines, we have selected the Sequential Minimal Optimization (SMO) algorithm [15] using Pearson VII function-based universal kernel [22]. From the decision trees, C4.5 algorithm [16] was chosen in our study. These classification algorithms constitute some of the most effective and widely utilized machine learning algorithms for classification [24] and are implemented in Java using WEKA Machine Learning Toolkit [23].

Table 2. Performance comparison of the weight-constrained neural network trained with WCNN$_1$, WCNN$_2$ and WCNN$_3$ against state-of-the-art classification algorithms, regarding F_1-score and accuracy

Algorithm	F_1-score	Accuracy
WCNN$_1$	77.18%	79.56%
WCNN$_2$	**79.04%**	**80.22%**
WCNN$_3$	79.17%	79.78%
Naive Bayes	63.82%	62.77%
kNN	71.33%	71.53%
SMO	74.67%	74.45%
C4.5	77.55%	77.37%

Table 2 presents the performance comparison of the weight-constrained neural networks, which were trained with all versions of WCNN against state-of-the-art classification algorithms, relative to F_1-score and accuracy. Notice that the best performance is highlighted in bold for each performance metric. Firstly, it is worth mentioning that the neural networks trained with WCNN$_2$ exhibited the highest average F_1-score. As regards the classification accuracy, the ANNs trained with all version of WCNN presented the best performance, outperforming all state-of-the-art classification algorithms.

Based on the above discussion, we are able to conclude out that the weight-constrained neural networks perform significantly better than any presented classification algorithm, reporting the best overall performance.

6   Conclusions

In this work, we evaluated the classification accuracy of weight-constrained neural networks for forecasting new product's sales increase. By placing constraints on the values of weights, the likelihood that some weights will *"blow up"* to unrealistic values is considerably reduced; thus all inputs and neurons of the network are efficiently explored. These modified prediction models are efficiently trained with a new training algorithm, called WCNN, which exploits a gradient-projection strategy for handling the bounds on the weights together with the numerical and theoretical advantages of the limited memory BFGS matrices. Our preliminary numerical experiments illustrate the classification efficiency of weight-constrained neural networks in terms of accuracy, compared to state-of-the-art machine learning prediction models.

Nevertheless, the a-priori determination of the optimal bounds on the weights of the networks is a rather challenging open problem; thus more research and experiments are needed. To this end, the question of what should be the values of the bounds for each benchmark or which additional constraints should be applied is still under consideration. Probably, the required research to answer these questions may reveal additional and crucial information and questions.

Our future work is concentrated on incorporating the proposed methodology to more advanced and complex neural network architectures. Additionally, since our experimental results are quite encouraging, a next step could be the evaluation of the proposed framework in challenging real-world regression problems.

References

1. Aha, D.: Lazy Learning. Springer, Heidelberg (2013). https://doi.org/10.1007/978-94-017-2053-3
2. Dolan, E., Moré, J.: Benchmarking optimization software with performance profiles. Math. Program. **91**, 201–213 (2002)
3. Domingos, P., Pazzani, M.: On the optimality of the simple Bayesian classifier under zero-one loss. Mach. Learn. **29**, 103–130 (1997)
4. Hagan, M., Menhaj, M.: Training feed-forward networks with the marquardt algorithm. IEEE Trans. Neural Netw. **5**(6), 989–993 (1994)
5. Hasin, M., Ghosh, S., Shareef, M.: An ANN approach to demand forecasting in retail trade in Bangladesh. Int. J. Trade Econ. Finan. **2**(2), 154 (2011)
6. Lee, W., Chen, C., Chen, K., Chen, T., Liu, C.: Comparative study on the forecast of fresh food sales using logistic regression, moving average and bpnn methods. J. Mar. Sci. Technol. **20**(2), 142–152 (2012)
7. Livieris, I.: Improving the classification efficiency of an ANN utilizing a new training methodology. Informatics **6**, 1 (2018)

8. Livieris, I., Drakopoulou, K., Pintelas, P.: Predicting students' performance using artificial neural networks. In: Information and Communication Technologies in Education, pp. 321–328 (2012)

9. Livieris, I., Pintelas, P.: An improved spectral conjugate gradient neural network training algorithm. Int. J. Artif. Intell. Tools **21**(01), 1250009 (2012)

10. Maren, A., Harston, C., Pap, R.: Handbook of Neural Computing Applications. Academic Press, Cambridge (2014)

11. Morales, J., Nocedal, J.: Remark on "Algorithm 778: L-BFGS-B: fortran subroutines for large-scale bound constrained optimization". ACM Trans. Math. Softw. (TOMS) **38**(1), 7 (2011)

12. Nguyen, D., Widrow, B.: Improving the learning speed of 2-layer neural networks by choosing initial values of the adaptive weights. In: International Joint Conference on Neural Networks, pp. 21–26. IEEE (1990)

13. Pathak, S.: Social implications of data mining techniques. J. Basic Appl. Eng. Res. (JBAER) **1**, 860 (2014)

14. Peattie, S.: Promotional competitions as a marketing tool in food retailing. Br. Food J. **100**(6), 286–294 (1998)

15. Platt, J.: Using sparseness and analytic QP to speed training of support vector machines. In: Kearns, M., Solla, S., Cohn, D. (eds.) Advances in Neural Information Processing Systems, pp. 557–563. MIT Press, Cambridge (1999)

16. Quinlan, J.: C4.5: Programs for Machine Learning. Morgan Kaufmann, San Francisco (1993)

17. Riedmiller, M., Braun, H.: A direct adaptive method for faster backpropagation learning: the RPROP algorithm. In: IEEE International Conference on Neural Networks, pp. 586–591. IEEE (1993)

18. Russell, S., Norvig, P.: Artificial Intelligence: A Modern Approach. Pearson Education Limited, Malaysia (2016)

19. Shanmuganathan, S., Samarasinghe, S. (eds.): Artificial Neural Network Modelling. SCI, vol. 628. Springer, Cham (2016). https://doi.org/10.1007/978-3-319-28495-8

20. Shukla, M., Jharkharia, S.: Applicability of ARIMA models in wholesale vegetable market: an investigation. Int. J. Inf. Syst. Supply Chain Manag. (IJISSCM) **6**(3), 105–119 (2013)

21. Tsoumakas, G.: A survey of machine learning techniques for food sales prediction. Artif. Intell. Rev. 1–7 (2018)

22. Üstün, B., Melssen, W., Buydens, L.: Facilitating the application of support vector regression by using a universal Pearson VII function based kernel. Chemometr. Intell. Lab. Syst. **81**(1), 29–40 (2006)

23. Witten, I., Frank, E., Hall, M., Pal, C.: Data Mining: Practical Machine Learning Tools and Techniques. Morgan Kaufmann, San Francisco (2016)

24. Wu, X., et al.: Top 10 algorithms in data mining. Knowl. Inf. Syst. **14**(1), 1–37 (2008)

25. Žliobaitė, I., Bakker, J., Pechenizkiy, M.: Beating the baseline prediction in food sales: how intelligent an intelligent predictor is? Expert Syst. Appl. **39**(1), 806–815 (2012)

Language Processing for Predicting Suicidal Tendencies: A Case Study in Greek Poetry

Alexandros Dimitrios Zervopoulos[✉], Evangelos Geramanis,
Alexandros Toulakis, Asterios Papamichail, Dimitrios Triantafylloy,
Theofanis Tasoulas, and Katia Kermanidis

Ionian University, Corfu, Greece
{p15zerv,p15gera,p15toul1,p15papa1,p15tria,p15taso,kerman}@ionio.gr

Abstract. Natural language processing has previously been used with fairly high success to predict a writer's likelihood of committing suicide, using a wide variety of text types, including suicide notes, micro-blog posts, lyrics and even poems. In this study, we extend work done in previous research to a language that has not been tackled before in this setting, namely Greek. A set of language-dependent (but easily portable across languages) and language-independent linguistic features is proposed to represent the poems of 13 Greek poets of the 20th century. Prediction experiments resulted in an overall classification rate of 84.5% with the C4.5 algorithm, after having tested multiple machine-learning algorithms. These results differ significantly from previous research, as some features investigated did not play as significant a role as was expected. This kind of task presents multiple difficulties, especially for a language where no previous research has been conducted. Therefore, a significant part of the annotation process was performed manually, which likely explains the somewhat higher classification rates compared to previous efforts.

Keywords: NLP · Suicide · Poetry

1 Introduction

A significant amount of research has been conducted on the topic of identifying mental health illnesses through the means of text analysis. For instance, such analysis has been used to predict various psychological states [1]. Being able to detect such psychological states in their early stages, through the means of Natural Language Processing (NLP) techniques could be of vital importance, before they lead to an unfortunate conclusion for the individual.

Furthermore, a great deal of effort has gone into discerning suicidal tendencies through the writer's language use, as suicide is a leading cause of death all

© IFIP International Federation for Information Processing 2019
Published by Springer Nature Switzerland AG 2019
J. MacIntyre et al. (Eds.): AIAI 2019 Workshops, IFIP AICT 560, pp. 173–183, 2019.
https://doi.org/10.1007/978-3-030-19909-8_15

over the world [2]. More specifically, there have been multiple recent attempts focusing on suicide notes. Pestian et al. [3] concluded that NLP could be used to differentiate between genuine and elicited suicide notes, by achieving a higher classification rate than mental health professionals. Many have tried to tackle the problem of emotion detection in suicide notes utilizing various methods, including entropy classification [4] and latent sequence models [5] in the pursuit of better understanding the suicidal mind.

Additionally, with the rise of the digital era and widespread use of the Internet, the phenomena of micro-blogging and social media emerged. This has resulted in an increasingly large proportion of people who use these means daily to express their feelings and opinions. Thus, there has been major interest in examining whether these can be useful in predicting suicidal ideation. Zhang et al. [6] deduced that such a task is realizable using the Chinese version of the Linguistic Inquiry and Word Count (LIWC), as well as Latent Dirichlet Allocation (LDA), on Chinese micro-blog users' data. Litvinova et al. [7] developed a mathematical model to predict suicidal tendencies based on Russian Internet texts, employing numerical rather than linguistic features. Burnap et al. [8] aimed to identify suicide related topics from posts on Twitter by training baseline classifiers, then improving upon them with an ensemble classifier.

It has been proven that suicide rates among artists, such as musicians and poets, are significantly higher than rates pertaining to the general population [9–11]. Lightman et al. [12] deployed Coh-Metrix and LIWC to contrast textual features of suicidal and non-suicidal songwriters. Mulholland and Quinn [13] composed a corpus consisting of songs from various English lyricists, which was comprised of a development, a training and a test set. This corpus was then used to derive lexical, syntactic, semantic class and n-gram features. These were then input into the Waikato Environment for Knowledge Analysis (Weka) to compare the performance of multiple machine learning algorithms in classifying whether or not the song was written by a suicidal lyricist. The algorithm that proved to have the highest classification rate was SimpleCart, with an overall accuracy of 70.6%. Pajak and Trzebiński [14] used LIWC to analyze Polish poems from six separate poets. Afterwards, ANOVA and logistic regression were used to extract the most prevalent features in identifying suicidal predisposition. They drew conclusions similar to those of previous works.

Perhaps one of the most influential contributions in the text analysis of poets is that of Stirman and Pennebaker [15], considering their results have been the basis of many different studies, such as [12–14]. The methodology they followed was the collection of 300 poems, and the study, with the aid of LIWC, of linguistic characteristics that could be distinguished between suicidal and non-suicidal poets. Furthermore, they investigated how such characteristics accord with the two most dominant suicide models, namely Durkheim's model [16], where suicide rate is linked to a society's integration level, and the hopelessness model [17], where an individual is overcome with negative emotions, such as hopelessness and helplessness, which ultimately drive them to suicide. These characteristics were then examined as to how they varied in different stages of the poets' careers.

It was concluded that suicide can in fact be predicted by their language use, finding stronger support for the social integration suicide model, and that there's no significant variation over time.

The purpose of this study is to train a machine learning model, which classifies a poem by the poet's proclivity towards suicide, based on textual features. In contrast to previous research in this area, the study will be focusing on Greek poetry of the 20th century, and aims to examine whether preceding results, derived mostly from English language works, can be verified. These include higher use of the first-person singular form, compared to the first-person plural form, more frequent use of death and sexual-related words, as well as fewer overall positive emotion words [15]. Overall, the methodology followed differs compared to previous efforts, given the lack of available tools for Greek, which resulted in the investigation of verb suffixes as features, as well as measuring in a novel manner the emotion of a poem's lyrics set in the range of $[0, 2]$, in hopes of increasing the overall reliability of the corpus' annotation. The algorithms used were for the most part examined in previous research, and have been shown to perform relatively well in these kinds of tasks.

The rest of this paper is organized as follows. Section 2 describes the collected data, as well as the process and criteria for gathering it. Section 3 presents the feature vector that represents each poem, and why the respective values were selected. In Sect. 4, the classification experiments are described in detail, including the algorithms used and their results. Section 5 illustrates some of the difficulties faced during the process of classifying a poet's suicidal ideation by their poem, especially in a language with a scarcity of processing tools. Finally, Sect. 6 presents future improvements that could be made and a conclusion of what was accomplished in this study.

2   Data Collection

A corpus of 90 poems was constructed, consisting of poems from 7 poets who committed suicide and 6 who did not. The number of poems is equally distributed between the two groups. Moreover, the number of poems from each poet ranges from 5 to 9. The vast majority of poets are male (with the exception of two female poets in the suicidal group), who lived in approximately the same period of time, i.e. in the early to mid 1900s. The rationale behind this requirement was for the poets to belong to the same phase of the Greek language history, as the writing style of Greek changed significantly during the second half of the 20th century. Specifically, Katharevousa was abolished as the official Greek language in 1976 and was replaced by Modern Greek.

It was of significant importance that the poets in the suicide group undoubtedly took their own life. Similarly, special attention was paid so that poets in the non-suicide group did not have a history of self-harm or suicide attempts. All of the above is illustrated in Table 1. The size of the poems varies between 80–300 words, with an average size of 155.35. For each poet, all poems were randomly selected, with no distinction as to the nature of their content, e.g. a poem particularly high in negative emotion was not specifically selected for a poet who committed suicide. The above criteria, combined with the overall low suicide rates of Greek poets, significantly restricted the size of the corpus.

Table 1. Composition of corpus

Poet	Poems	Year of death	Suicide
Giorgos Makris	7	1968	Yes
Kostas Karyotakis	5	1928	Yes
Alexis Traianos	5	1980	Yes
Minas Dimakis	5	1980	Yes
Katerina Gogou	8	1993	Yes
Napoleon Lapathiotis	7	1944	Yes
Koralia Andreadis	8	1976	Yes
George Seferis	9	1971	No
Tellos Agras	7	1944	No
Constantine P. Cavafy	7	1933	No
Kostis Palamas	8	1943	No
Nikolaos Kavvadias	7	1975	No
Odysseus Elytis	7	1996	No

The poems were stripped of all punctuation marks and accentuation using a Python script. This was required by certain parts of the annotation process described next, so that they could be automated.

3   Feature Description

Every poem is represented as a feature-value learning vector. The features that were selected for designing the vector are presented below. Some of these were based on the work of Kao and Jurafsky [18] as well as Stirman and Pennebaker [15], whereas others are novel, which are mostly applicable to the Greek language. A large number of features selected represent sums of occurence of linguistic characteristics of interest throughout the entire poem, which were normalized by the poem's length. These sum values for each poem were then normalized across the entire corpus using the well known normalization transformation of Eq. 1, where v is the initial feature value, v_{min} and v_{max} are the minimum and maximum values of the feature across all poems, and v_{norm} is the resulting normalized value.

$$V_{norm} = \frac{v - v_{min}}{v_{max} - v_{min}} \tag{1}$$

Overall, the number of features that were explored reached 37 in total.

3.1   Vocabulary Features

The vocabulary feature that was chosen is the type to token ratio (TTR), which is used as an indicator of the poem's richness in vocabulary [18].

3.2   Morphosyntactic Features

The social integration model suggests that individuals who commit suicide have failed to integrate with society, so they are expected to be more self-centered, which seems to be manifested through the use of more first-person singular words, as opposed to first-person plural words [15]. Based on that observation, the two morphosyntactic features that were selected were the count of occurrences of first-person singular and first-person plural verbs.

Due to the lack of reliable morphological analysis tools for Greek, especially for the historical phase of the language targeted herein, these counts were obtained using a set of predefined verb suffixes (Table 2), that constitute person and number morphemes. The core set of these suffixes was found in [19], and was subsequently enriched by the authors of this paper. Afterwards, a Python script was used to identify them in the poems. When any tense of a base suffix is found, it counts towards the base's occurrence, e.g. the occurrence of suffix ειρω is equivalent to that of ερνω. These bases are also used as features, to examine whether a subset of them are more prevalent in the process of the classification. All in all, these constitute 32 of the 37 features that were examined, 30 of which are the aforementioned suffixes.

3.3   Semantic Class Features

Suicidal poets are expected to deal more with negative emotion than with positive feelings, according to the hopelessness suicide model [17]. To test this, each verse was assigned a number ranging from 0 to 2 for the positive emotion it expressed, and 0 to 2 for the negative emotion. The range is overall lower than ones used in previous studies, as $[-5, 5]$ has been used for example in [20]. This was done to increase the overall reliability of the manual annotation. These numbers were then summed up for all verses of a poem, resulting in two features: one sum reflecting the positive, and one reflecting the negative emotion.

Additionally, sexual and death-related references were included as features, as has been suggested, in an ad-hoc analysis, that they can contribute to identifying suicidal tendencies [15]. For these features, the number of verses for each poem that were deemed to contain sexual or death references were summed up for each poem.

Each poem was annotated with the aforementioned semantic information by two Greek language native speakers. When a verse led to contrasting annotators' decisions, the feature value was decided upon by the majority vote of the authors of the present work.

Table 2. Suffixes used for the morphosyntactic features

Base Suffix	Different Tenses				
	Singular Active Construction				
αβω	αβω	αβα	αψα	αψω	
αζω	αζω	αζα	ασα	ασω	
αινω	αινω	αινα	ηνω		
εινω	εινω	εινα	εισα	εισω	
ερνω	ερνω	ερνα	ειρα	ερα	ειρω
ευω	ευω	ευα	εψα	εψω	
ηνω	ηνω	ηνα	ησα	ησω	
ιζω	ιζω	ιζα	ισα	ισω	
ινω	ινω	ινα	ωσα	ωσω	
λλω	λλω	λλα	ιλα	ιλω	
ττω	ττω	ττα	ξα	ξω	
ωνω	ωνω	ωνα	ωσα	ωσω	
ω					
	Plural Active Construction				
αβουμε	αβουμε	αβαμε	αψαμε	αψουμε	
αζουμε	αζουμε	αζαμε	ασαμε	ασουμε	
αινουμε	αινουμε	αιναμε	ησαμε	ησουμε	
εινουμε	εινουμε	ειναμε	εισαμε	εισουμε	
ευουμε	ευουμε	ευαμε	εψαμε	εψουμε	
ηνουμε	ηνουμε	ηναμε	ησαμε	ησουμε	
ιζουμε	ιζουμε	ιζαμε	ισαμε	ισουμε	
ινουμε	ινουμε	ιναμε	σαμε	σαμεν	σουμε
λλουμε	λλουμε	λλαμε	λαμε	λουμε	
ττουμε	ττουμε	τταμε	ξαμε	ξουμε	
	Singular Passive Construction				
αμαι	αμαι				
ουμαι	ουμαι	ουμουν			
ιεμαι	ιεμαι	ιομουν			
ομαι	ομαι	ομουν			
μαι	μαι	μουν	μουνα	ηκα	ηθω
	Plural Passive Construction				
ομαστε	ομαστε	ομασταν			
μαστε	μαστε	μασταν	ουμε	ηκαμε	

4   Prediction Results

Each poem was represented using the aforementioned features. The Weka machine learning workbench [21] was used for running prediction experiments pertaining to poets' suicidal tendencies. The baseline for our comparisons is the prediction accuracy of 50%, as the two groups are evenly split. Since the corpus was not divided into different sets for training and testing, Weka's k-fold cross validation functionality was used, for k = 5. A variety of tree and rule-based algorithms were compared as to their performance at accomplishing this task.

Table 3. Detailed accuracy for both classes by each algorithm

Algorithm	Precision	Recall	F-measure	Class
JIPPER (without pruning)	0.739	0.756	0.747	TRUE
	0.750	0.733	0.742	FALSE
JRIPPER (with pruning)	0.830	0.867	0.848	TRUE
	0.860	0.822	0.841	FALSE
Random forest	0.800	0.800	0.800	TRUE
	0.800	0.800	0.800	FALSE
Simple CART (with pruning)	0.784	0.889	0.833	TRUE
	0.872	0.756	0.810	FALSE
Simple CART (without pruning)	0.848	0.867	0.857	TRUE
	0.864	0.844	0.854	FALSE
C4.5 (with pruning)	0.830	0.867	0.848	TRUE
	0.860	0.822	0.841	FALSE
C4.5 (without pruning)	0.787	0.822	0.804	TRUE
	0.801	0.800	0.800	FALSE

The parameters used, which achieved the best results when running these tests, are described below. These are well-established algorithms in dealing with such tasks, JRIPPER was used in [3], C4.5 was used in [3] and [8] and finally Simple CART was used in [13].

The rule-based classifier tested was JRIPPER. This algorithm was run using 50 optimization runs, achieving a classification rate of 84.4% when making use of pruning. Afterwards, three different tree classifiers were tested, the first one being Simple CART. This resulted in an accuracy of 82.8%. Another tree based classifier used was RandomForest, which had a classification rate of 82.2%, after having performed 10,000 iterations. The last algorithm tested was C4.5 (known as J48 in Weka) classifying 84.5% of the instances correctly, with 0.25 as the confidence factor, performing pruning.

The algorithm that eventually achieved the highest classification rate was C4.5, reaching 84.5%. Various statistics are presented in Table 3 detailing some of the tests done, and the models derived from C4.5 are presented in Figs. 1 and 2.

The resulting models indicate that the overall classification result is largely based on the positive and negative emotion scores. At a first glance, and considering the researchers' lack of a professional literary background, the suffixes don't seem to form some clear pattern which could help identify suicidal ideation. However, it is evident that the results do differ based on the occurence of singular, as opposed to plural, verb suffixes, which does support Durkheim's model.

Tree and rule-based classifiers perform fairly well and result in simple models, which is in part attributed to the manual nature of the annotation process, as a result of the lack of reliable processing tools for the Greek language, as well as to

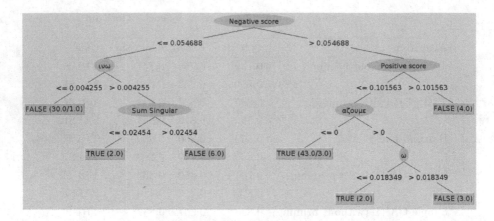

Fig. 1. The decision tree generated by C4.5 with pruning

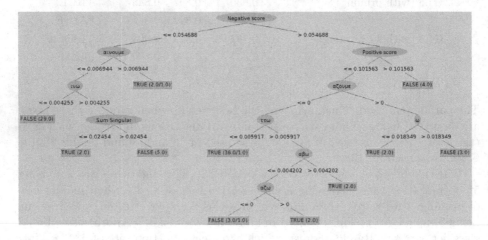

Fig. 2. The decision tree generated by C4.5 without pruning

the nature of the semantic features, which are of high-level linguistic knowledge. They have proven to perform fairly well in similar research conducted in the past as well. As a basis for comparison, the results of previous studies are presented in this paragraph. Pestian et al. [3] managed to accurately distinguish between elicited and genuine suicide notes 78% of the time. Litvinova et al. [7] reached a 71.5% classification rate of deciding whether Russian internet texts were suicidal or not. Mulholland and Quinn [13] achieved a performance of 70.6% in identifying suicidal tendencies of songwriters through their lyrics.

5   Discussion

Tackling the task of identifying suicidal ideation in poetry, particularly for a language where no previous research has been conducted, is certain to pose many difficulties. The construction of the corpus was largely difficult due to the strict criteria described in Sect. 2. It was hard to determine whether someone did not at least attempt to commit suicide in their lifetime, as it may not have necessarily become known to people outside their close social circle. Furthermore, in the case where it was ambiguous whether the cause of death was actually suicide, as is the case with Maria Polydouri, the poet was left out, which further shortened the number of candidate poems. Perhaps, one solution to this would have been to focus more on the few poets that have written a lot of poems. This does, however, introduce the risk of the classifier learning the patterns of those particular poets and being unable to accurately classify poems by others.

Additionally, and perhaps most importantly, the process of annotating the corpus was especially demanding, since the most prevalent tools used in previous research were not available for Greek. Such tools include LIWC, the UAM CorpusTool, various word-lists, such as AFINN and ANEW, used in sentiment analysis tasks, as well as corpora used in previous studies, which could have been used for comparison. This resulted in the manual annotation of a significant portion of the selected features. It was also a major restriction in the selection of the features, as the more sophisticated a feature is, the more rigorous the process of identifying it in the text needs to be. Not adhering to the appropriate level of rigorousness introduces further potential bias into the data, and given the annotators' lack of a professional literary background, this would have been an increasingly precarious task.

6 Conclusion and Future Work

In conclusion, a corpus of poems was composed to identify suicidal ideation in Greek poetry of the 20th century. This proved to be a challenging task, since there has not been any previous work done on the language that was selected. Nonetheless, the resulting classifier, C4.5, reached an accuracy of 84.4%. The features explored were mostly semantic in nature, while also utilizing morphosyntactic features, such as verb suffixes which are language specific and have not been investigated before. The results are overall promising and the features selected are easily portable across different strategies, which should allow future studies to confirm how successful our methodology was.

The construction of a properly annotated corpus proved to be the most challenging part of this task. Therefore, the development of such a corpus would be worth looking into, as it would greatly aid future efforts in studying NLP related topics for Greek texts. It is of critical importance, as has been showcased by the attempts in this study, to pay special attention when manually annotating data, and to adhere to best practices which have been studied extensively before, for example by Janyce et al. [22].

There's also a scarcity of available tools, which are often required in NLP related tasks, due to the complex structure of the Greek language. For example, tools for lemmatization and stemming are somewhat difficult to implement, partly due to punctuation and grammar rules. This indicates it would be meaningful to spend time developing such tools, before further progress into more intensive NLP tasks is made. Considering the above, any future advancements in the area will be interesting to behold, after this first attempt has been made, to keep track of how such difficulties are handled.

References

1. Pennebaker, J.W., King, L.A.: Linguistic styles: language use as an individual difference. J. Pers. Soc. Psychol. **77**(6), 1296 (1999)
2. Bertolote, J.M., Fleischmann, A.: A global perspective on the magnitude of suicide mortality. Oxford Textb. Suicidol. Suicide Prevent.: Glob. Perspect. 91–98 (2009)
3. Pestian, J., Nasrallah, H., Matykiewicz, P., Bennett, A., Leenaars, A.: Suicide note classification using natural language processing: a content analysis. Biomed. Inf. Insights **3**, BII.S4706 (2010). https://doi.org/10.4137/BII.S4706
4. Wicentowski, R., Sydes, M.R.: Emotion detection in suicide notes using maximum entropy classification. Biomed. Inf. Insights **5**, BII-S8972 (2012)
5. Cherry, C., Mohammad, S.M., Bruijn, B.D.: Binary classifiers and latentsequence models for emotion detection in suicide notes. Biomed. Inf. Insights **5s1**, BII.S8933 (2012). https://doi.org/10.4137/BII.S8933
6. Zhang, L., Huang, X., Liu, T., Li, A., Chen, Z., Zhu, T.: Using linguistic features to estimate suicide probability of chinese microblog users. In: Zu, Q., Hu, B., Gu, N., Seng, S. (eds.) HCC 2014. LNCS, vol. 8944, pp. 549–559. Springer, Cham (2015). https://doi.org/10.1007/978-3-319-15554-8_45
7. Litvinova, T.A., Seredin, P.V., Litvinova, O.A., Romanchenko, O.V.: Identification of suicidal tendencies of individuals based on the quantitative analysis of their internet texts. Computación y Sistemas **21**(2), 243–252 (2017)
8. Burnap, P., Colombo, W., Scourfield, J.: Machine classification and analysis of suicide-related communication on Twitter. In: Proceedings of the 26th ACM Conference on Hypertext and Social Media, pp. 75–84. ACM (2015)
9. Jamison, K.R.: Manic-depressive illness and creativity. Sci. Am.-Am. Edn. **276**, 44–52 (1997)
10. Raeburn, S.D.: Psychological issues and treatment strategies in popular musicians: a review, part I. Med. Probl. Perform. Artist. **14**, 171–179 (1999)
11. Stack, S.: Suicide among artists. J. Soc. Psychol. **137**(1), 129–130 (1997). https://doi.org/10.1080/00224549709595421. pMID: 9121137
12. Lightman, E.J., McCarthy, P.M., Dufty, D.F., McNamara, D.S.: Using computational text analysis tools to compare the lyrics of suicidal and non-suicidal songwriters. In: Proceedings of the Annual Meeting of the Cognitive Science Society, vol. 29, no. 29 (2007)
13. Mulholland, M., Quinn, J.: Suicidal tendencies: the automatic classification of suicidal and non-suicidal lyricists using NLP. In: Proceedings of the Sixth International Joint Conference on Natural Language Processing, pp. 680–684 (2013)
14. Pająk, K., Trzebiński, J.: Escaping the world: linguistic indicators of suicide attempts in poets. J. Loss Trauma **19**(5), 389–402 (2014). https://doi.org/10.1080/15325024.2013.794663
15. Stirman, S.W., Pennebaker, J.W.: Word use in the poetry of suicidal and nonsuicidal poets. Psychosom. Med. **63**(4), 517–522 (2001)
16. Durkheim, E.: Suicide: A Study in Sociology. Routledge, Abingdon (2005)
17. Petrie, K., Brook, R.: Sense of coherence, self-esteem, depression and hopelessness as correlates of reattempting suicide. Br. J. Clin. Psychol. **31**(3), 293–300 (1992)

18. Kao, J., Jurafsky, D.: A computational analysis of style, affect, and imagery in contemporary poetry. In: Proceedings of the NAACL-HLT 2012 Workshop on Computational Linguistics for Literature, pp. 8–17 (2012)
19. Wictionary. https://el.wiktionary.org/wiki/. Accessed 16 Mar 2019
20. Nielsen, F.Å.: A new ANEW: evaluation of a word list for sentiment analysis in microblogs. CoRR, vol. abs/1103.2903 (2011). http://arxiv.org/abs/1103.2903
21. Weka 3 - Data Mining with Open Source Machine Learning Software in Java. https://www.cs.waikato.ac.nz/ml/weka/
22. Wiebe, J., Wilson, T., Cardie, C.: Annotating expressions of opinions and emotions in language. Lang. Resour. Eval. **39**(2–3), 165–210 (2005)

Recognition of Urban Sound Events Using Deep Context-Aware Feature Extractors and Handcrafted Features

Theodore Giannakopoulos[1], Evaggelos Spyrou[1,2]([✉]), and Stavros J. Perantonis[1]

[1] National Center for Scientific Research - "Demokritos", Athens, Greece
{tyianak,espyrou,sper}@iit.demokritos.gr
[2] University of Thessaly, Lamia, Greece

Abstract. This paper proposes a method for recognizing audio events in urban environments that combines handcrafted audio features with a deep learning architectural scheme (Convolutional Neural Networks, CNNs), which has been trained to distinguish between different audio context classes. The core idea is to use the CNNs as a method to extract context-aware deep audio features that can offer supplementary feature representations to any soundscape analysis classification task. Towards this end, the CNN is trained on a database of audio samples which are annotated in terms of their respective "scene" (e.g. train, street, park), and then it is combined with handcrafted audio features in an early fusion approach, in order to recognize the audio event of an unknown audio recording. Detailed experimentation proves that the proposed context-aware deep learning scheme, when combined with the typical handcrafted features, leads to a significant performance boosting in terms of classification accuracy. The main contribution of this work is the demonstration that transferring audio contextual knowledge using CNNs as feature extractors can significantly improve the performance of the audio classifier, without need for CNN training (a rather demanding process that requires huge datasets and complex data augmentation procedures).

Keywords: Soundscape classification ·
Context-aware feature extractors · Convolutional Neural Networks

1 Introduction

Soundscape audio recordings capture the sonic environment of a particular time and location and it can be conceived as an "auditory landscape", either in an individual or common level. With the advances in audio signal processing and machine learning, it has become possible to automatically predict the content, the context [10,12,29,30] and even the quality [6] of the soundscape recordings. Automatic recognition of soundscapes is rather important in many emerging applications, such as surveillance, urban soundscape monitoring and noise source identification.

© IFIP International Federation for Information Processing 2019
Published by Springer Nature Switzerland AG 2019
J. MacIntyre et al. (Eds.): AIAI 2019 Workshops, IFIP AICT 560, pp. 184–195, 2019.
https://doi.org/10.1007/978-3-030-19909-8_16

An important problem in automatic soundscape classification is the diversity between different datasets and benchmarks, in terms of class taxonomy, dataset size and audio signal quality. In this work, we utilize the ability of deep neural networks to learn patterns in large datasets, capturing both spectral and temporal relations in audio signals. Towards this end, a deep learning network architecture is trained to distinguish between contextual classes (e.g., park, restaurant, library, metro station, etc). Then, this network is used as a supervised audio feature extractor in an urban classification task of urban audio events and in combination with handcrafted audio features. Extensive experimentation proves that this transfer of knowledge from an audio context domain, using deep neural networks, can boost the performance of the soundscape classification procedure, when handcrafted features are combined with the deep context-aware features.

The main contribution of this work is the experimental proof that audio contextual knowledge can be "transferred" through a CNN, which is trained in a scene-specific dataset, and that this scheme can be used to boost the performance of audio event classification based on typical handcrafted audio features. This has been experimentally demonstrated using two widely adopted benchmarks, even with a baseline classification approach and a standard early-fusion feature combination scheme.

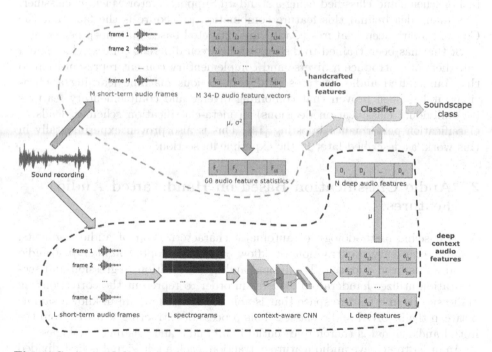

Fig. 1. Conceptual diagram of the proposed method. Two separate steps are adopted during in the analysis pipeline: hand-crafted-audio features are computed on the raw signal, as well as a supervised CNN trained to distinguish between different context classes is used as a feature extractor.

2   General Scheme

As illustrated in the general conceptual diagram of Fig. 1, we propose classifying unknown soundscape recordings using two distinct feature representation steps:

- **Handcrafted audio Features (HaF).** According to this widely-adopted approach, each signal is represented by a series of statistics computed over short-term audio features, either from the time or the frequency domain, such as signal energy, zero crossing rate and the spectral centroid. These features aim to represent the audio signal in a space that is discriminative with regards to the involved audio classes. This baseline audio representation methodology is described in more detail in Sect. 3.
- **Context-aware deep Features (CadF).** A supervised convolutional neural network is trained to discriminate between different audio urban context classes (such as park, restaurant, etc), based on spectrograms of short-term segments. The output of the last fully connected layer of this network is used as feature extractor in the initial soundscape classification task. This methodology is described in detail in Sect. 4.

The two different audio feature representations are then combined in an early-fusion scheme and classified using a standard Support Vector Machine classifier. The main idea behind this feature combination procedure is the fact that the Context-aware deep Features (CadF) are extracted based on a deep neural network that has been trained to distinguish between different context classes and can therefore introduce a diverse and complementary content representation to the Handcrafted audio Features (HaF). In various machine learning applications, it has been proven that combining diverse and complementary features (or individual classification decisions) in meta-classification schemes, leads to classification performance boosting [14]. This is also proven experimentally in this work, as described later in the experiments section.

3   Audio Classification Based on Handcrafted Audio Features

As a baseline methodology of automatic characterization of audio segments, a short-term feature extraction workflow of widely-adopted *handcrafted* audio features has been adopted. Traditional audio classification, regression and segmentation utilizes handcrafted features in order to represent the corresponding audio signals in a feature space that is able to discriminate an unknown sample between the involved audio classes. This process of extracting features from the initial audio signal is therefore essential in all audio analysis methodologies.

In order to achieve audio feature extraction, each audio signal is first divided to either overlapping or non-overlapping short-term windows (frames). Widely accepted short-term window sizes are 20 to 100 ms. Additionally, a widely adopted methodology in audio analysis is the processing of the feature sequence on a "mid-term basis", according to which the audio signal is first divided

Table 1. Handcrafted short-term audio features. In total, 34 audio features extracted from the time, spectral and cepstral domains are computed per short-term frame. This leads to a series of 34-dimensional feature vectors for each audio segment. At a second stage segment-level statistics (mean and standard deviation) are computed for the whole audio segment, leading to a 68-dimensional representation.

Index	Name	Description
1	Zero crossing rate	Rate of sign-changes of the signal during the duration of a particular frame
2	Energy	(Normalized) sum of squares of the signal values
3	Entropy of energy	Entropy of sub-frames' normalized energies
4	Spectral centroid	Center of gravity of the spectrum
5	Spectral spread	Second central moment of the spectrum
6	Spectral entropy	Entropy of the normalized spectral energies for a set of sub-frames
7	Spectral flux	Squared diffs between the normalized magnitudes of the spectra of the two successive frames
8	Spectral rolloff	Frequency below which 90% of the magnitude distribution of the spectrum is concentrated
9–21	MFCCs	Mel frequency cepstral coefficients
22–33	Chroma vector	A 12-element representation of the spectral energy using a semitone spacing
34	Chroma deviation	Standard deviation of the 12 chroma coefficients

into mid-term windows (segments), which can be either overlapping or non-overlapping. For each segment, the short-term processing process, described above, is carried out and the feature sequence from each mid-term segment, is used for computing feature statistics (e.g. the average value of the zero crossing rate). Therefore, each mid-term segment is represented by a set of statistics. Typical values of the mid-term segment size can be 1 to 10 s [5,11,28].

Table 1 shows the adopted handcrafted audio features. In this work, two mid-term statistics have been adopted, namely the average value and the standard deviation of the respective short-term features. This means that the final signal representation using these handcrafted feature statistics is a $34 \times 2 = 68$ feature vector. The pyAudioAnalysis library has been adopted for implementing these audio features [4]. Each unknown audio file is therefore represented using the aforementioned procedure and it is classified using a Support Vector Machine classifier with an RBF kernel. More details on the classification scheme of the handcrafted audio features are given in the experiments section. pyAudioAnalysis has been widely used in several audio classification tasks in the bibliography (e.g., [16,27]) and it implements most basic audio features. In addition, in this paper it has been chosen for its Pythonic implementation that makes it easier to combine with the deep learning - related experiments implemented in Keras and Tensorflow.

4 Context-Aware Deep Learning

4.1 Convolutional Neural Networks

As with most machine learning application domains, audio analysis has significantly benefited by the recent advances that *deep learning* has offered. Most of the research efforts towards this direction have focused on employing audio features in deep learning schemes for speech recognition [3,8], generic audio analysis [15] and music classification [22]. Also, inspired by the outstanding results of convolutional neural networks (CNNs) in image classification [13], a few research efforts have also focused on particular audio analysis tasks by representing the audio signal as a 2-D time-frequency representation, mainly for musical signal analysis applications [2,7,23,24,31] and speech emotion recognition [9]. In general, such deep-architectures and especially deep CNNs are well known for their ability to autonomously learn highly-invariant feature representations, extracted from complex images.

CNNs have been widely adopted as deep architectures. They are actually a subcategory of traditional neural-networks (ANNs). However, in CNNs, (convolutional) neurons in one or more layers are applied to a small "region" of the layer input, emulating the response of an individual neuron to visual stimuli. These layers are called convolutional and are usually deployed in the beginning of the architectural scheme. CNNs in general use one or more convolutional layers, usually followed by a subsampling step and at the end by one or more fully connected layers, similar to the ones used in traditional multilayer neural networks. CNNs have been proven to achieve the training of computationally large model with very robust feature representations especially in difficult multi-class image classification tasks.

4.2 Context-Aware Deep Audio Feature Extractors

Signal Representation. In this work, we propose using CNNs as estimators of contextual audio classes. Towards this end, instead of using handcrafted audio features, the audio signal is first represented by its **spectrogram**: in particular, a Short-Term FFT (applied on the hanning-windowed version of each raw audio signal) is used to estimate the audio signal's spectrum, using a short-term window of 20 ms with 50% overlap (i.e. the short-term window's size is 10 ms). It has to be noted, that before the spectrogram calculation, the signal is resampled to 16 KHz and stereo signals are converted to single-channel. In addition, after the spectrogram calculation, only the first 100 frequency bins are kept. Since each short-term window is 20 ms long, this actually means that only frequencies up to 5000 Hz are kept, i.e. 62.5% of the total spectral distribution. The spectrogram process calculation is performed for each 200 ms mid-term segment. Therefore,

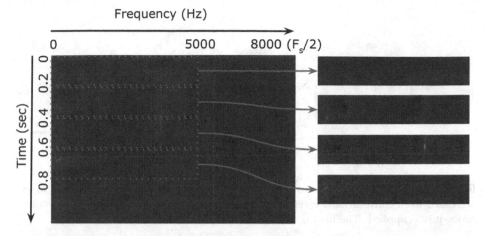

Fig. 2. Signal representation adopted in the deep learning scheme: each 19×100 spectrogram representation (corresponding to a 200 ms segment) is fed as input to the context-aware CNN model

for each individual audio segment the respective time-frequency spectrogram representation corresponds to an image of 19×100 resolution. Figure 2 illustrates the adopted process that leads to the signal representation used by the convolutional neural network. Each individual 19×100 spectrogram representation (corresponding to a 200 ms segment) is fed as input to the context-aware CNN described in the next section.

CNN Architecture. The aforementioned 19×100 spectrogram image is fed as input to the proposed CNN architecture. As shown in Fig. 3, the convolutional neural network that is trained to recognize audio context classes has first a convolutional layer that takes the initial spectrogram image (19×100) and uses 64 convolutional nodes (3×3 each). This is also followed by a batch normalization and a RELU activation stage [25]. Then a similar 2nd convolutional layer is used with the same number of nodes, followed by a maxpooling and a dropout step. Maxpooling is actually a sub-sampling layer that changes the resolution of its input, in order to facilitate the discovery of more abstract features and avoid overfitting. In this architecture, maxpooling size is set equal to 1×2, in order to only subsample the representation dimensions that correspond to the frequency domain. Dropout layers are used in an additional effort to avoid overfitting [26]. According to the dropout technique, at each training stage, individual nodes are "dropped out" of the net with a particular probability. Incoming and outgoing edges to a dropped-out node are also removed. Dropout is set equal to 0.2 in our system.

The group of these two convolutional layers and the maxpooling layer is then repeated at a second group of layers. Finally, a fully connected (dense) layer that maps the (flat) representation is generated by the last pooling layer to a

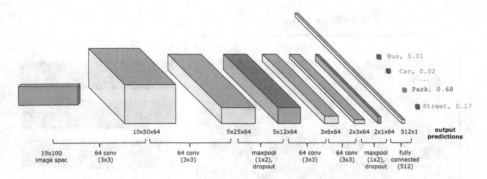

Fig. 3. Adopted CNN architecture. In general, two groups of two convolutional layers are used. Each convolutional layer has 64 nodes, while after each group a maxpooling procedure is applied. The final dense layer has 512 nodes

high-dimensional (512) flat representation. The final output of the network is the prediction of the adopted audio scene classes as described in the sequel. The adopted CNN architectural scheme has resulted after a parameter optimization procedure where the number of convolutional layers, the number of convolutional neurons at each layer and the size of the dense layer have been used as parameters, where performance measures from the TUT dataset have been used (not the final evaluation datasets).

CNN Training Procedure. In this work, it is our goal to extract audio context-aware knowledge through the utilization of a CNN that has been trained to distinguish between acoustic scene classes. Towards this end, the aforementioned network has been trained using the TUT Acoustic scene classification dataset [17]. This is a widely adopted benchmark of almost 5000 audio segments of 10 s each. The segments have been annotated to 15 scene classes that describe the recording context such as: bus, car, city center, home, metro station, residential area, train etc. The adopted CNN scheme has been trained on several non-overlapping 200-ms spectrograms of the aforementioned audio segments of the TUT dataset. In total, around 200 thousand spectrograms have been used to train the CNN. The resulting CNN is used as a feature extractor, i.e. the last output layer is omitted in the overall system.

Both the network and the training procedure has been implemented using the Tensorflow [1] and Keras (keras.io) frameworks. The training procedure has been carried out in a Linux workstation equipped with a Tesla K40c GPU, which achieved a 15x speed boosting, compared to the CPU-based training procedure.

Using CNN as a Feature Extractor. As soon as the CNN is trained as described above, the input values of its last dense layer (i.e. the 512 values of the respective fully connected layer) are adopted as deep features for each 0.2 s audio segment. These 512 feature sequences are then used to produce long-term averages. Note, that this corresponds to the statistic calculation substage of the handcrafted feature extraction described in Sect. 3. However, in the case of the CNN-based feature extractor, only means of the short-term features are extracted, due to the fact that the CNN training phase has also taken into consideration the temporal evolution of the audio signal (through one of the two dimensions of the spectrogram), so there is no obvious need for further using standard deviation or some other statistic, apart from the mean value.

Therefore, during the audio event recognition phase, each audio recording is represented by 512 averages of the respective 512 short-term sequences of the deep context-aware features. Finally, these 512 features are merged with the 68 handcrafted audio feature statistics, leading to a early fusion feature vector of 580 dimensions in total, for each audio recording.

5   Experimental Evaluation

5.1   Sound Event Datasets

The TUT dataset described in Sect. 4.2 has been used to train the adopted CNN scheme to distinguish between audio scenes that characterize the "context" of the audio signal. In order to evaluate the performance of the final classification approach, two audio event datasets have been utilized:

- The Urban Soundcape Dataset 8K (U-8K) [21], contains 8732 labeled sound excerpts (all less or equal to 4s of length) of urban sounds from 10 audio event classes: air conditioner, car horn, children playing, dog bark, drilling, engine idling, gun shot, jackhammer, siren, and street music. The average classification accuracy obtained is 68% for the baseline audio classification method.
  The ESC-50 dataset [19] has also been used in various audio classification papers as a benchmark. This is a public labeled dataset of 2000 environmental recordings with 50 audio event classes, 40 sound files per class, 5 s per file. The number of classes is much higher in this dataset, therefore the classification accuracy of the reported baseline method is around 44%.

5.2   Experimental Results

Table 2 presents the classification results for all three methods on both datasets: baseline (BL, as described in the corresponding dataset descriptions, i.e., [21] and [19]), Handcrafted audio features (HaF), context-aware deep features (CadF) and combination (HaF + CadF). Note that the HaF results correspond to a tuning procedure in terms of short-term window size and step. The best performance has been reported for a 40 ms frame of 50% overlap (i.e. 20 msec step) and a non-overlapping 2-s segment size. The C parameter of the SVM classifier has been selected in the context of a cross-validation pipeline from the range 0.01 to 50. The selected C value was 10 for both tasks and the respective training errors were 65% and 82% which does not indicate a significant overfitting state. Also, it

Table 2. Classification accuracy for all audio feature methods: baseline, handcrafted audio features, context-aware deep features and combination. The performance boosting offered by the combination classification method has been found to be statistically significant ($p < 0.05$)

Method	ESC50	U-8K
BL	44	68
HaF	46.6 ± 2.5	69.4 ± 6.6
CadF	44.2 ± 1.8	65.1 ± 5.2
HaF + CadF	52.2 ± 2	73.1 ± 6.2

has to be noted that melgrams have also been evaluated as an alternative signal representation method and they did not lead to performance improvement (they were on average 1% less accurate for both methods).

It can be seen that the HaF method slightly outperforms the CadF feature extraction approach, however the two feature methodologies combined lead to a relative performance boosting of 11% and 5% for the ESC50 and the U-8K datasets respectively. This performance boosting, despite the fact that the CadF method alone hardly outperforms the baseline approach, is a rather important finding. Note that all classification results presented here are for the best Support Vector Machine classifier, with a RBF kernel, where the C parameter has been tuned in a cross-validation procedure. Other widely used classifiers such as random forests and extra trees have been also evaluated but achieved lower classification rates, when used both in the individual feature representation feature methods and in their combinations.

The goal of this paper is to demonstrate the ability of the "context-aware" CNNs to provide an alternative feature representation that boosts the performance of handcrafted audio features. The aforementioned results prove that, even with a baseline classification and fusion approach the combination of the two feature representation methodologies lead to significant performance boosting. Despite the fact that a simple workflow has been used in the classification stage, the overall method achieves comparable results for the U-8K dataset (74% in [18] and 75% in [10]), even if such methods adopt complex deep learning classification schemes that usually require laborious data augmentation procedures and respective parameter tuning [20].

6   Conclusions

In this paper we have demonstrated the utilization of Convolutional Neural Networks that have been trained to distinguish between acoustic scene (context) classes, in a framework for classifying urban audio events. Towards this end, handcrafted audio features as well as features extracted from the proposed CNN are combined in an early fusion approach and classified using a baseline classifier. Extensive experimentation has proven that this combination leads to a relative performance boosting of up to 11%, despite the fact that the performance of the CNN-generated features alone is hardly baseline-equivalent. This is due to the fact that the CNN introduces highly diverse representation, which is not modelled in the handcrafted features.

The contribution of this work is focused in the fact that it experimentally proves that the transfer of contextual knowledge using a CNN trained in a scene-specific dataset can lead to significant performance boosting when combined with typical handcrafted (manually designed) audio features. However, this performance boosting has been demonstrated using a very simple classification scheme (i.e. SVMs performed on simple long-term feature statistics). Our ongoing and future work aims to combine this contextual knowledge in the context of a deep learning framework that will replace the simple feature merging (early fusion) and the (meta)classification technique adopted in this paper.

Acknowledgment. We acknowledge support of this work by the project SYNTELE-SIS "Innovative Technologies and Applications based on the Internet of Things (IoT) and the Cloud Computing" (MIS 5002521) which is implemented under the "Action for the Strategic Development on the Research and Technological Sector", funded by the Operational Programme "Competitiveness, Entrepreneurship and Innovation" (NSRF 2014-2020) and co-financed by Greece and the European Union (European Regional Development Fund).

References

1. Abadi, M., et al.: TensorFlow: large-scale machine learning on heterogeneous distributed systems. arXiv preprint arXiv:1603.04467 (2016)
2. Choi, K., Fazekas, G., Sandler, M.: Explaining deep convolutional neural networks on music classification. arXiv preprint arXiv:1607.02444 (2016)
3. Dahl, G.E., Yu, D., Deng, L., Acero, A.: Context-dependent pre-trained deep neural networks for large-vocabulary speech recognition. IEEE Trans. Audio Speech Lang. Process. **20**(1), 30–42 (2012)
4. Giannakopoulos, T.: pyaudioanalysis: an open-source python library for audio signal analysis. PloS One **10**(12), e0144610 (2015)
5. Giannakopoulos, T., Pikrakis, A.: Introduction to Audio Analysis: A MATLAB® Approach. Academic Press, Cambridge (2014)
6. Giannakopoulos, T., Siantikos, G., Perantonis, S., Votsi, N.E., Pantis, J.: Automatic soundscape quality estimation using audio analysis. In: Proceedings of the 8th ACM International Conference on PErvasive Technologies Related to Assistive Environments, p. 19. ACM (2015)
7. Grill, T., Schluter, J.: Music boundary detection using neural networks on spectrograms and self-similarity lag matrices. In: 2015 23rd European Signal Processing Conference (EUSIPCO), pp. 1296–1300. IEEE (2015)
8. Hinton, G., et al.: Deep neural networks for acoustic modeling in speech recognition: the shared views of four research groups. IEEE Signal Process. Mag. **29**(6), 82–97 (2012)
9. Huang, Z., Dong, M., Mao, Q., Zhan, Y.: Speech emotion recognition using CNN. In: Proceedings of the 22nd ACM International Conference on Multimedia, pp. 801–804. ACM (2014)

10. Huzaifah, M.: Comparison of time-frequency representations for environmental sound classification using convolutional neural networks. arXiv preprint arXiv:1706.07156 (2017)
11. Hyoung-Gook, K., Nicolas, M., Sikora, T.: MPEG-7 Audio and Beyond: Audio Content Indexing and Retrieval. Wiley, Hoboken (2005)
12. Khunarsal, P., Lursinsap, C., Raicharoen, T.: Very short time environmental sound classification based on spectrogram pattern matching. Inf. Sci. **243**, 57–74 (2013)
13. Krizhevsky, A., Sutskever, I., Hinton, G.E.: ImageNet classification with deep convolutional neural networks. In: Advances in Neural Information Processing Systems, pp. 1097–1105 (2012)
14. Kuncheva, L.I., Whitaker, C.J.: Measures of diversity in classifier ensembles and their relationship with the ensemble accuracy. Mach. Learn. **51**(2), 181–207 (2003)
15. Lee, H., Pham, P., Largman, Y., Ng, A.Y.: Unsupervised feature learning for audio classification using convolutional deep belief networks. In: Advances in Neural Information Processing Systems, pp. 1096–1104 (2009)
16. Mesaros, A., et al.: DCASE 2017 challenge setup: tasks, datasets and baseline system. In: DCASE 2017-Workshop on Detection and Classification of Acoustic Scenes and Events (2017)
17. Mesaros, A., Heittola, T., Virtanen, T.: TUT database for acoustic scene classification and sound event detection. In: 2016 24th European Signal Processing Conference (EUSIPCO), pp. 1128–1132. IEEE (2016)
18. Piczak, K.J.: Environmental sound classification with convolutional neural networks. In: 2015 IEEE 25th International Workshop on Machine Learning for Signal Processing (MLSP), pp. 1–6. IEEE (2015)
19. Piczak, K.J.: ESC: dataset for environmental sound classification. In: Proceedings of the 23rd ACM International Conference on Multimedia, pp. 1015–1018. ACM (2015)
20. Salamon, J., Bello, J.P.: Deep convolutional neural networks and data augmentation for environmental sound classification. IEEE Signal Process. Lett. **24**(3), 279–283 (2017)
21. Salamon, J., Jacoby, C., Bello, J.P.: A dataset and taxonomy for urban sound research. In: Proceedings of the 22nd ACM international conference on Multimedia, pp. 1041–1044. ACM (2014)
22. Scardapane, S., Comminiello, D., Scarpiniti, M., Uncini, A.: Music classification using extreme learning machines. In: 2013 8th International Symposium on Image and Signal Processing and Analysis (ISPA), pp. 377–381. IEEE (2013)
23. Schlüter, J., Böck, S.: CNN-based audio onset detection mirex submission
24. Schlüter, J., Böck, S.: Musical onset detection with convolutional neural networks. In: 6th International Workshop on Machine Learning and Music (MML), Prague, Czech Republic (2013)
25. Schmidhuber, J.: Deep learning in neural networks: an overview. Neural Netw. **61**, 85–117 (2015)
26. Srivastava, N., Hinton, G.E., Krizhevsky, A., Sutskever, I., Salakhutdinov, R.: Dropout: a simple way to prevent neural networks from overfitting. J. Mach. Learn. Res. **15**(1), 1929–1958 (2014)
27. Subramaniam, A., Patel, V., Mishra, A., Balasubramanian, P., Mittal, A.: Bimodal first impressions recognition using temporally ordered deep audio and stochastic visual features. In: Hua, G., Jégou, H. (eds.) ECCV 2016. LNCS, vol. 9915, pp. 337–348. Springer, Cham (2016). https://doi.org/10.1007/978-3-319-49409-8_27

28. Theodoridis, S., Koutroumbas, K.: Pattern Recognition, 4th edn. Academic Press, Cambridge (2008)
29. Thorogood, M., Fan, J., Pasquier, P.: Soundscape audio signal classification and segmentation using listeners perception of background and foreground sound. J. Audio Eng. Soc. **64**(7/8), 484–492 (2016)
30. Ye, J., Kobayashi, T., Murakawa, M.: Urban sound event classification based on local and global features aggregation. App. Acoust. **117**, 246–256 (2017)
31. Zhang, C., Evangelopoulos, G., Voinea, S., Rosasco, L., Poggio, T.: A deep representation for invariance and music classification. In: 2014 IEEE International Conference on Acoustics, Speech and Signal Processing (ICASSP), pp. 6984–6988. IEEE (2014)

Studying the Spatialities of Short-Term Rentals' Sprawl in the Urban Fabric: The Case of Airbnb in Athens, Greece

Konstantinos Gourzis[1]($\boxtimes$), Georgios Alexandridis[2], Stelios Gialis[1],
and George Caridakis[2]

[1] Department of Geography, University of the Aegean, Mytilene, Greece
gourzisk@gmail.com, stgialis@aegean.gr
[2] Intelligent Interaction Research Group, Cultural Technology Department,
University of the Aegean, Mytilene, Greece
{gealexandri,gcari}@aegean.gr
https://ii.ct.aegean.gr/

Abstract. This work constitutes a theoretically-informed empirical analysis of the spatial characteristics of the short-term rentals' market and explores their linkage with shifts in the wider housing market within the context of a south-eastern EU metropolis. The same research objective has been pursued for a variety of international paradigms; however, to the best of our knowledge, there has not been a thorough and systematic study for Athens and its neighborhoods. With a theoretical framework that draws insight from the political-economic views of Critical Geography, this work departs from an assessment of Airbnb listings, and proceeds inquiring the expansion of the phenomenon with respect to the rates of long-term rent levels in the neighborhoods of Central Athens, utilizing relevant data. The geographical framework covers the City of Athens as a whole, an area undergoing profound transformations in recent years, stemming from diverse factors that render the city one of the most dynamic destinations of urban tourism and speculative land investment. The analysis reveals a prominent expansion of the short-term rental phenomenon across the urban fabric, especially taking ground in hitherto underexploited areas. This expansion is multifactorial, asynchronous and exhibits signs of positive relation with the long-term rentals shifts; Airbnb not only affects already gentrifying neighborhoods, but contributes to a housing market disruption in non-dynamic residential areas.

Keywords: Airbnb · Gentrification · Housing markets · Spatio-temporal humanities

1 Introduction

The expansion of *short-term rental* (STR) markets in recent years is a reality that definitely affects living conditions, especially in urban areas. This fact can

© IFIP International Federation for Information Processing 2019
Published by Springer Nature Switzerland AG 2019
J. MacIntyre et al. (Eds.): AIAI 2019 Workshops, IFIP AICT 560, pp. 196–207, 2019.
https://doi.org/10.1007/978-3-030-19909-8_17

be attributed to a number of characteristics of STRs, like their ability to take advantage of local landmarks (more than hotels do) because of their capacity to expand in already built-up areas, without the need of specific permits or being subject to land use zoning [6]. This is exceptionally important in the context of urban tourism, a rapidly growing part of the tourism industry, affecting mainly lower-end hotels and those not targeting affluent business travelers [7]. The increasing number of STR listings has generated controversies on several issues of regulation, housing markets and various other spatio-temporal effects [17]. Thus, it calls for urgent research attention based on, among other things, the perspective of humanistic data mining.

Within the STR market, *Airbnb*[1], an online *peer-to-peer* (P2P) accommodation platform, holds a prominent share. Airbnb is a global phenomenon; since its emergence in 2007, it has managed to expand to 81 thousand cities across 191 countries, currently counting more than 6 million listings. While linkages between the spatial characteristics of the platform's listings and shifts in the housing market have been studied for a variety of cities, like New York [15], Boston [8] or even Barcelona [14], there has not been, to the best of our knowledge, a thorough study for a south-eastern EU metropolis, like Athens and its neighborhoods.

The main aim of the current research is to tentatively discuss the consolidation of Airbnb in the city of Athens and associate it with several socio-economic aspects in specific city areas. The expansion of STRs is viewed as an outcome of several processes, needs and antinomies; i.e through the lens of transnational capital flows into the housing market of a dynamic city. Departing from an analysis of STRs listings (number, density) within the context of the biggest Greek city, we proceed by relating their expansion with an increase in *long-term rental* (LTR) prices. Specifically, it is highlighted how STRs might put pressure on other forms of housing, causing rents and property values to rise, as residences become "cash cows" [8] and reinforce gentrification [11].

2   The Spatialities of Short-Term Rentals

At the global scale, the Airbnb "community" sprawls in a heterogeneous fashion [9], being mainly used in macro-peripheries where tourism is already a prominent industry, boasts dynamic development overall and the population is "technologically savvy" [7]. The majority of entries regard entire house renting, indicating that the commercial use of Airbnb is pervasive, rendering the platform a rental marketplace rather than a true sharing economy mediator. This reality is further characterized by the heavy involvement of business operators whose presence is obscured by the use of "front men". In 2017, it was found that almost 70% of all listings globally referred to entire apartments/houses [9], while in 2016 almost half of the lodgings researched in 5 global cities referred to traditional holiday businesses [5]. Additionally, Airbnb functions often as a mechanism that allows middle and upper-class homeowners to consolidate their position in expensive

---

[1] https://airbnb.com/.

housing markets, in addition to being a channel of extra income for the urbanities of lower classes, who experience an exacerbated vulnerability amid conditions of low affordable housing stock and high tourist demand [5].

One of the earliest arguments in favor of Airbnb was that it would disperse the supply of tourism-oriented accommodation, relieving areas receiving heavy visitor flows. Nevertheless, an analysis for Barcelona [13] concluded that Airbnb functions as a force concentrating supply rather than decentralizing it. On top of that, the way listings unravel follows a pattern that derives from a specific sociocultural profile regarding both hosts and guests [13].

Apart from Barcelona, STR listings in Europe show significant concentrations in Paris, London, and Rome. Athens also exhibits high concentrations relative to its population, even though it is not among the European cities with the largest number of Airbnb entries. In the US, most Airbnb activity is located in five specific cities: New York, Los Angeles, San Francisco, Miami and Boston [10].

Specifically, New York holds a prominent position in the relevant literature, boasting an exceptionally consolidated activity of the STR market. At the same time, it shows concrete signs of ongoing dynamism and expansion (followed by San Francisco, Miami, Oakland and Oahu [7]) but it also exhibits falling rates of profitability in relation to LTRs. Listings are again mainly located in downtown areas, even though lately they tend to expand to hitherto under-exploited, residential areas [4], resonating with the recent situation in Barcelona as well [6]. In poorer areas, Airbnb seems to be reaffirming its original purpose as a niche sharing economy, with private rooms - which stand for a more casual use of the platform - holding a disproportionate presence [4].

3 The Impact on Long-Term Rentals

The second issue relevant to our research, is the effect of Airbnb – and the STR phenomenon in general – on housing availability and affordability, specifically on LTR levels. There are arguments postulating against such a linkage, as in many cases the P2P accommodation market is very small in comparison to that of LTRs; the reliance of landlords upon long-term tenants, and the falling rates of STRs [4] could be strong factors towards this direction. Another issue keeping short-term and LTRs' markets afar is the extensive use of housing units that would have remained out of circulation had they not been Airbnb entries; this is particularly the case with spare rooms, that could not be rented out to regular tenants [3]. In some cases, this connection could even be reversed, with STRs causing rents' decrease, due to the overuse of commons by more people and the negative externalities the higher densities in uses and human flows the rise of P2P accommodation brings [15]. However, there are clear indications linking the STR phenomenon with rents' inflation [13]; the mobilization of tourism-oriented companies, which in many cases spread their investments across multiple geographical localities and pour a large number of listings into the P2P accommodation market, the stagnation of rent levels even amid recessive pressures that would normally cause shrinkage, or more importantly, the multiple cases where cities experience stark rates of rising rents, such as in San Francisco - which, ironically, is the home city of the Airbnb company itself. Most conducted studies conclude that a link between rising rents and STRs expansion is intuitively relevant and "straightforward" [15].

More specifically, one of the first works that theorized in a systematic way upon the aforementioned connection, identified two mechanisms that distort the housing market and limit the supply of affordable housing [11]. The first refers to the "simple conversion" of houses previously rented out long-term into Airbnb entries year-round. This mechanism generates a relatively insignificant rise in rents citywide, that mainly affects already gentrifying and affluent neighborhoods, as well as downtown areas where the rental market is tighter. However, the impact of the second mechanism is argued to be more severe, and it refers to cases where landlords decide to turn whole buildings into Airbnb listings [16]. In these instances of "hotelization", the supply of housing is significantly shrunk, spurring displacement and gentrification.

Today, it is widely believed that the link between STRs and rent-inflation is tangible and severely affects contemporary cities [11,18]. Empirically, existing research has managed to correlate a specific level of rents inflation to the expansion of STR markets in New York [15], Boston [8] and Barcelona [14].

4   The Case of Athens, Greece

4.1   Data

Airbnb does not, so far, provide any data on the spread of its platform on the various cities it operates. Therefore, in order to examine its influence, external sources had to be used, like *Inside Airbnb*[2], a website providing both relevant data dumps and tools for downloading the desired information directly from Airbnb. More specifically, Inside Airbnb collects and publishes data dumps of the listings that appear on the P2P platform for various cities and on various dates (recently, it has been collecting data on an almost monthly basis). Each dump consists of a number of files that provide insight on different aspects of the phenomenon; describing in detail the collected listings, designating when each listing is available for rental on the platform and finally containing the reviews it has received so far.

LTR prices, on the other hand, are provided by *RE/MAX* [1], a private agency conducting surveys on the real estate market in Greece. RE/MAX releases data on LTRs and mean prices per neighborhood, which are conducted on an annual basis and regard the whole domestic market. It should be noted that the spatial boundaries of the neighborhoods in RE/MAX reports are different from the ones Airbnb uses. Figure 1 shows Athens' neighborhoods as designated in the Airbnb platform. In order to achieve a controlled comparison between the data on short and long-term rentals, the neighborhoods from the private firm have been adapted to the Airbnb neighborhood format (as shown in Fig. 4).

---

[2] http://insideairbnb.com.

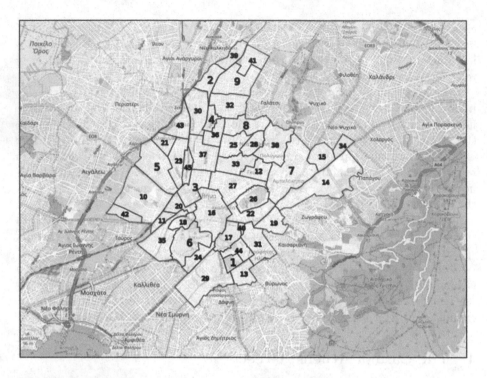

Fig. 1. List of Athens' neighborhoods (numbering is according to Table 1)

In order to more thoroughly interpret the temporal as well as the spatial effect of STRs on LTRs within the City of Athens, two data dumps that have been obtained in the same month three years apart, were scrutinized (July 17th, 2015 and July 16th, 2018). The analysis mainly focused on the available listings. Initially, the number of listings per neighborhood have been examined, along with their relative change between 2015 and 2018 (Table 1). Then, the *density* (number of listings per km^2 - Fig. 2) and its change throughout the study period have been calculated (Fig. 3). Additionally, the *location quotient* (LQ), a metric originating from the area of economic development has been computed for all neighborhoods. LQ is related to density and is used to determine the concentration of a characteristic in a particular area with respect to a wider area. In this case, it was defined as the ratio of a neighborhood's density to the overall density of the City of Athens (Table 1).

Apart from the expansion of STRs in terms of magnitude and density, the interrelation between short and long-term rentals has been explored. Specifically, the above results have been compared with the changes in rent prices per neighborhood (Fig. 4), while at the same time it has been accounted for what they might mean for the wider area of Athens. It should also be noted that the followed analyis scheme, based on the spatial comparison of absolute numbers

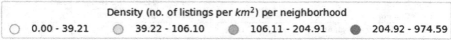

Fig. 2. Density (number of listings per km^2) across Athens' neighborhoods as of July 16, 2018

and densities for Airbnb listings, albeit a preliminary one, in accordance with relevant research [11,18].

4.2 Discussion

The most obvious observation of our analysis is that Airbnb listings are increasing in skyrocketing rates, following the general trend of the "sharing economy". In the field of daily economic life in Athens, such an increase has come as an outlet for many landlords seeking to increase their earnings, avoid the risks of long-term tenancy (damages, unpaid bills etc.) or even allowing for segments of homeowners to continue living in rapidly appreciating housing markets [12]. Our analysis reveals that these astonishing expansion tendencies in the STR market are geographically uneven. The overall increase in the number of listings between 2015 and 2018 is above 300% (Table 1), whereas in specific neighborhoods the increments are much sharper. The results are deemed as expected, with central areas presenting the highest numbers, densities of listings and concentration of activity (LQs); apart from Koukaki-Makrygianni, a neighborhood among the

Table 1. Change in the number of Athens neighbourhoods' listings on Airbnb and the respective location quotients between July 17th, 2015 and July 16th, 2018

Id	Neighbourhood	Number of listings			Location quotient	
		2015 July 17th	2018 July 16th	Change	2015 July 17th	2018 July 16th
1	1o Nekrotafeio	15	46	207%	0.98	0.71
2	Agios Eleftherios	10	32	220%	0.31	0.24
3	Agios Konstantinos-Plateia Vathis	64	484	656%	1.31	2.34
4	Agios Nikolaos	11	54	391%	0.64	0.74
5	Akadimia Platonos	13	71	446%	0.15	0.20
6	Akropoli	69	331	380%	0.96	1.09
7	Ambelokipi	96	377	293%	0.76	0.71
8	Ano Kypseli	31	78	152%	0.66	0.39
9	Ano Patisia	23	77	235%	0.33	0.26
10	Ellinoroson	6	52	767%	0.17	0.35
11	Emporiko Trigono-Plaka	308	1,179	283%	3.51	3.17
12	Gazi	27	84	211%	1.80	1.32
13	Goudi	48	116	142%	0.35	0.20
14	Gouva	23	67	191%	0.78	0.54
15	Gyzi	27	96	256%	0.92	0.77
16	Ilisia	61	201	230%	1.78	1.38
17	Keramikos	62	217	250%	2.63	2.17
18	Kolokynthou	3	12	300%	0.13	0.12
19	Kolonaki	93	318	242%	2.16	1.74
20	Kolonos	10	84	740%	0.22	0.44
21	Koukaki-Makrygianni	117	723	518%	4.51	6.57
22	Kypseli	54	229	324%	1.45	1.45
23	Lykavittos	42	127	202%	1.04	0.75
24	Mouseio-Exarcheia-Neapoli	164	790	382%	2.41	2.74
25	Nea Kypseli	17	69	306%	0.70	0.67
26	Neos Kosmos	146	635	335%	1.29	1.32
27	Nirvana	16	96	500%	0.27	0.39
28	Pangrati	132	476	261%	2.46	2.10
29	Patisia	33	107	224%	0.61	0.47
30	Pedio Areos	20	87	335%	0.49	0.50
31	Pentagono	3	6	100%	0.17	0.08
32	Petralona	83	285	243%	1.25	1.01
33	Plateia Amerikis	30	114	280%	1.12	1.00
34	Plateia Attikis	66	424	542%	1.18	1.79
35	Polygono	11	30	173%	0.16	0.11
36	Prombona	4	13	225%	0.15	0.11
37	Rigillis	2	12	500%	0.53	0.75
38	Rizoupoli	5	19	280%	0.14	0.12
39	Rouf	-	-	-	-	-
40	Sepolia	5	21	320%	0.13	0.12
41	Stadio	46	223	385%	1.83	2.09
42	Stathmos Larisis	8	58	625%	0.42	0.72
43	Thiseio	60	266	343%	3.06	3.20
44	Votanikos	19	77	305%	0.15	0.14
45	Zappeio	33	105	218%	0.96	0.72
	Total	**2,116**	**8,968**	**324%**	-	-

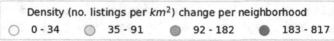

Density (no. listings per km^2) change per neighborhood

◯ 0 - 34   ◔ 35 - 91   ● 92 - 182   ● 183 - 817

Fig. 3. Density (number of listings per km^2) change across Athens' neighborhoods between 2015 and 2018.

most noteworthy in terms of Airbnb activity at a global scale, listings are concentrated in the areas of the Emporiko Trigono-Plaka, Thiseio, Kerameikos and Mouseio-Exarcheia-Neapoli.

Airbnb follows a multifactorial pattern of expansion; some areas appear exceptionally lucrative to visitors due to their vicinity to important landmarks, others for their central location, being at a walking distance from most entertainment and cultural spots and some for their convenient position within public transport networks. Koukaki-Makrygianni and Thiseio reflect the first case, exhibiting the biggest densities and concentrations (LQs) during the research period, as most of the apartments listed offer a direct view on the Acropolis, with the neighborhood being in close distance to the Museums of Acropolis and of Modern Art. Emporiko Trigono-Plaka embodies the second case; a visitor choosing a place there is within the most vibrant part of the city. On the other hand, neighborhoods like Pangrati represent a convenient option, being close to the subway and boasting its own local mix of restaurants and bars, due to gentrifying processes in the recent years.

Percentage change in mean price (in €) per month, m^2 and neighborhood for LTRs

○ 11% - 19%   ○ 20% - 24%   ● 25% - 31%   ● 32% - 59%

Fig. 4. Percentage change in the mean price (in €) per month and m^2 for LTRs across Athens' neighborhoods between 2016 and 2018

Airbnb's expansion is also asynchronous; traditionally dynamic areas in the STRs market, such as Emporiko Trigono-Plaka mentioned above, show stagnation signs, with steady rates of density and concentration. The market appears to be expanding outwards, as [14] noted for Barcelona as well, with underexploited central and western zones presenting noteworthy changes. The areas around Agios konstandinos-Plateia Vathis and Plateia Attikis show off their dynamism, experiencing sharp increases in STR volume, even if they do not constitute the safest parts of Athens.

In general, online P2P accommodation platforms have unlocked an array of cheaper choices in comparison to the price range in the regular hospitality industry for tourists and visitors alike, accommodating a more authentic experience that simulates a local way of living. Tourism boom in many geographical contexts can be directly attributed to the emergence of such platforms [14], because, apart from more affordable choices, they offer an unmatched convenience of booking a room or a house and directly check a wider spectrum of prices and choices. Such choices can be divided into two categories: the cheap and the vibrant, "real-feel" neighborhoods. Plateia Attikis is a peripheral, not expensive neighborhood, with a notably high concentration of Airbnb activity, and the 542% increase in platform entries within the last 3 years is surely eye-catching. The area even though is one of the cheapest options, is close to public transit networks (Attikis Station). Exarcheia, on the other hand, is a neighborhood that attracts an alternative crowd of urban dwellers and the same has started being the case with tourists from abroad. Besides a diverse and vibrant downtown neighborhood, Exarcheia will be part of a forthcoming subway line, drawing the attention of international capital from China, Russia and Israel, which is invested in "ghost hotels" [16]. Such investments can be seen as a logical market response within a context of rampant expanse, with investors and homeowners exploring their options even in areas that, albeit central, had not shown signs of increased activity until recently. Such areas represent a promise of higher yields; leaving the operation of unsafe, informal hotels - hidden as mere listings - aside, the above designate a moving away of Airbnb from the "casual entrepreneurship" of its first years and a formalization of its activities, as the very recent acquisition of HotelTonight by Airbnb has shown.

Lastly, the platform's expansion has been found to be relevant with significant rent hikes, turning housing in Athens less affordable. This is particularly evident in the areas mentioned above for their high Airbnb listings' densities and LQs: Koukaki-Makrygianni, Pangrati and Mouseio-Exarcheia-Neapoli. There - and especially in the first two - the increments are almost 50% within a 3-year span (Fig. 4). More specifically, it has been observed in the data that the said hike in LTR prices is highly correlated to the increased Airbnb activity over the studied period, as measured by three distinct *correlation coefficients*; the *Pearson's* r (0.76), the *Spearman's* ρ (0.74) and the *Kendall's* τ (0.67).

Overall, the rental market in Athens shows worrying signs of inflation. This reality is attributed to two main reasons; the available housing stock for renting has significantly shrunk and the LTRs receive heavy pressure from the STRs, as the conversion of rented apartments to Airbnb listings constitute an attractive choice for landlords. Furthermore, Airbnb in particular, has been identified in numerous reports and surveys as a crucial factor of reversing the negative climate of the whole Greek real estate market after 2017. At that point, the rental market stopped shrinking and started exhibiting signs of expansion, which are expected to intensify [1,2]. However, we should not attribute such rent increases solely to the negative externalities of the STRs market. We must identify, for the context of Athens, and the "positive cycle" as well [8]; the necessary renovations done to the existing housing stock, in order to be more attractive for the Airbnb users and the emerging array of local businesses that are positively affected by the increased pedestrian traffic (grocery stores, cafes - mainly those offering breakfast - services directed to urban tourists - such as luggage storage places) lead to an overall upgrading of the economic base and physical environment of these areas and to higher rents.

5   Conclusions

In this work, a preliminary study of the effect of STRs and more specifically those originating from the Airbnb P2P online platform, has been attempted. The increase in the number of listings within the City of Athens and its neighborhoods has been evaluated both quantitatively and qualitatively over a period spanning three years, during which the capital of Greece showed signs of reverting recession and growth, with respect to the real estate market. Emphasis has been placed on the spatial characteristics of the STR phenomenon, in terms of neighborhood density and LQ, with the findings being on a par with similar research studying the dynamics of the city. Additionally, an initial evaluation of the linkages between the spatial characteristics of Airbnb listings and shifts in the housing market has been affirmed, with the observed LTR hikes exhibiting a highly positive correlation with Airbnb expansion, as measured by three distinct correlation coefficients.

The obtained results are very informative and call for a more in-depth analysis of STR development in other dimensions as well. One such direction worth exploring is the fluctuation in STR prices in a temporal (e.g. time of the year) as well as a spatial context. The aforementioned analysis, could be further enhanced through the inclusion of more parameters (like house size, facilities, etc) that would most likely lead to the discovery of very interesting underlying characteristics.

Acknowledgments. This research work has been supported by the General Secretariat for Research and Technology (GSRT) of the Ministry of Education of the Hellenic Republic, under T1EDK-03470.

References

1. Panhellenic survey for property rentals in 2018 (in Greek). Technical report, RE/MAX, September 2018. https://www.remax.gr/news/485
2. Antonakakis, I., Liapikos, I.: Property market annual report 2017 Greece. Technical report, MRICS, March 2018. https://gr.eurobankpropertyservices.net/-/media/eps/reports/annual-real-estate-report_2017.pdf
3. Barron, K., Kung, E., Proserpio, D.: The sharing economy and housing affordability: evidence from airbnb. In: Proceedings of the 2018 ACM Conference on Economics and Computation, EC 2018, p. 5. ACM, New York (2018). https://doi.org/10.1145/3219166.3219180
4. Coles, P.A., Egesdal, M., Ellen, I., Li, X., Sundararajan, A.: Airbnb usage across New York City neighborhoods: geographic patterns and regulatory implications. SSRN Electron. J. (2017). https://doi.org/10.2139/ssrn.3048397
5. Crommelin, L., Troy, L., Martin, C., Pettit, C.: Is airbnb a sharing economy superstar? Evidence from five global cities. Urban Policy Res. **36**(4), 429–444 (2018). https://doi.org/10.1080/08111146.2018.1460722

6. Gutiérrez, J., García-Palomares, J.C., Romanillos, G., Salas-Olmedo, M.H.: The eruption of airbnb in tourist cities: comparing spatial patterns of hotels and peer-to-peer accommodation in Barcelona. Tourism Manag. **62**, 278–291 (2017). https://doi.org/10.1016/j.tourman.2017.05.003. http://www.sciencedirect.com/science/article/pii/S0261517717301036

7. Heo, C.Y., Blengini, I.: A macroeconomic perspective on airbnb's global presence. Int. J. Hospitality Manag. **78**, 47–49 (2019). https://doi.org/10.1016/j.ijhm.2018.11.013. http://www.sciencedirect.com/science/article/pii/S0278431918304882

8. Horn, K., Merante, M.: Is home sharing driving up rents? Evidence from airbnb in Boston. J. Hous. Econ. **38**, 14–24 (2017). https://doi.org/10.1016/j.jhe.2017.08.002. http://www.sciencedirect.com/science/article/pii/S1051137717300876

9. Ke, Q.: Sharing means renting? An entire-marketplace analysis of airbnb. In: Proceedings of the 2017 ACM on Web Science Conference, WebSci 2017, pp. 131–139. ACM, New York (2017). https://doi.org/10.1145/3091478.3091504

10. Lane, J., Woodworth, R.M.: The sharing economy checks. In: An Analysis of Airbnb in the United States. Technical report, CBRE Hotels' Americas Research (2016)

11. Lee, D.: How airbnb short-term rentals exacerbate Los Angeles's affordable housing crisis: analysis and policy recommendations. Harv. L. Pol'y Rev. **10**, 229 (2016)

12. Rousanoglou, N.: Foreign investor invation in downtown Athens. Kathimerini Newspaper, September 2018. (in Greek). http://www.kathimerini.gr/986258/article/oikonomia/real-estate/eisvolh-ependytwn-sto-kentro-ths-a8hnas

13. Sans, A.A., Quaglieri, A.: Unravelling airbnb: urban perspectives from Barcelona. In: Reinventing the Local in Tourism: Producing, Consuming and Negotiating Place, vol. 73, p. 209. Channel View Publications (2016)

14. Segú, M.: Do short-term rent platforms affect rents? Evidence from airbnb in Barcelona. MPRA Paper 84369, University Library of Munich, Germany, February 2018. https://ideas.repec.org/p/pra/mprapa/84369.html

15. Sheppard, S., Udell, A.: Do airbnb properties affect house prices? Department of economics working papers 2016-03, Department of Economics, Williams College (2016). https://EconPapers.repec.org/RePEc:wil:wileco:2016-03

16. Sideris, S.: Mapping the dominance of airbnb in Athens: the world's most popular short-term rental platform and how it is affecting our neighborhoods explained visually, August 2018. https://medium.com/athenslivegr/mapping-the-dominance-of-airbnb-in-athens-4cb9e0657e80

17. Slee, T.: What's Yours Is Mine: Against the Sharing Economy. OR Books, New York City (2015). http://www.jstor.org/stable/j.ctt1bkm65n

18. Wachsmuth, D., Chaney, D., Kerrigan, D., Shillolo, A., Basalaev-Binder, R.: The high cost of short-term rentals in New York City. Technical report, Urban Politics and Governance Research Group, School of Urban Planning, McGill University (2018)

A Brief Overview of Dead-Zone Pattern Matching Algorithms

Miznah Alshammary[1]([⊠]), Mai Alzamel[1]([⊠]), Costas Iliopoulos[1]([⊠]),
Richard E. Watson[2]([⊠]), and Bruce W. Watson[2]([⊠])

[1] Department of Informatics, King's College London, London, UK
{miznah.alshammary,mai.alzamel,c.iliopoulos}@kcl.ac.uk
[2] Department of Information Science, Stellenbosch University,
Stellenbosch, South Africa
bruce@fastar.org

Abstract. Within the last decades, the *dead-zone* algorithms have emerged as being highly performant on certain types of data. Such algorithms solve the keyword exact matching problem over strings, though extensions to trees and two-dimensional data have also been devised. In this short paper, we give an overview of such algorithms.

1 Introduction and Related Work

In this paper, we present a new family of algorithms solving the single keyword string pattern matching problem. This particular pattern matching problem can be described as follows: given an input string S and a keyword p, find all occurrences of p as a continuous substring of S. The field of string pattern matching is generally well-studied (some thought it to be exhausted by the end of the 1970's), however, it continues to yield new and exciting algorithms, as was seen in annual conferences such as *Combinatorial Pattern Matching* and *Stringology*. In [8] (a dissertation by the last author of this paper), a taxonomy of existing algorithms was presented, along with a number of new algorithms. Any given algorithm may have more than one possible derivation, leading to different classifications of the algorithm in a taxonomy[1]. Many of the new derivations can prove to be more than just an educational curiosity, possibly leading to interesting new families of algorithms. This paper presents one such family, with some new algorithms and also some alternative derivations of existing ones. The algorithms presented in this paper have been extended to handle some more complex pattern matching problems, including multiple keyword pattern matching, regular pattern matching and multi-dimensional pattern matching. For some recent examples of this, see [9–12].

---

[1] This is precisely what happened with the Boyer-Moore type algorithms as presented in the dissertation [8].

© IFIP International Federation for Information Processing 2019
Published by Springer Nature Switzerland AG 2019
J. MacIntyre et al. (Eds.): AIAI 2019 Workshops, IFIP AICT 560, pp. 208–218, 2019.
https://doi.org/10.1007/978-3-030-19909-8_18

2   Mathematical Preliminaries

While most of the mathematical notation and definitions used in this paper are is described in detail in [4], here we present some more specific notations. Indexing within strings begins at 0, as in the C and C++ programming languages. We use ranges of integers throughout the paper which are defined by (for integers i and j):

$$[i,j) = \{\, k \mid i \leq k < j \,\}$$
$$(i,j] = \{\, k \mid i < k \leq j \,\}$$
$$[i,j] = [i,j) \cup (i,j]$$
$$(i,j) = [i,j) \cap (i,j]$$

In addition, we define a *permutation* of a set of integers to be a bijective mapping of those integers onto themselves.

3   The Problem and a First Algorithm

Before giving the problem specification (in the form of a postcondition to the algorithms), we define a predicate which will make the postcondition and algorithms easier to read. Keyword p (with the restriction that $p \neq \varepsilon$, where ε is the empty string) is said to *match* at position j in input string S if $p = S_{j\cdots j+|p|-1}$; this is restated in the following predicate:

Definition 3.1 (Predicate *Matches*): We define predicate *Matches* as

$$Matches(S,p,j) \equiv (p = S_{j\cdots j+|p|-1})$$

□

The pattern matching problem requires us to compute the set of all matches of keyword p in input string S. We register the matches as the set O (for "output") of all indices j (in S) such that $Matches(S,p,j)$ holds.

Definition 3.2 (Single keyword pattern matching problem): Given a common alphabet V, input string S, and pattern keyword p, the problem is defined using postcondition PM:

$$O = \{\, j \mid j \in [0,|S|) \wedge Matches(S,p,j) \,\}$$

Note that this postcondition implicitly depends upon S and p, even though we do not make that explicit.   □

We can now present a nondeterministic algorithm which keeps track of the set of possible indices (in S) at which a match might still be found (indices at which we have not yet checked for a match). This set is known as the *live zone*. Those indices not in the live zone are said to be in the *dead zone*. This give us our first algorithm (presented in Dijkstra's pseudocode [1,3,6]).

Algorithm 3.3:

$live, dead := [0, |S|), \emptyset;$
$O := \emptyset;$
{ invariant: $live \cup dead = [0, |S|) \wedge live \cap dead = \emptyset$
$\qquad \wedge O = \{ j \mid j \in dead \wedge Matches(S, p, j) \} \}$
do $live \neq \emptyset \rightarrow$
$\quad$ **let** $j : j \in live;$
$\quad live, dead := live \setminus \{j\}, dead \cup \{j\};$
$\quad$ **if** $Matches(S, p, j) \rightarrow O := O \cup \{j\}$
$\quad \| \quad \neg Matches(S, p, j) \rightarrow$ **skip**
$\quad$ **fi**
od{ postcondition: *PM* }

$\square$

The invariant specifies that *live* and *dead* are disjoint and account for all indices in S; additionally, any match at an element of *dead* has already been registered. Thanks to this relationship between *live* and *dead*, we could have written the repetition condition $live \neq \emptyset$ as $dead \neq [0, |S|)$, and the j selection condition $j \in live$ as $j \notin dead$. It should be easy to see that the invariant and the termination condition of the repetition implies the postcondition—yielding a correct algorithm. Note that this algorithm is highly over-specified by keeping both variables *live* and *dead* to represent the live and dead zones, respectively. For efficiency, only one of these sets would normally be kept, as is seen in [9–11].

Some of the rightmost positions in S cannot possibly accommodate matches—no match can be found at any point $j \in [|S| - |p| + 1, |S|)$ since $|S_{j \cdots |S|-1}| \leq |S_{|S|-|p|+1 \cdots |S|-1}| < |p|$ (the match attempt begins too close to the end of S for p to fit). For this reason, we safely change the initializations of *live* and *dead* to

$$live, dead := [0, |S| - |p|], [|S| - |p| + 1, |S|)$$

In the next section, give a more deterministic (more realistically implemented) version of the last algorithm.

4 A More Deterministic Algorithm

In the last algorithm, our comparison of p with $S_{j \cdots j+|p|-1}$ is embedded within the evaluation of predicate *Matches*. In this section, we make this comparison explicit. We begin by noting that $p = S_{j \cdots j+|p|-1}$ is equivalent to comparing the individual symbols p_k of p with the corresponding symbols S_{j+k} of S (for $k \in [0, |p|)$). In fact, we can consider the symbols in any order whatsoever. To determine the order in which they will be considered, we introduce *match orders*:

Definition 4.1 (Match order): We define a match order *mo* as a permutation on $[0, |p|)$. $\qquad\qquad\qquad\qquad\qquad\qquad\qquad\qquad\qquad\qquad\qquad\qquad\qquad \square$

Using *mo*, we can restate our match predicate.

Property 4.2 (Predicate *Matches*): Predicate *Matches* is restated as

$$Matches(S, p, j) \equiv (\forall\, i : i \in [0, |p|) : p_{mo(i)} = S_{j+mo(i)})$$

□

This rendition of the predicate will be evaluated by a repetition which uses a new integer variable i to step from 0 to $|p| - 1$, comparing $p_{mo(i)}$ to the corresponding symbol of S. As i increases, the repetition has the following invariant:

$$(\forall\, k : k \in [0, i) : p_{mo(k)} = S_{j+mo(k)})$$

and terminates as early as possible.

In the following algorithm, we use the match order mo, the new repetition and our previous optimization to the initializations of *dead* and *live*.

Algorithm 4.3:

```
live, dead := [0, |S| − |p|], [|S| − |p| + 1, |S|);
O := ∅;
{ invariant: live ∪ dead = [0, |S|) ∧ live ∩ dead = ∅
            ∧ O = { j | j ∈ dead ∧ Matches(S, p, j) } }
do live ≠ ∅ →
   let j : j ∈ live;
   live, dead := live \ {j}, dead ∪ {j};
   i := 0;
   { invariant: (∀ k : k ∈ [0, i) : p_mo(k) = S_j+mo(k)) }
   do i < |p| cand p_mo(i) = S_j+mo(i) →
      i := i + 1
   od;
   { postcondition: (∀ k : k ∈ [0, i) : p_mo(k) = S_j+mo(k))
                   ∧ (i < |p| ⇒ p_mo(i) ≠ S_j+mo(i)) }
   if i = |p| → O := O ∪ {j}
   ‖ i < |p| → skip
   fi
od{ postcondition: PM }
```

□

The operator P **cand** Q appears in the guard of the inner loop of the above algorithm. This operator is similar to conjunction $P \wedge Q$ except that if the first conjunct evaluates to *false* then the second conjunct is not even evaluated. This proves to be a useful property in cases such as the loop guard since, if the first conjunct $(i < |p|)$ is *false* (hence $i >= |p|$, and indeed $i = |p|$), then the term $mo(i)$ appearing in the second conjunct is not even defined. Note that the implication within the second conjunct of the loop postcondition is derived from the loop guard, forcing the implication operator to be conditional as well (that is, if $i < |p|$ is determined to be *false*, then $p_{mo(i)} \neq S_{j+mo(i)}$ is not even evaluated).

5   Reusing Match Information

On each iteration of the outer repetition, index j is chosen and eliminated from the live zone in the statement:

$$live, dead := live \setminus \{j\}, dead \cup \{j\}$$

The performance of the algorithm can be improved if we remove more than just j in some of the iterations. To do this, we can use some of the match information, such as i, which indicates how far through mo the match attempt proceeded before finding a mismatching symbol. The information most readily available is the postcondition of the inner repetition:

$$(\forall \ k : k \in [0, i) : p_{mo(k)} = S_{j+mo(k)}) \wedge (i < |p| \Rightarrow p_{mo(i)} \neq S_{j+mo(i)})$$

We denote this postcondition by $Result(S, p, i, j)$. Since this postcondition holds, we may be able to deduce that certain indices in S cannot possibly be the site of a match. It is such indices which we could also remove from the live zone. They are formally characterized as:

$$\{ x \mid x \in [0, |S|) \wedge (Result(S, p, i, j) \Rightarrow \neg Matches(S, p, x)) \} \tag{1}$$

Determining this set at pattern matching time is inefficient and not easily implemented. We wish to derive a safe approximation of this set which can be precomputed, tabulated and indexed (at pattern matching time) by i. In order to precompute it, the approximation must be independent of j and S. We wish to find a strengthening of the range predicate since this will allow us to still remove a safe set of elements from set $live$, thanks to the property that, if $P \Rightarrow Q$ (P is a *strengthening* of Q, and Q is a *weakening* of P), then

$$\{ x \mid P(x) \} \subseteq \{ x \mid Q(x) \}$$

As a first step towards this approximation, we can normalize the ideal set (Eq. (1) above), by subtracting j from each element. The resulting characterization will be more useful for precomputation reasons:

$$\{ x \mid x \in [-j, |S| - j) \wedge (Result(S, p, i, j) \Rightarrow \neg Matches(S, p, j + x)) \}$$

Note that this still depends upon j, however, it will make some of the derivation steps shown shortly in Sect. 5.1 easier. Because those steps are rather detailed, they are presented in isolation. Condensed, the derivation appears as:

$$(Result(S, p, i, j) \Rightarrow \neg Matches(S, p, j + x))$$
$$\Leftarrow \qquad \{ \text{Section 5.1} \}$$
$$\neg((\forall \ k : k \in [0, i) \wedge mo(k) \in [x, |p| + x) : p_{mo(k)} = p_{mo(k)-x})$$
$$\wedge (i < |p| \wedge mo(i) \in [x, |p| + x) \Rightarrow p_{mo(i)} \neq p_{mo(i)-x}))$$
$$\equiv \qquad \{ \text{De Morgan's Law} \}$$

$$\neg(\forall\, k : k \in [0, i) \wedge mo(k) \in [x, |p| + x) : p_{mo(k)} = p_{mo(k)-x})$$
$$\vee\, \neg(i < |p| \wedge mo(i) \in [x, |p| + x) \Rightarrow p_{mo(i)} \neq p_{mo(i)-x})$$

$\equiv$ { De Morgan's Law on the universal quantification }

$$(\exists\, k : k \in [0, i) \wedge mo(k) \in [x, |p| + x) : p_{mo(k)} \neq p_{mo(k)-x})$$
$$\vee\, \neg(i < |p| \wedge mo(i) \in [x, |p| + x) \Rightarrow p_{mo(i)} \neq p_{mo(i)-x})$$

$\equiv$ { De Morgan's Law on the implication, which is conditional }

$$(\exists\, k : k \in [0, i) \wedge mo(k) \in [x, |p| + x) : p_{mo(k)} \neq p_{mo(k)-x})$$
$$\vee\, (i \geq |p| \vee mo(i) \notin [x, |p| + x)\ \mathbf{cor}\ p_{mo(i)} \neq p_{mo(i)-x})$$

$\equiv$ { define the predicate $Approximation(p, i, x)$ }

$Approximation(p, i, x)$

Note that we define the predicate $Approximation(p, i, x)$ which depends only on p and i and hence can be precomputed and tabulated. It should be mentioned that this is one of several possible useful strengthenings which could be derived. We could even have used the strongest predicate, *false*, instead of $Approximation(p, i, x)$. This would yield the empty set, $\varnothing$, to be removed from *live* in addition to j (as in the previous algorithm).

We can derive a smaller range predicate of x for which we have to check if $Approximation(p, i, x)$ holds. Notice that choosing and x such that $[x, |p| + x) \cap [0, |p|) = \varnothing$ has two important consequences:

- The range of the quantification in first conjunct of $Approximation(p, i, x)$ is empty (hence this conjunct is *true*, by the definition of universal quantification with an empty range).
- The range condition of the second conjunct (the 'implicator') is *false*—hence the whole of the second conjunct is *true* since *false* $\Rightarrow P$ for all predicates P.

With this choice of x, we see that predicate $Approximation(p, i, x)$ always evaluates to *false*, in which case we need not even consider values of x such that $[x, |p| + x) \cap [0, |p|) = \varnothing$. As a result, we characterize those x for which $[x, |p| + x) \cap [0, |p|) \neq \varnothing$ as follows:

$$[x, |p| + x) \cap [0, |p|) \neq \varnothing$$

$\equiv$ { for integers u, v, y, z: $[u, v) \cap [y, z) = \varnothing \equiv (v - 1 < y \vee u > z - 1)$ }

$$\neg(|p| + x - 1 < 0 \vee x > |p| - 1)$$

$\equiv$ { arithmetic }

$$\neg(x < 1 - |p| \vee x > |p| - 1)$$

$\equiv$ { De Morgan's Law }

$$x \geq 1 - |p| \wedge x \leq |p| - 1$$

$\equiv$ { definition of ranges }

$$x \in [1 - |p|, |p| - 1]$$

Clearly we can use the restriction $x \in [1 - |p|, |p| - 1]$. Intuitively (and information theoretically), we know that there must be such a range restriction since we can not possibly know from a current match attempt whether or not we will find a match of p in S more than $|p|$ symbols away.

Finally we have the following algorithm (in which we have added the additional update of *live* and *dead* below the inner repetition). Note that we introduce the set *nogood* to accumulate the indices for which $Approximation(p, i, x)$ holds. Also note that we renormalize the set *nogood* by adding j to each of its members and ensuring that it is within the valid range of indices, $[0, |S|)$.

Algorithm 5.1:

$live, dead := [0, |S| - |p|], [|S| - |p| + 1, |S|);$
$O := \emptyset;$
$\{$ invariant: $live \cup dead = [0, |S|) \wedge live \cap dead = \emptyset$
          $\wedge\ O = \{\, l \mid l \in dead \wedge Matches(S, p, l) \,\} \}$
do $live \neq \emptyset \rightarrow$
   let $j : j \in live;$
   $live, dead := live \setminus \{j\}, dead \cup \{j\};$
   $i := 0;$
   $\{$ invariant: $(\forall\, k : k \in [0, i) : p_{mo(k)} = S_{j+mo(k)}) \}$
   do $i < |p|$ **cand** $p_{mo(i)} = S_{j+mo(i)} \rightarrow$
        $i := i + 1$
   od;
   $\{$ postcondition: $Result(S, p, i, j) \}$
   if $i = |p| \rightarrow O := O \cup \{j\}$
   $[\!] \ i < |p| \rightarrow$ **skip**
   fi;
   $nogood := (\{\, x \mid x \in [1 - |p|, |p| - 1] \wedge Approximation(p, i, x) \,\} + j) \cap [0, |S|);$
   $live := live \setminus nogood;$
   $dead := dead \cup nogood$
od$\{$ postcondition: $PM \}$

□

5.1   Range Predicate Strengthening

Here, we present the derivation of a strengthening of the range predicate

$$Result(S, p, i, j) \Rightarrow \neg Matches(S, p, j + x)$$

Being more comfortable with weakening steps, we begin with the negation of part of the above range predicate, and proceed by weakening:

   $\neg(Result(S, p, i, j) \Rightarrow \neg Matches(S, p, j + x))$
$\equiv$ $\{$ definition of $\Rightarrow \}$
   $\neg(\neg Result(S, p, i, j) \vee \neg Matches(S, p, j + x))$
$\equiv$ $\{$ De Morgan's Law $\}$
   $Result(S, p, i, j) \wedge Matches(S, p, j + x))$
$\equiv$ $\{$ definition of $Result$ and $Matches \}$
   $(\forall\, k : k \in [0, i) : p_{mo(k)} = S_{j+mo(k)}) \wedge (i < |p| \Rightarrow p_{mo(i)} \neq S_{j+mo(i)})$
   $\wedge\ (\forall\, k : k \in [0, |p|) : p_{mo(k)} = S_{mo(k)+j+x})$
$\equiv$ $\{$ change range predicate in second quantification and definition of $mo \}$
   $(\forall\, k : k \in [0, i) : p_{mo(k)} = S_{j+mo(k)}) \wedge (i < |p| \Rightarrow p_{mo(i)} \neq S_{j+mo(i)})$

$\land \ (\forall \ k : mo(k) \in [0, |p|) : p_{mo(k)} = S_{mo(k)+j+x})$

$\Rightarrow$ { change dummy $(mo(k') = mo(k) + x)$, restrict range }

$(\forall \ k : k \in [0, i) : p_{mo(k)} = S_{j+mo(k)}) \land (i < |p| \Rightarrow p_{mo(i)} \neq S_{j+mo(i)})$

$\land \ (\forall \ k' : mo(k') - x \in [0, |p|) : p_{mo(k')-x} = S_{mo(k')+j})$

$\equiv$ { simplify range predicate of second quantification }

$(\forall \ k : k \in [0, i) : p_{mo(k)} = S_{j+mo(k)}) \land (i < |p| \Rightarrow p_{mo(i)} \neq S_{j+mo(i)})$

$\land \ (\forall \ k' : mo(k') \in [x, |p| + x) : p_{mo(k')-x} = S_{mo(k')+j})$

$\Rightarrow$ { one-point rule: second conjunct and second quantification }

$(\forall \ k : k \in [0, i) : p_{mo(k)} = S_{j+mo(k)})$

$\land \ ((i < |p| \land mo(i) \in [x, |p| + x)) \Rightarrow p_{mo(i)} \neq p_{mo(i)-x})$

$\land \ (\forall \ k' : mo(k') \in [x, |p| + x) : p_{mo(k')-x} = S_{mo(k')+j})$

$\Rightarrow$ { combine two quantifications and remove dependency on S and transitivity of $=$ }

$(\forall \ k : k \in [0, i) \land mo(k) \in [x, |p| + x) : p_{mo(k)} = p_{mo(k)-x})$

$\land \ ((i < |p| \land mo(i) \in [x, |p| + x)) \Rightarrow p_{mo(i)} \neq p_{mo(i)-x})$

6   Choosing j from the Live Zone

In this section, we discuss strategies for choosing the index j (from the live zone) at which to make a match attempt. In the last algorithm, the way in which j is chosen from set *live* is nondeterministic. This leads to the situation that *live* (and, of course, *dead*) is fragmented, meaning that an implementation of the algorithm would have to maintain a set of indices for live. If we can ensure that *live* is contiguous, then an implementation would only need to keep track of the (one or two) boundary points between *live* and *dead*. There are several ways to do this, and we discuss some of them in the following subsections section. Each of these represents a particular *policy* to be used in the selection of j.

6.1   Minimal Element—Towards the Classical Boyer-Moore Algorithm

We could use the policy of always taking the minimal element of *live*. In that case, we can make some simplifications to the algorithm (which, in turn, improve the algorithm's performance):

- We need only store the minimal element of *live*, instead of sets *live* and *dead*. We use $\widetilde{live}$ to denote the minimal element.
- The dead zone update could be modified as follows: we will have considered all of the positions to the left of j and so we can ignore the negative elements of the update set:

$$\{ x \mid x \in [1 - |p|, 0) \land Approximation(p, i, x) \}$$

Indeed, we can just add the maximal element (which is still contiguously in the update set and greater than j) of the update set to $\widehat{live}$ for the new version of our new update of *live* and *dead*.

Depending upon the choice of weakening, and the choice of match order, the above policy yields variants of the classical Boyer-Moore algorithm (see [2,7,8]):

Algorithm 6.1:

$\widehat{live} := 0;$
$O := \emptyset;$
do $\widehat{live} \leq |S| - |p| \rightarrow$
   $j := \widehat{live};$
   $\widehat{live} := \widehat{live} + 1;$
   $i := 0;$
   $\{$ invariant: $(\forall\, k : k \in [0, i) : p_{mo(k)} = S_{j+mo(k)})\, \}$
   do $i < |p|$ **cand** $p_{mo(i)} = S_{j+mo(i)} \rightarrow$
     $i := i + 1$
   od;
   $\{$ postcondition: $Result(S, p, i, j)\, \}$
   if $i = |p| \rightarrow O := O \cup \{j\}$
   $\|\ i < |p| \rightarrow$ **skip**
   fi;
   $\widehat{nogood} := (\textbf{MAX}\ x : x \in [0, |p| - 1] \wedge (\forall\, h : h \in [0, x] : Approximation(p, i, x)) : x);$
   $\widehat{live} := \widehat{live} + \widehat{nogood}$
od$\{$ postcondition: $PM\, \}$

$\square$

6.2   Recursion

We could also devise a recursive version of the algorithm as a procedure. This procedure receives a contiguous range of live indices (*live*)—initially consisting of the range $[0, |S| - |p|]$.

If the set it receives is empty, the procedure immediately returns. If the set is non-empty, j is chosen so that the resulting dead zone would appear reasonably close to the middle of the current live zone[2]. This ensures that we discard as little information as possible from the *nogood* index set. After the match attempt, the procedure recursively invokes itself twice, with the two reduced live zones on either side of the new dead zone. This yields the following procedure:

---

[2] The algorithm given in this section makes a simple approximation by taking the middle of the live zone it receives, and subtracting $\lfloor |p|/2 \rfloor$.

Algorithm 6.2:

$\quad$ **proc** $mat(S, p, live, dead) \rightarrow$
$\qquad$ { $live$ is contiguous }
$\qquad$ **if** $live = \varnothing \rightarrow$ **skip**
$\qquad$ ‖ $\quad live \neq \varnothing \rightarrow$
$\qquad$ $live\_low := (\textbf{MIN}\ k : k \in live : k);$
$\qquad$ $live\_high := (\textbf{MAX}\ k : k \in live : k);$
$\qquad$ $j := \lfloor (live\_low + live\_high - |p|)/2 \rfloor;$
$\qquad$ $i := 0;$
$\qquad$ { invariant: $(\forall\ k : k \in [0, i) : p_{mo(k)} = S_{j+mo(k)})$ }
$\qquad$ **do** $i < |p|$ **cand** $p_{mo(i)} = S_{j+mo(i)} \rightarrow$
$\qquad\qquad$ $i := i + 1$
$\qquad$ **od**;
$\qquad$ { postcondition: $Result(S, p, i, j)$ }
$\qquad$ **if** $i = |p| \rightarrow O := O \cup \{j\}$
$\qquad$ ‖ $\quad i < |p| \rightarrow$ **skip**
$\qquad$ **fi**;
$\qquad$ $new\_dead := (\{\, x \mid x \in [1 - |p|, |p| - 1] \wedge Approximation(p, i, x) \,\} + j) \cap [0, |S|);$
$\qquad$ $dead := dead \cup new\_dead;$
$\qquad$ $mat(S, p, [live\_low, (\textbf{MIN}\ k : k \in new\_dead : k)), dead);$
$\qquad$ $mat(S, p, ((\textbf{MAX}\ k : k \in new\_dead : k), live\_high], dead)$
$\quad$ **fi**
$\quad$ **corp**

$\hfill \square$

This procedure is used in the algorithm:

Algorithm 6.3:

$\quad O := \varnothing;$
$\quad mat(S, p, [0, |S| - |p|], [|S| - |p| + 1, |S|))$
$\quad$ { postcondition: PM }

$\hfill \square$

Naturally, for efficiency reasons, the set *live* can be represented by its minimal and maximal elements (since it is contiguous). Note that the *dead zone* need not be contiguous. This recursive algorithm is presented in [9], and with benchmarking data in [10].

7 Conclusions

We have shown that there are still many interesting algorithms to be derived within the field of single keyword pattern matching. The correctness preserving derivation of am entirely new family of such algorithms demonstrates the use of formal methods and the use of predicates, invariants, postconditions and preconditions. It is unlikely that such a family of algorithms could have be devised without the use of formal methods.

References

1. Cohen, E.: Programming in the 1990s. Springer, New York (1990). https://doi.org/10.1007/978-1-4613-9706-9
2. Crochemore, M., Rytter, W.: Text Algorithms. Oxford University Press, Oxford (1994)
3. Dijkstra, E.W.: A Discipline of Programming. Prentice Hall, Englewood Cliffs (1976)
4. Gries, D., Schneider, F.B.: A Logical Approach to Discrete Math. Springer, New York (1993). https://doi.org/10.1007/978-1-4757-3837-7
5. Gries, D.: The Science of Programming. Springer, New York (1981). https://doi.org/10.1007/978-1-4612-5983-1
6. Kourie, D.G., Watson, B.W.: The Correctness-by-Construction Approach to Programming. Springer, New York (2012). https://doi.org/10.1007/978-3-642-27919-5
7. Hume, S.C., Sunday, D.: Fast string searching. Softw. Pract. Exp. **21**(11), 1221–1248
8. Watson, B.W.: Taxonomies and toolkits of regular language algorithms, Ph.D dissertation, Faculty of Mathematics and Computing Science, Eindhoven University of Technology, Eindhoven, The Netherlands, September 1995. ISBN 90-386-0396-7
9. Watson, B.W., Kourie, D.G., Strauss, T.: A sequential recursive implementation of dead-zone single keyword pattern matching. In: Arumugam, S., Smyth, W.F. (eds.) IWOCA 2012. LNCS, vol. 7643, pp. 236–248. Springer, Heidelberg (2012). https://doi.org/10.1007/978-3-642-35926-2_26
10. Mauch, M., Kourie, D.G., Watson, B.W., Strauss, T.: Performance assessment of dead-zone single keyword pattern matching. In: Proceedings of the South African Institute for Computer Scientists and Information Technologists Conference, pp. 59–68 (2012)
11. Watson, B.W., Cleophas, L.G., Kourie, D.G.: Using correctness-by-construction to derive dead-zone algorithms. In: Prague Stringology Conference, pp. 84–95 (2014)
12. Daykin, J.W., et al.: Three strategies for the dead-zone string matching algorithm. In: Prague Stringology Conference, p. 117 (2018)

On the Cyclic Regularities of Strings

Oluwole Ajala[1($\boxtimes$)], Miznah Alshammary[1($\boxtimes$)], Mai Alzamel[1($\boxtimes$)], Jia Gao[1($\boxtimes$)],
Costas Iliopoulos[1($\boxtimes$)], Jakub Radoszewski[2($\boxtimes$)], Wojciech Rytter[2($\boxtimes$)],
and Bruce Watson[3($\boxtimes$)]

[1] Faculty of Natural and Mathematical Sciences, King's College London,
London, UK
{oluwole.ajala,miznah.alshammary,mai.alzamel,jia.gao,
c.ilioupoulos}@kcl.ac.uk
[2] Faculty of Mathematics, Informatics and Mechanics, University of Warsaw,
Warsaw, Poland
{jrad,rytter}@mimuw.edu.pl
[3] Faculty of Informatics Science, Stellenbosch University,
Stellenbosch, South Africa
bwwatson@sun.ac.za

Abstract. Regularities in strings are often related to periods and covers, which have extensively been studied, and algorithms for their efficient computation have broad application. In this paper we concentrate on computing cyclic regularities of strings, in particular, we propose several efficient algorithms for computing: (i) cyclic periodicity; (ii) all cyclic periodicity; (iii) maximal local cyclic periodicity; (iv) cyclic covers.

Keywords: Cyclic regularities · Periods · Covers

1 Introduction and Related Work

A fundamental concept of repeating patterns or *regularities* is that of periods (also known as powers). A period of order k is defined by a concatenation of k identical blocks of symbols. The study of periods can be traced to as far back as the early 1900s with the work of [9], who researched a set of strings that do not contain any substrings that are periods. Periods in diverse forms gained prominence, when they became key structures in computational biology, where they are associated with various regulatory mechanisms and play an important role in genomic fingerprinting [6].

In regularities in strings, one of the most general notions is related to period or power, for instance, given a string x of length n, a period k of a string x is a sub string of x, if it can be decomposed into equal length blocks of symbols, such that $x = u^k u'$, where u' is a prefix of u. However, for simplicity we will discard u' and only consider u^k.

So far, regularities in strings related with periods and powers, which have been extensively studied, [3–5,8] and algorithms for their efficient computation

© IFIP International Federation for Information Processing 2019
Published by Springer Nature Switzerland AG 2019
J. MacIntyre et al. (Eds.): AIAI 2019 Workshops, IFIP AICT 560, pp. 219–224, 2019.
https://doi.org/10.1007/978-3-030-19909-8_19

220   O. Ajala et al.

have broad applications. In this paper, we study cyclic factors of strings. The motivation of cyclic factors comes from viruses. The viruses are circular strings, for example Escherichia coli (E.coli) has 154 bases and it is circular [12] (Fig. 1). Formally, the viruses break up at any point of the circle, for example, that can appear in the DNA sequence as $x_\delta \ldots x_n x_1 \ldots x_{\delta-1}$ breaking up at position δ (Fig. 2). Now, we propose several efficient algorithms for computing: (i) cyclic periodicity; (ii) all cyclic periodicity; (iii) maximal local cyclic periodicity; (iv) cyclic covers.

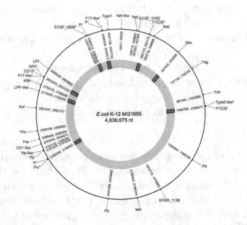

Fig. 1. The E. coli K-12 MG1655 chromosome (outer black ring) was used as a reference map to visualise the locus position of 30 chromosome-borne CU fimbrial types. Types highlighted in blue are present in E. coli K-12 MG1655, types in red are absent in this strain. Fimbrial types associated with PAIs are indicated by an asterisk. A number of PAI associated fimbrial gene clusters occupy different locus positions relative to the MG1655 genome. tRNA sites that flank CU-containing PAIs are indicated on the inner blue ring [12]. (Color figure online)

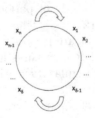

Fig. 2. Circular pattern.

2   Preliminaries

A *string* x of length $|x| = n$ over an alphabet Σ of size σ can be denoted as $x[1..n] = x[1]x[2]\ldots x[i]\ldots x[n]$, where $1 \le i \le n$ and the *i-th letter* of x is denoted by $x[i] \in \Sigma$. The empty string ϵ is the string of length 0. The string x^R is the *reverse* of string x. And $x[i..j]$, $1 \le i \le j \le n$, denotes the contiguous substring (or factor) of letters, such as $x[i]x[i+1]x[i+2]\ldots x[j]$. A substring $x[i..j]$ is a suffix of x, if $j = n$ and a substring $x[i..j]$ is a prefix of x, if $i = 1$. Given a cyclic factor u of length k, $1 \le k \le n$, we denote by $c(u)$, for instance, $u = ababc$, $c(u)$ is one of the following rotations: $ababc$, $babca$, $abcab$, $bcaba$, $cabab$. Moreover, we say $u = u_1u_2\ldots u_n$, $c_\delta(u) = u_\delta \ldots u_n u_1 \ldots u_{\delta-1}$.

In this paper, suffix trees are used extensively as computation tools. For a general introduction to suffix trees, see [2,7,10,11].

K-CYCLIC PERIOD
Input: Given a string x of length n, and an integer $k < n$, compute k-cyclic-period ℓ of x, where $x = u_1u_2\ldots u_\ell$, $u_i = c(u_j)$, $|u_i| = |u_j| = k$, $\forall\ i,j$, $1 \le i \le \ell$, $1 \le j \le \ell$, and $k \times \ell = n$.
Output: k-cyclic-period ℓ of x

Example 1. Consider a string $x = aaabaabaabaabaaa =: u_1u_2u_3u_4$, where $u_1 = aaab$, $u_2 = aaba$, $u_3 = abaa$, $u_4 = baaa$ and $k = 4$, $\ell = 4$. Therefore x has a period of length ℓ.

Definition 1. *A cyclic periodic array A of a string x of length n is defined to be as follows: $A[i] := \ell$, $1 \le i \le n$, if and only if $x[1..i]$ has cyclic periodicity ℓ by a string u and there no u', with $|u'| \le |u|$ that is a cyclic period of $x[1..i]$.*

Example 2. Consider a string $x = aababa$ of length 6, a cyclic periodic array A as follows:

$$x[1] = a \implies A[1] := 1 \qquad\qquad x[1..4] = aaba \implies A[4] := 1$$
$$x[1..2] = a\,a \implies A[2] := 2 \qquad\quad x[1..5] = aabab \implies A[5] := 1$$
$$x[1..3] = aab \implies A[3] := 1 \qquad\quad x[1..6] = aab\,aba \implies A[6] := 2$$

Definition 2. *We define maximal local k-cyclic periodicity of a string x, if a substring y is cyclic periodic and y is not a substring of another cyclic periodic strings.*

Example 3. Consider a string $x = aaaababaaab$, $\Sigma = \{a,b\}$, and a substring $y = aabababaa$ is 3-cyclic periodic and substring $y\alpha = aabababaaa$, $\alpha \in \Sigma$, is not cyclic periodic, and substring $\beta y = aaabababaa$, $\beta \in \Sigma$ is not cyclic periodic. Therefore, the substring $y = aabababaa$ is maximal local 3-cyclic periodic in string $x = aaaabababaaa$.

Definition 3. *We say that a string x of length n is cyclic-coverable by a string u of length k', if and only if, for every position i of x, the following condition holds $x[\beta..\gamma] = c(u)$, $1 \le \beta \le i \le \gamma \le n$.*

Example 4. Consider a string $x = aababaa = u_1 u_2$, $u_1 = aaba$, $u_2 = abaa$, $k' = 4$, $\gamma = 2$, is cyclic coverable by a string u, for every position i of x, $x[1..4] = x[4..7] = c(u)$.

Definition 4. *Compute all cyclic covers of a given string x, that is for all possible length cyclic covers.*

Example 5. Consider a string $x = ababbaba$, then ab, $abab$, $ababb$, $ababbab$ are cyclic covers of x.

3 Computing k-cyclic Periodicity

Theorem 1. *Given a string x of length n and an integer k, $1 \leq k \leq n$, test whether it is k-cyclic periodic; this can be determined in $\mathcal{O}(n/k)$ time and $\mathcal{O}(n)$ space.*

Proof. We construct the suffix tree of x (see [7,10,11]). We let $u = x[1 \ldots k]$, then let ℓ_m denote the depth of the lowest common ancestor of $x[1..n]$ (see [1]), and $x[i_m..n]$. We compute the LCA ℓ_m of $x[1..n]$ and $x[i_m..n]$ for $i_m = 2k, 3k, \ldots$, and $\ell_k = n - k$, if $\ell_m = 1$ for some m, then x is not k-cyclic periodic string. Now consider $C_m^{rignt} = (u_{\ell_m+1} \ldots u_k)^R$, compute the ℓ'_m the LCA of u^R and C_m^{right}. If $\ell'_m \geq \ell_m$ for all m, then x is k-cyclic periodic. □

4 Computing All Cyclic Periodicities

Theorem 2. *Given a string x of length n, test whether it is k-cyclic periodicity for all $1 \leq k \leq n$, this can be determined in $\mathcal{O}(n \log n)$ time and $\mathcal{O}(n)$ space.*

Proof. We apply the algorithm of Theorem 1 for $k = 1, 2, \ldots, n$ and we test all cyclic periods of length k. The construction of the suffix tree of string x and x^R is done once costing $\mathcal{O}(n)$. The total cost is

$$\mathcal{O}(n) + \mathcal{O}(\sum_{k=1}^{n} n/k) = \mathcal{O}(n \log n)$$

□

Lemma 1. *Compute the cyclic period of x.*

Proof. The smallest cyclic-period of x is the cyclic-period of x. □

5   Computing Maximal Local k-cyclic Periodicity

Theorem 3. *We can compute all k-cyclic periodicity of x in $\mathcal{O}(n \log n)$ time.*

Proof. We apply the algorithm for $k = 1, 2, \ldots, n$ and in this case, extend it to cyclic periods of length $k + 1$, where $|y| = m$ is cyclic periodic and $y\alpha = m + 1$ is not cyclic periodic. Next, we perform this algorithm on string x^R as $\mathcal{T}(x^R)$, where $|y| = m$, again is cyclic periodic and $\beta y = m + 1$ is not cyclic periodic.

The construction of the suffix tree of string x is done once. The total cost is

$$\mathcal{O}(\sum_{k=1}^{n} n/k) = \mathcal{O}(n \log n)$$

$\square$

Lemma 2. *Compute maximal local k-cyclic periodicity of x.*

Proof. We compute and merge the arrays for $y\alpha$ and βy of x. That is the maximal local k-cyclic periodicity of x. $\square$

6   Computing k'-cyclic Coverability

Theorem 4. *Given a string x of length n and an integer k', $1 \leq k' \leq n$, test whether it is k'-cyclic coverable, this can be determined in $\mathcal{O}(n)$ time and $\mathcal{O}(n)$ space.*

Proof. We compute the suffix tree of string x as $\mathcal{T}(x)$, and also we compute the suffix tree of string x^R as $\mathcal{T}(x^R)$.

Then we check $x[1, k']$ with each one of $x[n - k' + 1, n]$, $x[n - k', n - 1]$, $x[n - k' - 1, n - 2] \ldots x[2, k' + 1]$, together with the reverse pairs in $T(x^R)$. This way we build a collection of cyclic covers if there is one.

The construction of the suffix tree costs $\mathcal{O}(n)$; checking of equality costs $\mathcal{O}(1)$ and there are n factors. The total time is $\mathcal{O}(n)$. $\square$

7   Computing All Cyclic Coverability

Theorem 5. *Given a string x of length n, test whether it is k'-cyclic coverable for $1 \leq k' \leq n$, this can be determined in $\mathcal{O}(n^2)$ time and $\mathcal{O}(n)$ space.*

Proof. We apply the algorithm for $k' = 1, 2, \ldots, n$ and we compare all cyclic coverable of length k'. The construction of the suffix tree of string x is done once. The total cost is

$$\mathcal{O}(\sum_{k'=1}^{n} n) = \mathcal{O}(n^2)$$

$\square$

Lemma 3. *Compute the cyclic coverability of x.*

Proof. The smallest cyclic coverable of x is the all the cyclic coverable of x. $\square$

8   Conclusions and Open Problems

In this paper, we defined k-cyclic periodicity, we presented several efficient algorithms for computing: (i) cyclic periodicity; (ii) all cyclic periodicity; (iii) maximal local cyclic periodicity; (iv) cyclic covers.

Future work will be focused on computing the cyclic-periodic array, that is the cyclic periodicity of every prefix of string x and computing the cyclic-coverability array, that is testing each prefix of x, for cyclic-coverability. Finally, we will extend the cyclic periodicity to cover the case $u_1 u_2 u_2 \ldots u_k u^1$, where $u_i = c(u_j) \ \forall \ i, j$ and u^1 is a substring of some u_i.

References

1. Bender, M.A., Farach-Colton, M.: The LCA problem revisited. In: Gonnet, G.H., Viola, A. (eds.) LATIN 2000. LNCS, vol. 1776, pp. 88–94. Springer, Heidelberg (2000). https://doi.org/10.1007/10719839_9
2. Crochemore, M., Hancart, C., Lecroq, T.: Algorithms on Strings. Cambridge University Press, New York (2007)
3. Defant, C.: Anti-power prefixes of the Thue-Morse word. arXiv preprint arXiv:1607.05825 (2016)
4. Erdős, P., et al.: Anti-ramsey theorems (1973)
5. Fujita, S., Magnant, C., Ozeki, K.: Rainbow generalizations of ramsey theory: a survey. Graphs Comb. **26**(1), 1–30 (2010)
6. Kolpakov, R., Bana, G., Kucherov, G.: mreps: efficient and flexible detection of tandem repeats in DNA. Nucleic Acids Res. **31**(13), 3672–3678 (2003)
7. McCreight, E.M.: A space-economical suffix tree construction algorithm. J. ACM (JACM) **23**(2), 262–272 (1976)
8. Narayanan, S.: Functions on antipower prefix lengths of the Thue-Morse word. arXiv preprint arXiv:1705.06310 (2017)
9. Thue, A.: Uber unendliche zeichenreihen. Norske Vid Selsk. Skr. I Mat-Nat Kl. (Christiana) **7**, 1–22 (1906)
10. Ukkonen, E.: Constructing suffix trees on-line in linear time. In: Proceedings of the IFIP 12th World Computer Congress on Algorithms, Software, Architecture-Information Processing 1992, Volume 1-Volume I, pp. 484–492. North-Holland Publishing Co. (1992)
11. Weiner, P.: Linear pattern matching algorithms. In: 14th Annual Symposium on Switching and Automata Theory, SWAT 1973, pp. 1–11. IEEE (1973)
12. Wurpel, D.J., Beatson, S.A., Totsika, M., Petty, N.K., Schembri, M.A.: Chaperone-usher fimbriae of Escherichia coli. PloS one **8**(1), e52835 (2013)

Paid Crowdsourcing, Low Income Contributors, and Subjectivity

Giannis Haralabopoulos[1]([✉])(iD), Christian Wagner[1], Derek McAuley[1],
and Ioannis Anagnostopoulos[2]

[1] University of Nottingham, Nottingham, UK
{giannis.haralabopoulos,christian.wagner,derek.mcauley}@nottingham.ac.uk
[2] University of Thessaly, Volos, Greece
janag@dib.uth.gr

Abstract. Scientific projects that require human computation often resort to crowdsourcing. Interested individuals can contribute to a crowdsourcing task, essentially contributing towards the project's goals. To motivate participation and engagement, scientists use a variety of reward mechanisms. The most common motivation, and the one that yields the fastest results, is monetary rewards. By using monetary, scientists address a wider audience to participate in the task. As the payment is below minimum wage for developed economies, users from developing countries are more eager to participate. In subjective tasks, or tasks that cannot be validated through a right or wrong type of validation, monetary incentives could contrast with the much needed quality of submissions. We perform a subjective crowdsourcing task, emotion annotation, and compare the quality of the answers from contributors of varying income levels, based on the Gross Domestic Product. The results indicate a different contribution process between contributors from varying GDP regions. Low income contributors, possibly driven by the monetary incentive, submit low quality answers at a higher pace, while high income contributors provide diverse answers at a slower pace.

Keywords: Crowdsourcing · Demographics · Monetary rewards · Subjectivity

1 Introduction

Crowdsourcing is the process where a number of non expert people collectively perform a task. The task is presented to a wide group of internet users via an online platform and each user provides their unique input. The collection of inputs from the crowd is aggregated to provide information necessary for the task at hand. The users are referred as workers or contributors and the person that requests the crowdsourcing is known as requester.

As more and more requesters create tasks for workers, new tasks must provide incentives for participation. Money is the most common crowdsourcing incentive,

© IFIP International Federation for Information Processing 2019
Published by Springer Nature Switzerland AG 2019
J. MacIntyre et al. (Eds.): AIAI 2019 Workshops, IFIP AICT 560, pp. 225–231, 2019.
https://doi.org/10.1007/978-3-030-19909-8_20

and the one that yields the fastest results, but of varying quality [1]. Gamification of crowdsourcing tasks, i.e. the use of game elements such as point ladders and rewards, is another way of keeping workers interested and engaged in the task [8].

A crowdsourcing task is split in small micro tasks. Each micro task requires some seconds (on rare occasions minutes) to be completed, therefore the monetary incentive per micro task is usually low. The minimum allowed per micro task is 0.01$ in most crowdsourcing platforms[1,2]. This results in a low salary per hour, which according to Horton and Chilton [5], has a median of 1.38$/h.

Studies have showed that workers from Europe and America provide higher quality contributions than workers from Asia [6,7]. In addition, it is also shown that per task payment reduces contributor productivity [13] and monetary rewards negatively influence answers quality [14]. Considering that Asia's mean GDP per capita is almost 26% of Europe's, less than 14% of North America's[3], and the fact that participation incentives exist due monetary rewards, could there be a link between income and quality of crowdsourcing contributions?

During the analysis of the crowdsourcing results from one of our recent studies [9,12], we found evidence of high percentage of spam or dishonest contribution from workers originating from low income countries. Participants that deliver systematically the same contributions were identified as dishonest contributors, with high certainty. We hypothesize that workers from low income countries are mainly motivated by the monetary incentive, rather than the contribution to the crowdsourcing task.

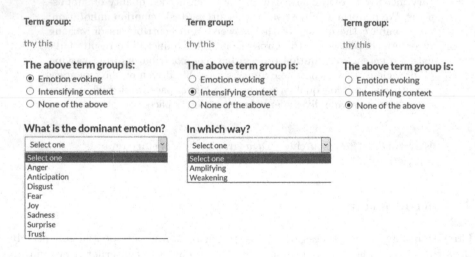

Fig. 1. Micro-task structure

---
[1] https://www.figure-eight.com/.
[2] https://www.mturk.com/.
[3] http://www.imf.org/external/datamapper/NGDPDPC@WEO/OEMDC/ADVEC/
     WEOWORLD.

2   Task

The crowdsourcing task, as described in [9,12], requires workers to choose from one of the three main classes and then select the most appropriate subclass. As seen in Fig. 1, workers select the appropriate class with a radio button, and unless the class selection is none, a drop-down menu appears that requires a single selection.

The use of fixed radio and drop-down selections, allows the requester to capture and filter out spamming behavior. This type of behavior is easy to capture when a dishonest worker is constantly selecting the same options over and over again, but undetectable if a dishonest user utilizes more elaborate methods of spamming, such as automated mouse movement applications. The inclusion of quality control questions [10], which usually appear at the start of the task, forces workers to adopt a cautious behavior early on the task, and then proceed to provide dishonest contributions at a higher pace. In addition, the nature of a subjective task, such as the emotional annotation of terms, doesn't provide a solid basis for quality control questions that use predefined answers.

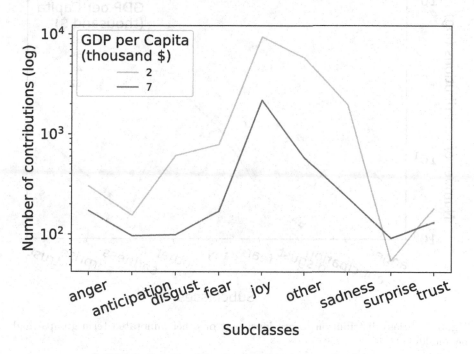

Fig. 2. Subclass distribution (low income levels)

In this subjective crowdsourcing task, each term group was annotated by 6 separate workers, and each worker was not able to annotate more than 1% of the corpus. The subclass distribution of the contributions, as seen in Fig. 2, was comprised of mostly joy annotated term groups. The nine subclasses, visible in

Figs. 2 and 3, represent the eight emotions, while the subclass "other" refers to either intensifiers and negators, or term groups that are not emotion evocative and not intensifying. Ninety and seventy two percent of workers from countries with GDP income per capita of less than 10K$ annotated term groups exclusively with joy or none. This high annotation percentage in a single subclass, of a random distribution of terms, is strong indication of spam and dishonesty.

Although this behavior was verified manually by the authors at a term level, where we analysed individual terms to determine whether they were evoking any emotion, in large scale crowdsourcing tasks there is no need for manual verification. The probability of annotation workers constantly encountering terms of the same emotion would be extremely low. E.g. if the combined probability of a term group being none or joy was 99%, the probability of encountering six hundred exclusively none or joy term groups would only be 0.2405%. Thus the probability that a worker honestly annotated a diverse corpus of words only with a single emotion is very close to zero.

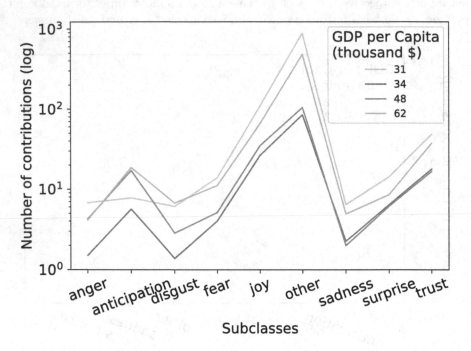

Fig. 3. Subclass distribution in previously joy or other annotated term groups (high income levels)

3   Quality of Workers and Contributions

The requested task had both a set of test questions, that would say if a term was an intensifier or emotion evoking, and a distribution control of contributions was applied. However, a high number of test questions would appear during the initial stages of the task, something that workers were aware of and could easily exploit. The distribution control worked well on identifying spammers, but it required a minimum number of answers from each worker before excluding workers that constantly annotated a single emotion.

The distribution threshold was set at 40%, which is approximately double the highest occurrence of a single emotion in another similar study [11]. After filtering out workers that had more than 40% of their total annotations in a single subclass, we end up with a smoother distribution of annotations, but strictly bound to the threshold. From the total one hundred eighty seven participating workers, only thirty six were identified as eligible based on the 40% filtering process. This in turn, reduced the number of total annotations deemed valid, from more than fifty thousands to less than eleven thousands. The percentage of invalidated annotations and the originating country of the contributors are the basis of our hypothesis.

4   Testing the Hypothesis

Our hypothesis is that workers from low income countries are motivated from the monetary incentive, rather than contributing to the task. A direct implication of this hypothesis is that monetary incentivised workers provide low quality answers. In order to test this hypothesis we used 1555 term groups as annotated strictly to joy or none, prior to the filtering process, with a majority higher than 80% of the total annotations. Six annotations per term group were required, with the same test questions for workers as before. The task was requested in the same platform, with the exact same settings, but only allowed workers from countries with GDP per capita higher then 30K$ to participate.

In the high income task, workers annotated term groups diversely, and the previously dominant joy emotion is the third most frequently occurring subclass. Additionally, strong majority agreement (over 80%) over joy and none subclasses is lower, with 42 term groups annotated as joy and 181 as none, compared to 1055 and 500 respective term groups of the initial task.

In total group of 112 contributors in the hypothesis group, 32 were flagged as eligible by our 40% single annotation check. A slightly lower eligibility over assessment than the initial task, due to the fact that hypothesis term groups were biased towards joy and none. However, workers annotated term groups in all of the possible subclasses, and only 4% and 36.2% of the term groups were still majorly annotated as joy and none respectively.

None was the most common occurring annotation post-filter, and the only subclass affected by the single annotation check. It's challenging to determine honesty post-annotation with an unsupervised method, more so on a monetary incentivised subjective task.

5   Conclusion

The results suggest that income is an important factor in crowdsourcing participation. As the particular crowdsourcing task is mainly of subjective nature, the validation of the hypothesis can only be based on the diversity of the provided contributions, compared to the initially single subclass accumulated contributions. In an objective task, quality questions and distribution filtering are sufficient measures to prevent dishonesty. Modern crowdsourcing platforms[4] provide ethical rewards and worker demographic pre-screening, empowering requesters and workers alike.

We are studying the subjective aspects of crowdsourcing, and our goal is to address the evaluation of subjective contributions with objective criteria in future publications. Additionally, in purely subjective crowdsourcing tasks, demographics like age, sex, or education levels, should be further studied to better understand crowd's performance [2,3]. Our preliminary findings are in line with research that suggests voluntary crowdsourcing provides highest quality contributions than paid crowdsourcing [1]. Workers participating voluntarily are only motivated by their desire to contribute, which can be supplemented by a range of non monetary incentives to improve engagement. Apart from voluntary participation, a critical mass of honest participators [4] can function as a self-maintained filter for dishonesty and spamming in both objective and subjective tasks.

References

1. Mao, A., et al.: Volunteering versus work for pay: incentives and tradeoffs in crowdsourcing. In: First AAAI Conference on Human Computation and Crowdsourcing (2013)
2. Pavlick, E., Post, M., Irvine, A., Kachaev, D., Callison-Burch, C.: The language demographics of Amazon mechanical turk. Trans. Assoc. Comput. Linguist. **2**, 79–92 (2014)
3. Ross, J., Irani, L., Silberman, M., Zaldivar, A., Tomlinson, B.: Who are the crowdworkers?: shifting demographics in mechanical turk. In: Extended Abstracts on Human Factors in Computing Systems, CHI 2010, pp. 2863–2872. ACM (2010)
4. Sharma, A.: Crowdsourcing critical success factor model: strategies to harness the collective intelligence of the crowd. London School of Economics (LSE), London (2010)
5. Horton, J.J., Chilton, L.B.: The labor economics of paid crowdsourcing. In: Proceedings of the 11th ACM Conference on Electronic Commerce, pp. 209–218 (2010)
6. Rogstadius, J., Kostakos, V., Kittur, A., Smus, B., Laredo, J., Vukovic, M.: An assessment of intrinsic and extrinsic motivation on task performance in crowdsourcing markets. In: ICWSM, vol. 11, pp. 17–21 (2011)
7. Kazai, G., Kamps, J., Milic-Frayling, N.: The face of quality in crowdsourcing relevance labels: demographics, personality and labeling accuracy. In: Proceedings of the 21st ACM International Conference on Information and Knowledge Management, pp. 2583–2586. ACM (2012)

---

[4] https://prolific.ac/.

8. Hamari, J., Koivisto, J., Sarsa, H.: Does gamification work? – a literature review of empirical studies on gamification. In: 2014 47th Hawaii International Conference on System Sciences (HICSS), pp. 3025–3034. IEEE (2014)

9. Haralabopoulos, G., Simperl, E.: Crowdsourcing for beyond polarity sentiment analysis a pure emotion lexicon. arXiv preprint arXiv:1710.04203 (2017)

10. Allahbakhsh, M., Benatallah, B., Ignjatovic, A., Motahari-Nezhad, H.R., Bertino, E., Dustdar, S.: Quality control in crowdsourcing systems: issues and directions. IEEE Internet Comput. **17**(2), 76–81 (2013)

11. Mohammad, S.M., Turney, P.D.: NRC emotion lexicon. NRC Technical report (2013)

12. Haralabopoulos, G., Wagner, C., McAuley, D., Simperl, E.: A multivalued emotion lexicon created and evaluated by the crowd. In: 2018 Fifth International Conference on Social Networks Analysis, Management and Security (SNAMS), pp. 355–362. IEEE, October 2018

13. Ikeda, K., Bernstein, M.S.: Pay it backward: per-task payments on crowdsourcing platforms reduce productivity. In: Proceedings of the 2016 CHI Conference on Human Factors in Computing Systems. ACM (2016)

14. Acar, O.A.: Harnessing the creative potential of consumers: money, participation, and creativity in idea crowdsourcing. Mark. Lett. **29**(2), 177–188 (2018)

Predicting Secondary Structure for Human Proteins Based on Chou-Fasman Method

Fotios Kounelis[1], Andreas Kanavos[1,2], Ioannis E. Livieris[2(✉)],
Gerasimos Vonitsanos[1], and Panagiotis Pintelas[3]

[1] Computer Engineering and Informatics Department, University of Patras,
Patras, Greece
{kounelis,kanavos,mvonitsanos}@ceid.upatras.gr
[2] Computer and Informatics Engineering Department,
Technological Educational Institute of Western Greece, Antirrio, Greece
livieris@teiwest.gr
[3] Department of Mathematics, University of Patras, Patras, Greece
ppintelas@gmail.com

Abstract. Proteins are constructed by the combination of a different number of amino acids and thus, have a different structure and folding depending on chemical reactions and other aspects. The protein folding prediction can help in many healthcare scenarios to foretell and prevent diseases. The different elements that form a protein give the secondary structure. One of the most common algorithms used for secondary structure prediction constitutes the Chou-Fasman method. This technique divides and in following analyses each amino acid in three different elements, which are α-helices, β-sheets and turns based on already known protein structures. Its aim is to predict the probability for which each of these elements will be formed. In this paper, we have used Chou-Fasman algorithm for extracting the probabilities of a series of amino acids in FASTA format. We make an analysis given all probabilities for any length of a human protein without any restriction as other existing tools.

Keywords: Protein structure prediction ·
Computational structural biology · Human proteins ·
Secondary structure prediction · Protein folding

1 Introduction

Proteins form one or more determined conformations guided by a number of complicated and reversible non-covalent interactions in order to unfold their biological functions. Although determining the structure of a protein can be obtained by time-consuming as well as relatively expensive techniques such as crystallography, dual polarization interferometry and nuclear-magnetic resonance spectroscopy, new techniques based on the area of bioinformatics have

ⓒ IFIP International Federation for Information Processing 2019
Published by Springer Nature Switzerland AG 2019
J. MacIntyre et al. (Eds.): AIAI 2019 Workshops, IFIP AICT 560, pp. 232–241, 2019.
https://doi.org/10.1007/978-3-030-19909-8_21

been developed. These techniques aim to compute and in following predict protein structures based on their amino acid sequences.

Amino acids are one of the main components that form proteins [26,27]. They are encoded directly from the genetic code through the transcript-RNA. These specific components contain functional groups of amine and carboxyl as well as side chains. Twenty different amino acids are encoded from the genetic code, although a lot more have naturally occurred [28]. Using different techniques, additional amino acids which generate proteins with newly enhanced properties [29] are genetically encoded.

Protein structure can be predicted with the use of structure analysis and prediction tools according to their amino-acid sequences. More specifically, solving the structure of a given protein can be considered as highly important in medicine (another example is the drug design) and biotechnology (an example constitutes the design of novel enzymes). Thus, the area of computational protein structure prediction is constantly evolving, by following the development of intelligent algorithms and more important, by taking advantage of the increase in computational power of machines.

Regarding the protein structure prediction, the primary structure is employed to predict secondary as well as tertiary structures. The primary structure consists of the linear sequence of amino acids [4,21]. There are twenty different amino acids, that their occurrence in the sequence and the position or positions they occur, will form a different protein.

Furthermore, the different elements that form a protein as well as their 3D structure give the secondary structure [19]. α-helices, β-sheets, turns, and omega loops are the elements that occur in the secondary structure of a protein and the ones that our paper predicts.

After the above elements are formed and in following are combined in the 3D space, the tertiary structure of the protein is shaped [2]. This structure has one or more secondary structures and may have interactions and bonds with amino acid side chains. The tertiary structure is considered as the highest structure of a protein, where all the protein subunits are arranged and numbered [11].

In the present manuscript, we have employed the Chou-Fasman method, an algorithm used for secondary structure prediction. With this method, we aim to divide and analyse each amino acid in three different elements, namely α-helices, β-sheets and turns based on already known protein structures to predict the probability for each one of these elements. There are also other tools to implement the Chou-Fasman method but they lack in different aspects that we overcome.

The first obstacle is the size limit of online tools. Our implementation predicts the secondary structure for any length of sequence. Furthermore, our implementation provides the probabilities for all three different elements that the Chou-Fasman algorithm can predict. This part of our paper overcomes the problem of other tools that don't predict the probabilities for turns. Even if turns have the lowest probabilities, it is yet a very useful part of the secondary structure of a protein.

The second contribution of the proposed work deals with the proteins we study. We aim at the human proteins and their probabilities so that we can primarily understand what is the performance of this method in this specific type of proteins. This will allow us in the future to build a more robust map for human proteins that are produced from different chromosomes and check the performance of different algorithms on this kind of map.

The remainder of the paper is organized as follows. Section 2 presents a brief survey of recent studies concerning protein structure prediction, homology modeling and protein fold recognition. Section 3 presents a reference to the prediction tools and methods and introduces the Chou-Fasman method while in Sect. 4, we present our experimental results. Finally, Sect. 5 discusses our concluding remarks, the open problems as well as our future work.

2   Background Topics

Regarding protein structure prediction, several methods and techniques have been proposed with the aim of attempting to specify the structure and bonds of an amino acid sequence [12,24]. As a result, the knowledge of the protein structure is critical and thus, several determinants can be considered as important; the bond angle stresses, the electrostatic interactions, the hydrogen and covalent bonds, the hydrophobicity and hydrophilicity of residues, the van der Waals interactions, as well as the enthalpy and the entropy.

Regarding protein structure determinants, there are two important aspects as well; initially, the information about them, and as a result, the information regarding the structure of a protein is entirely contained within the sequence (in addition to knowledge of the solvent). In following, these determinants can also be considered as measurements of physical properties. Without the aid protein chaperones, we can assume that proteins can take their native conformation in a solvent; then enough information for predicting protein structures ab initio (from basic principles) can be considered. However, many of the determinants are not precisely known or may be too compute-intensive and computationally non-tractable.

Protein structure prediction has resorted to knowledge-based methods, since there is lack of feasible ab initio methods. Specifically, homology modeling [6] as well as protein fold recognition methods [13] constitute the two major and complementary approaches that were taken.

2.1   Homology Modeling

In terms of homology modeling, the amino acid sequence of a protein with unknown structure is aligned against sequences of proteins with known structures. Furthermore, high degrees of homology (very similar sequences across and between the proteins) can be used for determining the global structure of the corresponding protein and in turn for placing it into a certain fold category. On the other hand, lower degrees of homology may be still used in order to determine local structures, with an example being the Chou-Fasman method [8,16] for predicting secondary structure. An advantage for homology modeling methods is the lack of dependence on the knowledge of physical determinants.

Every homology modeling process consists of four steps which are always the same [17]. Firstly, the homologous template proteins of already known proteins should be gathered. Secondly, the best set of templates should be selected. In following, this set will be used in order to optimize the multiple sequence alignment for the query. Finally, the model that will be as close as possible to the structure of the templates, will be built. These steps can be repeated until a satisfying model finally occurs [22].

More to the point, homology modeling constitutes a very important tool for 3D protein structure models. This is the reason why web-based integrated systems have been built. SWISS-MODEL [2,5,22] is considered as such a workspace, where for any queries, a library is searched for suitable templates. This tool is very reliable as it depends on sequence alignment for predicting the structure of the protein.

Homology modeling can be further utilized for the correct prediction of quaternary protein structure [1]. The researchers in this work used homology to fill the gap of non-structural experimental evidence for the 3D multimeric assemblies. Apart from that, homology modeling can be also used for large proteins too. In [23], an approach for the structure prediction of large proteins is described. In this work, an alignment method, which exploits bioinformatics algorithms to match values from a database to experimental data, is produced.

2.2 Protein Fold Recognition

Fold recognition methods take a complementary approach. In these methods, structures, not sequences, are aligned. If the sequence of a protein has an unknown structure, with the method called "threading", it undertakes the conformation of the backbone (protein sans side chains) of a known structure. For each attempt, higher physical determinants produce a more complete score for the alignment. These methods tend to be more computational-intensive than homology modeling methods, but they give more confidence in the physical viability of the results.

One of the major contributions is Phyre2 [15]; a suite of tools available on the web to predict and analyse protein structure, function and mutations. The focus of Phyre2 is to provide biologists with a simple and intuitive interface to state-of-the-art protein bioinformatics tools.

A recent work [7] has improved Chou-Fasman method in three aspects; authors replaced the nucleation regions with extreme values of coefficients calculated by the continuous wavelet transform, in following substituted the original secondary structure conformational parameters with folding type-specific secondary structure propensities and finally modified Chou-Fasman rules.

In a more recent work, authors in [20] present a detailed overview of the molecular, functional, and structural characteristics of collagenase from

Pseudomonas aeruginosa which might be helpful for understanding the possible structure and functions of unknown proteins.

3 Prediction Tools and Methods

A great number of structure prediction software tools are developed for dedicated protein features, some among which are disorder prediction, dynamics prediction, structure conservation prediction, etc. Homology modeling, protein threading, ab initio methods, secondary structure prediction, and transmembrane helix and signal peptide prediction are approaches that help.

Each method uses a different level of the protein structure to predict another one. The primary structure is based on the amino acids linear sequence, which when combined in different places and varying numbers, form a different protein. In our paper, we deal with the secondary structure prediction. Regarding the tools used for predicting the secondary structure of a protein, they are based on the primary structure. In following, we analyze the secondary structure prediction and especially, the method for predicting the secondary structure on the human proteins in a more detailed way.

3.1 Secondary Structure Prediction

The prediction of local secondary structures is facilitated via these tools. These structures are solely based on the amino acid sequence of the protein and their prediction is afterwards compared to DSSP (Define Secondary Structure of Proteins) score [14], which is calculated based on the crystallographic structure of the protein [3, 18]. It is the standard method used to assign secondary structure annotations to a protein structure. In addition, it calculates all DSSP entries from PDB (Protein Data Bank). DSSP utilizes the atomic coordinates of a structure to assign the secondary codes, but is not a secondary structure prediction tool.

Neural nets and support vector machines comprise modern machine learning methods on which prediction methods for secondary structure rely on. Taking into consideration databases of known protein structures along with these methods is an optimal combination.

More specifically, the secondary structure prediction problem for a protein sequence is to predict for each amino acid, whether it appears in α-helix, β-sheets or any other team. There are several prediction algorithms, which provide such probabilities to solve the problem [10, 30, 31]. One of the most well-known and pioneer method is the Chou-Fasman technique. This method provides probabilities of amino acids whether they appear in α-helix, β-sheets or turns.

3.2 Chou-Fasman Method

The Chou-Fasman method exports the probabilities for a block of amino acids to be shown in each one of the three elements. Based on the frequencies that are calculated from observation for each amino acid, the probability for the whole sequence is predicted. When the method predicts helices and sheets, it works on a similar way; it has a window sliding on the frequency and upon meeting a high probability, it gets extended until the probability is under the predefined threshold.

On the other hand, even if turns have the same length of windows as in helices, the procedure is different due to the fact that many turn regions may occur in both helices and sheets. In order to predict a turn, its probability should be greater than helix or sheet as well as the same probability should be greater than a predefined threshold.

$$p(t) = p_t(j) \times p_t(j+1) \times p_t(j+2) \times p_t(j+3) \tag{1}$$

In formula (1), we can see this probability which explains why it is lower than the probabilities of helices and turns in all our experiments, where j is the position of each amino acid in the positions of the window with length equal to four.

There have been found that different amino acids have a higher tendency to occur in a certain secondary structure class, for example, alanine is known to appear in a helix form. The Chou-Fasman technique is based on statistical data and rules to provide such probabilities. When the method was introduced not many things were known about protein structure and as a result, the accuracy of the method was lower than it is nowadays.

Lab experiments can clearly prove which of the predicted probabilities of this technique are true and which are not. This allows the methods that produce their probabilities from already known structures, such as Chou-Fasman, to improve. As a result, we examine this method on the latest prediction updates. This will allow us to compare these results in later research, with probabilities that either have been collected in the past with the same method or by other modern methods. In the following section, we will analyze the proteins that were used and their form, as well as explain the methodically exported data.

4   Experimental Methodology

In order to gain a deeper insight on the elements that are analyzed, we present the following results that portray the distributions for secondary structure prediction.

The Chou-Fasman algorithm was implemented and run for ten different human proteins. These ten proteins as depicted in Tables 1 and 2 as *Apolipoprotein C-I, Casein Kinase 2, Disulphide Isomerase, Glutaredoxin, Insuline like 3, Intereleukin6, Lysozyme C, Major prion Protein, Prion like Protein Dropel* and *S100-D*. Each protein was split in five continuous amino acid blocks. For each block, the three different probabilities for each structure that will be formed, is produced. In order to understand and explain these data in a more rigorous way, we have Fig. 1 to illustrate them. The three different lines represent the structures; while in y axis, the percentage is represented and in x axis, the different blocks in a consecutive order for each protein, are represented.

Table 1. Human proteins details 1/2

	Apolipo-protein C-I	Casein-Kinase 2	Disulphide isomerase	Glutare-doxin	Insuline like 3
Chromosome	19	20	16	5	19
Number of amino acids	83	391	525	106	131
Most frequently appearing amino acids	Leu(L)	Leu(L)	Leu(L)	Leu(L), Gln(Q)	Leu(L)
Number of most frequently appearing amino acids	12	33	63	12	22
Percentage of most frequently appearing amino acids	14.5%	8.4%	12%	11.3%	16.8%
Instability index	30.79	48.79	46.79	43.72	53.10
Stable/Unstable	Stable	Unstable	Unstable	Unstable	Unstable
Non appearing amino acids	Pyl(P), Sec(S)	Pyl(P), Sec(S)	Pyl(P), Sec(S)	Pyl(P), Sec(S)	Pyl(P), Sec(S)

In following, we analyze the results of the ten proteins that were used in the Chou-Fasman technique. All these proteins belong to the human organism (Homo Sapiens). The human organism has 23 pairs of chromosomes and in the first row, we can see the number of the chromosomes in which each protein is deployed. The proteins are constructed from several amino acids. In the second row, we can see their number of amino acids. We can observe diversity in this specific characteristic as for example, the number of amino acids in protein S100-B is 92, whereas in Disulphide isomerase, the number of amino acids is 525. This diversity gives us a better insight to check the probability spectrum of the Chou-Fasman technique.

In the third, fourth and fifth lines, the most appeared amino acids as well as their percentage in the whole sequence are presented. We notice that Leucine (Leu) is the most common amino acid, which exists in almost all the proteins; specifically, this happens in seven out of the total ten proteins. However, even if Leucine is the most common amino acid in Casein Kinase 2 protein, the percentage remains low; this makes the deduction that all of the amino acids which occur share the same percentage, but this one is slightly larger.

Furthermore, the sixth line presents the instability index. This metric informs us whether a protein will be stable in a protein tube. In order to be stable, a protein should have an instability index of less than 40. As we can see, the four out of the total ten proteins are stable where Prion-like Protein Dropel is the most stable of all and the Casein Kinase 2 is the most unstable. Finally, in

Table 2. Human proteins details 2/2

	Intere-leukin 6	Lyso-zyme C	Major prion protein	Prion like protein dropel	S100-B
Chromosome	7	12	20	20	21
Number of amino acids	211	148	253	176	92
Most frequently appearing amino acids	Leu(L)	Ala(A)	Gly(G)	Leu(L)	Glu(E)
Number of most frequently appearing amino acids	28	15	45	20	16
Percentage of most frequently appearing amino acids	13.3%	10.11%	17.8%	11.4%	17.4%
Instability index	37.38	27.71	43.11	23.06	36.45
Stable/Unstable	Unstable	Stable	Unstable	Stable	Stable
Non appearing amino acids	Pyl(P), Sec(S)	Pyl(P), Sec(S)	Pyl(P), Sec(S)	Pyl(P), Sec(S)	Pyl(P), Sec(S)

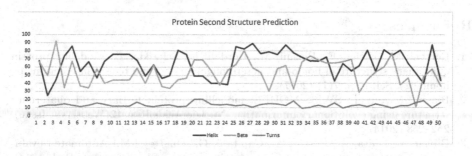

Fig. 1. The different probabilities for the three structures in all amino acid blocks

all of these proteins, two amino acids never occur inside the sequence, namely Pyrrolysine (Pyl) and Selenocysteine (Sec).

As we can see in Fig. 1, both α-helices and β-sheets have for each block a greater probability than turns. Concretely, α-helices have in more than half the blocks a greater probability than β-sheets. Our first remark from the figure is that for all the blocks in these ten human proteins, these amino acids are more possible to form an α-helix structure.

A second observation that follows the previous one, is that there are whole proteins, like the third (*Casein Kinase 2*) and the sixth (*Prion like Protein Dropel*) for the amino acid blocks 11–15 and 26–30 respectively, that have bigger probability of forming an α-helix. This means that these two proteins, in their whole sequence, according to the Chou-Fasman algorithm, will have a structure of an α-helix. This is not usual regarding the corresponding proteins, as only the two out of ten have this probability.

5   Conclusions and Future References

In this paper, we analysed the problem of the secondary structure prediction for human proteins. Chou-Fasman is a method which solves this problem by predicting the structure in which a block of amino acids will be formed. Depending on the probability of each amino acid that will appear in α-helices, β-sheets, or turns, this method produces the output. We used this method for ten human proteins to predict their secondary structure form.

Chou-Fasman method achieves success rate equal to 50%–60%, while other more modern secondary structure prediction methods, like GOR [9] or Porter 5 [25] achieve better results. As an open problem for research will be to implement other modern methods and make a comparative study between these methods and thus, discuss their differences in human proteins. Furthermore, it would be of great interest to implement those methods for proteins that are coded from different human chromosomes. This could potentially create a hybrid model for the use of different prediction methods depending on the chromosome from which a protein is derived of.

References

1. Bertoni, M., Kiefer, F., Biasini, M., Bordoli, L., Schwede, T.: Modeling protein quaternary structure of homo-and hetero-oligomers beyond binary interactions by homology. Sci. Rep. **7**(1) (2017)
2. Biasini, M., et al.: SWISS-MODEL: modelling protein tertiary and quaternary structure using evolutionary information. Nucleic Acids Res. **42**(Webserver-Issue), 252–258 (2014)
3. Bliven, S., Lafita, A., Parker, A., Capitani, G., Duarte, J.M.: Automated evaluation of quaternary structures from protein crystals. PLoS Comput. Biol. **14**(4), e1006104 (2018)
4. Bock, J.R., Gough, D.A.: Predicting protein-protein interactions from primary structure. Bioinformatics **17**(5), 455–460 (2001)
5. Bordoli, L., Kiefer, F., Arnold, K., Benkert, P., Battey, J.N.D., Schwede, T.: Protein structure homology modeling using SWISS-MODEL workspace. Nat. Protoc. **4**(1), 1–13 (2008)
6. Cavasotto, C.N., Phatak, S.S.: Homology modeling in drug discovery: current trends and applications. Drug Discovery Today **14**(13), 676–683 (2009)
7. Chen, H., Gu, F., Huang, Z.: Improved Chou-Fasman method for protein secondary structure prediction. BMC Bioinform. **7**(S-4) (2006)
8. Chou, P.Y., Fasman, G.D.: Empirical predictions of protein conformation. Annu. Rev. Biochem. **47**(1), 251–276 (1978)
9. Garnier, J., Gibrat, J.F., Robson, B.: GOR method for predicting protein secondary structure from amino acid sequence, vol. 266, pp. 540–553 (1996)
10. Ito, M., Matsuo, Y., Nishikawa, K.: Prediction of protein secondary structure using the 3D-1D compatibility algorithm. Comput. Appl. Biosci. **13**(4), 415–424 (1997)

11. Janin, J., Bahadur, R.P., Chakrabarti, P.: Protein-protein interaction and quaternary structure. Q. Rev. Biophys. **41**(2), 133–180 (2008)
12. Jiménez-Montaño, M.A., de la Mora-Basáñez, C.R., Pöschel, T.: The hypercube structure of the genetic code explains conservative and non-conservative aminoacid substitutions in vivo and in vitro. BioSystems **39**(2), 117–125 (1996)
13. Jones, D., Taylor, W., Thornton, J.: A new approach to protein fold recognition. Nature **358**, 86–89 (1992)
14. Joosten, R.P., et al.: A series of PDB related databases for everyday needs. Nucleic Acids Res. **39**(Database Issue), 411–419 (2011)
15. Kelley, L.A., Mezulis, S., Yates, C.M., Wass, M.N., Sternberg, M.J.: The Phyre2 web portal for protein modeling, prediction and analysis. Nat. Protoc. **10**(6), 845 (2015)
16. Kumar, T.A.: CFSSP: Chou and Fasman secondary structure prediction server. Wide Spectr. **1**(9), 15–19 (2013)
17. Meier, A., Söding, J.: Automatic prediction of protein 3D structures by probabilistic multi-template homology modeling. PLoS Comput. Biol. **11**(10), e1004343 (2015)
18. Palczewski, K., et al.: Crystal structure of rhodopsin: a G protein-coupled receptor. Science **289**(5480), 739–745 (2000)
19. Perticaroli, S., Nickels, J.D., Ehlers, G., O'Neill, H., Zhang, Q., Sokolov, A.P.: Secondary structure and rigidity in model proteins. Soft Matter **9**(40), 9548–9556 (2013)
20. Rani, S., Pooja, K.: Elucidation of structural and functional characteristics of collagenase from Pseudomonas aeruginosa. Process Biochem. **64**, 116–123 (2018)
21. Sanger, F.: The arrangement of amino acids in proteins. Adv. Protein Chem. **7**, 1–67 (1952)
22. Schwede, T., Kopp, J., Guex, N., Peitsch, M.C.: SWISS-MODEL: an automated protein homology-modeling server. Nucleic Acids Res. **31**(13), 3381–3385 (2003)
23. Shen, Y., Bax, A.: Homology modeling of larger proteins guided by chemical shifts. Nat. Methods **12**(8), 747–750 (2015)
24. Siman, R., Noszek, J.C.: Excitatory amino acids activate calpain I and induce structural protein breakdown in vivo. Neuron **1**(4), 279–287 (1988)
25. Torrisi, M., Kaleel, M., Pollastri, G.: Porter 5: fast, state-of-the-art ab initio prediction of protein secondary structure in 3 and 8 classes. bioRxiv (2018)
26. Vickery, H.B.: The history of the discovery of the amino acids II. A review of amino acids described since 1931 as components of native proteins. In: Advances in Protein Chemistry, vol. 26, pp. 81–171 (1972)
27. Vickery, H.B., Schmidt, C.L.: The history of the discovery of the amino acids. Chem. Rev. **9**(2), 169–318 (1931)
28. Wagner, I., Musso, H.: New naturally occurring amino acids. Angewandte Chemie International Edition in English **22**(11), 816–828 (1983)
29. Xie, J., Schultz, P.G.: Adding amino acids to the genetic repertoire. Curr. Opin. Chem. Biol. **9**(6), 548–554 (2005)
30. Yavuz, B.C., Yurtay, N., Özkan, Ö.: Prediction of protein secondary structure with clonal selection algorithm and multilayer perceptron. IEEE Access **6**, 45256–45261 (2018)
31. Zhou, Z., Yang, B., Hou, W.: Association classification algorithm based on structure sequence in protein secondary structure prediction. Expert Syst. Appl. **37**(9), 6381–6389 (2010)

Author Index

Printed in the United States
By Bookmasters